Desecrate

Knights of Eternity: Book Two

Rachel Ní Chuirc

Copyright © 2024 by Rachel Ni Chuirc

Published through The Legion Publishers Ltd

Editing by Anna Johnstone

Editing by Judy Roth

Cover by Rashed Alakroka

Typography by May Dawney Designs

Formatting and additional editing by Christine Cajiao

All rights reserved. This book or any portion thereof may not be reproduced in any manner whatsoever without the

express written permission of the author/publisher except for the use of brief quotations in a book review.

This is a work of fiction.

THANKS!

Woof! How are we on the second book already? Just yesterday I was thanking people for their help with the first KoE, and now here you are, sitting there with your beautiful eyebrows, ready to read the sequel (and they truly are magnificent eyebrows!).

As always, I have many people to thank: Aisling O'Connell, Ilya Voulis, and Ruairí Moore for reading through an early version of this book and catching my (many) mistakes. The Legion beta readers for their amazing feedback. The Legion Publishers: Jez, Chrissy, and Geneva for their constant kindness and support. My family for always having time to talk. And by talk, I mean listen to me yell about vaxion, molger, and MUSHROOMS! (This makes sense in the book... probably.) And as always, I need to thank you (and your eyebrows), for picking up this book. I've learned a lot since book one, and Zara the Fury took me on a *hell* of a journey for this one. I hope you enjoy reading about the vaxion muscle mommy as much as I enjoyed writing about her.

Love,

Rachel Ní Chuirc
CHAOS GREMLIN

P.S My last name is pronounced "knee-kirk." If you forget how to say it, picture kneeing Captain Kirk in the face, and you've got it!

Contents

THANKS!	3
Contents	4
Prologue	7
Chapter One	9
Chapter Two	13
Chapter Three	19
Chapter Four	23
Chapter Five	30
Chapter Six	35
Chapter Seven	41
Chapter Eight	46
Chapter Nine	50
Chapter Ten	56
Chapter Eleven	61
Chapter Twelve	68
Chapter Thirteen	73
Chapter Fourteen	78
Chapter Fifteen	83
Chapter Sixteen	87
Chapter Seventeen	93
Chapter Eighteen	98
Chapter Nineteen	106
Chapter Twenty	111
Chapter Twenty-One	115
Chapter Twenty-Two	122
Chapter Twenty-Three	127

Chapter Twenty-Four	133
Chapter Twenty-Five	138
Chapter Twenty-Six	142
Chapter Twenty-Seven	147
Chapter Twenty-Eight	152
Chapter Twenty-Nine	157
Chapter Thirty	164
Chapter Thirty-One	170
Chapter Thirty-Two	177
Chapter Thirty-Three	182
Chapter Thirty-Four	187
Chapter Thirty-Five	193
Chapter Thirty-Six	200
Chapter Thirty-Seven	206
Chapter Thirty-Eight	211
Chapter Thirty-Nine	218
Chapter Forty	223
Chapter Forty-One	228
Chapter Forty-Two	233
Chapter Forty-Three	239
Chapter Forty-Four	245
Chapter Forty-Five	251
Chapter Forty-Six	258
Chapter Forty-Seven	265
Chapter Forty-Eight	272
Chapter Forty-Nine	278
Chapter Fifty	283
Chapter Fifty-One	289

Chapter Fifty-Two	296
Chapter Fifty-Three	304
Chapter Fifty-Four	310
Chapter Fifty-Five	315
Chapter Fifty-Six	320
Chapter Fifty-Seven	325
Chapter Fifty-Eight	332
Chapter Fifty-Nine	339
Chapter Sixty	344
Chapter Sixty-One	351
Epilogue	359
END OF BOOK TWO	367
REVIEWS	368
WANDERING WARRIOR	369
QUEST ACADEMY	370
SCARLET CITADEL	371
ARISE ALPHA	372
SOMNIA ONLINE	373
FACEBOOK AND SOCIAL MEDIA	374
LITRPG!	375
LITRPG LEGION	376

Prologue

The twin suns of the Void, its home and prison, grew hot—the red sands beneath it fire to its flesh. But the entity did not care.

It could no longer burn.

It pulled against its chains, the manacles that bound it cracking with every tug. The board was set, the pieces it had spent decades setting up finally in play.

It was *time*.

***

In the cold dark of the forest, Magnus screamed. Ropes bound him to a solitary tree where urine soaked his trousers. A rag had been shoved into his mouth, making him gag, and he couldn't feel his legs. But that wasn't why he screamed.

The voice was here. And it was *angry*. Tears ran down his cheeks, but he didn't cry for himself. He cried for Zara the Fury.

A decade ago, he'd left the Ivory Keep at his master's behest, setting up in a castle at the edge of Navaros where he slowly amassed gold, grain, and mercenaries. In time, friends stopped calling, his family quietly wrote him out of the will, and even the gossip mill ceased churning out rumors about the eccentric mage and his betrothed. Magnus didn't care. He was a man driven by a singular purpose—to serve. He thought that was all he needed.

But as he screamed, he found his mind kept going back to her. To Zara. To his Fury. Despite the cauterized stump that was once his right arm, her parting gift, he missed her with a ferocity that rivaled his willingness to serve. His master had given her to him as a tool. Something to aid him as he carried out the voice's will. Yet as she grew, as he remade her time and again, she became so much more than that.

His master's rage was a twitching blade in his skull, each twist threatening to rend it in two. Only the image of Zara and her fanged smile kept him sane. *I am nothing.* He pleaded as the voice grew louder. *I am the festering maggots in the skulls of your enemies.*

I am the worms that writhe in the soil beneath your feet. There is nothing I wouldn't do, wouldn't give, to please you.

This seemed to calm the voice, and the pain briefly abated. Magnus sagged against the ropes that bound him, cold sweat pouring from him. An image grew in his mind, blurry at first, but the edges sharpened like a blade on a whetstone. Realization made Magnus lift his head for the first time in hours. He smiled, cracked lips filling with blood. How foolish he'd been to doubt.

It had been written in the stars all along.

Chapter One

Noah was twelve years old. He liked video games, chocolate and banana sandwiches, and going to the arcade with his aunt, [SYSTEM ERROR]. Even though [SYSTEM ERROR] was his aunt, she felt more like a big sister. She was five years and eleven months older than him (he'd counted) and had shown him the best game ever—*Knights of Eternity*. It was an old arcade game, with janky 8-bit sounds and big blocky pixels, but it was tougher than anything he'd ever played.

One of his favorite things to do, when not playing *Knights of Eternity*, was *thinking* about *Knights of Eternity*. He had notebooks full of ideas and strategies. Was it better, for instance, to charge through the many-armed Sucklers using Marito's *Heroic Strength* or to slip past them with Lazander's *Hunter's Shadow*? Or maybe he could total them in one fell swoop with Gabriel's *Feast of Shadows*—the mage's dark magic blasting everything to pieces.

But time and again, Noah found himself going back to the Prince of Navaros, and leader of the Gilded Knights—Valerius. With his shiny white armor, massive shield, and killer one-liners—"Justice waits for no man!"—it was hard to imagine a more perfect knight.

He didn't just think about Valerius when it came to games though. Whenever Noah got sad, or angry, he'd ask himself, "What would Valerius do?" He was wondering about it now as his mom cried in the bathroom.

It was his fault. Dad's six-month anniversary was coming up, and she wanted to go to his grave together. Smiling, she talked about picking out some flowers and bringing tools to tidy it up—like it'd be fun. A "treat" for them both.

"What's the point? Dad's dead," he told her, "and stupid flowers aren't going to change that." Her lip had quivered, and he knew he'd gone too far. She'd turned without a word, slamming the bathroom door shut.

In minutes he heard her sobbing.

Valerius wouldn't have made her cry, he thought, picking at the last of his Mighty Crunch Munch cereal—his dinner that night. He'd go in, tell her he was sorry, and that he'd love to go to Dad's grave with her.

But he couldn't do it.

His phone bleeped, and he checked it, dribbling milk on himself. It was a message from [SYSTEM ERROR] asking if he wanted to go to the arcade. He almost smiled. He never talked about Mom with her. About how much she cried. But [SYSTEM ERROR] always seemed to know. He grabbed his bag and yelled that he was going out. He didn't wait for his mom to reply.

The arcade was downtown, sandwiched between an old car part factory that had been shut down before Noah was born and a bar that always had motorcycles outside of it. [SYSTEM ERROR] held him close, talking loudly about the *arcade* and how it was owned by *Uncle Jacobi* until they reached the peeling paint of the double doors.

He pushed past her, throwing the doors open. The glow of endless arcade machines, the thrum of cheesy pop music, and the smell of popcorn made him breathe deeply, a smile on his face.

Home—*this* was home.

[SYSTEM ERROR] bought him a soda, even though he was only supposed to have them on Saturdays. The arcade screen lit up in time with Noah's smile, and soon he forgot about his dad's anniversary, the fight with his mom, and the fact that some nights the only way he could fall asleep was to cry until he couldn't feel anything anymore.

This is it, he had decided, cracking his knuckles as he slipped a token into *Knights of Eternity*. Today was the day he was going to beat her—his arch-nemesis, Zara the Fury.

Zara had fangs and claws and an ultimate spell called *Inferno* that totaled his party, even with Valerius as his avatar. He'd never managed to get past her third stage—what first act boss had *three* health bars?—but with a soda in one hand and a bag of tokens in the other, he was going to do it.

At least, that's what he thought.

He didn't think that anymore.

Now he wished he hadn't come to the arcade at all. He wished he'd told [SYSTEM ERROR] he was tired and just sat at the kitchen table and done his math homework. But he hadn't.

And now [SYSTEM ERROR] was lying on the ground, covered in blood.

The arcade was empty. Everyone but Noah and Adrian had run when the shooting started. Adrian had his phone in hand, and someone on loudspeaker—a man with a strong, stern voice like a teacher. The man was saying things like "check for an exit wound" and "put pressure on it," but the words and their meaning kept slipping past Noah.

Adrian held out a hand, yelling something about Noah's school sweater. It was a dark blue scratchy thing that was too small for Noah, let alone Adrian. Why did he want it? When Noah shook his head, confused, Adrian grabbed the edges of his sweater and yanked it over Noah's head. He folded it roughly, pressing it to [SYSTEM ERROR]'s chest.

Oh, Noah thought, remembering all the hospital programs his mom and [SYSTEM ERROR] liked to watch. *That's why*.

Adrian was telling him something but the words were mushy one second and too quick for him the next. His ears were still ringing long after the last gunshots had echoed through the empty arcade. With a frustrated sigh, Adrian grabbed Noah—spinning him around as he pointed to someone on the floor behind them.

Uncle Jacobi.

The big man with the big laugh and bigger hugs. Who always slipped Noah extra tokens at the arcade. Who cooked dinner for him and his mom whenever she was too sad. His white shirt, always clean and pressed, had two splotches of blood the size of Noah's palms on the back. They looked like drops of the red slushies Jacobi sold. He always said they were the best in the city.

"Damn it, Noah, check if Jacobi is breathing!" Adrian said, his voice suddenly too loud. Noah looked at Adrian with his floppy hair that was always styled with too much gel and his big smile that made [SYSTEM ERROR] sigh like a lovesick puppy. Only Adrian wasn't smiling now. His hands and t-shirt were covered in blood, and there was something wrong with one of his ears. Blood and strips of flesh hung from where it used to be.

Whatever Adrian saw on Noah's face made him stop. "I'm sorry. I'm sorry, you—you press down hard on this, okay? I'm going to check on Jacobi."

He grabbed Noah's limp and useless hands, forcing them onto the rough scratchy sweater. It felt wet and warm under his hands. He thought of the last time he saw his dad. How his dad had hugged him and whispered in his ear to look after his mom.

Tears sprang to Noah's eyes.

He stared at [SYSTEM ERROR]'s face. The little scar on her lip from where she'd fought pirates, or so she'd told him. The dimple on her right cheek that deepened when she smiled. He remembered how she'd moved in after the funeral. How she made chocolate and banana sandwiches for breakfast for him when his mom couldn't get out of bed. How she'd be waiting for him when she got home from school, even though she was supposed to be in class.

"Be okay," he whispered. "Please, be okay. *Please.*" It was a prayer, a wish, a *plea* to the universe to not do this, to not take his best friend away from him.

And then he saw something that made his hope vanish.

"Adrian. *Adrian!*" he screamed. "[SYSTEM ERROR] isn't breathing!"

Chapter Two

The sun was setting when they found the bodies. Streaks of red and orange cast long shadows on the Captain's Barracks—fresh scars from a long and bloody fight marking the stone and earth. When the Gilded Knights left the Ivory Keep in pursuit of the traitor Magnus, they'd gathered a small but impressive company of knights and mages. Many had fought with the Gilded Knights for years, aiding Navaros' finest warriors on countless missions. They had felt confident, some might even say arrogantly so, that they would be more than enough for a single rogue mage.

They were wrong.

Kilin was the only mage left. When Gabriel had chosen Farah, a master of illusions and obscura, to enter the barracks he'd been hurt. The castle was surrounded by Calix Rings, a complex barricade he'd studied intensively. Did Gabriel think he couldn't handle it? That he hadn't *trained* for this?

Then Merrin, Lazander's hawk and constant companion, had shown up at camp—squawking and flapping her wings in blind terror. And Kilin suddenly understood why Gabriel left him behind.

Knights clanked at his back, trying and failing not to crowd him as they rushed to the first of the six rings. He slapped his hands against the barricade, trying to focus on dispelling the magic as quickly as possible. But he kept getting distracted by the knights' whispering.

"… Magnus was alone, that's what the spymaster's shadows said…"

"… in the bloody hell happened in there?"

"… someone must be hurt. Or worse. Who do you think…"

He punched his fist through the Calix Rings, choosing brute force over subtlety as he flooded the barrier with magic. Had Gabriel suspected something would happen? That the mission would go wrong? It must be. Other than Gabriel, he was the only one who could get through.

He felt the knights at his back jump in surprise, and one of them, an older woman with hard eyes, laid a hand on his shoulder.

"Steady, Kilin," Mara said quietly. "We might need your magic inside."

He nodded stiffly, trying to quell the rapid-fire questions that plagued his mind. He needed to focus, but he couldn't stop picturing the horrors they'd find. Who, or what, could hurt the Gilded Knights?

***

They found Corym first.

Eighteen years of age, this had been his first mission with the Gilded Knights and his hero, Valerius. When not hanging on to the prince's every word, he'd pepper the others in the company with questions: How many hours did Valerius sleep at night? How did he take his breakfast? Did they think Valerius would ever spar with Corym, or would that be too much to ask?

Mara took her sword—a beloved weapon that had saved her life countless times. She drove it into the spot where they'd found Corym, running a finger along its edge, and pressed a bloodied index and thumb to her eyes.

"Gallow, God of Judgment, remember his sacrifice," she whispered.

They found Farah and Gabriel next.

Kilin was inconsolable, gripping the cold hands of his master and fellow student as he sobbed. He wouldn't leave, not even when the spymaster's shadows arrived to examine the bodies. It was only when one of them leaned down and broke their code of silence, whispering they would do whatever it took to get the bastard who did this, did Kilin nod and let the shadows take his friends away.

A stunned silence enveloped Marito's corpse.

His skull had partially caved from the fall from the tower, the spark of life, of mischief, gone from his eyes. Despite the blood that pooled about him, the knights kept expecting him to sit up and proclaim, "It is but a scratch, my good sers!"

He didn't.

Every knight in the company drew their swords—some hard-worn gifts from the Ivory Keep, others family heirlooms passed on for generations. They drove their blades into the thick, heavy soil that surrounded Marito, burying them deep to form a circle—a memorial for where the greatest of them had fallen.

No sword was driven into the ground for Valerius.

Kilin and his fellow knights searched the Captain's Barracks from top to bottom, but they could find neither sight nor sound of the prince. Nor the villain who had murdered their companions in cold-hearted blood.

For Magnus was gone.

They found a chair by an overflowing chamber pot, the smell strong enough to make Mara's eyes water. She picked up two lengths of frayed rope, turning them over in her hands. Snapping them outward, she measured them against her own chest and the arms of the chair. As she'd guessed, it was only enough to tie up someone slim… and with one arm—*Magnus*. The blood and spittle on the rope suggested he'd used his teeth to tear his bindings and escape. The chamber pot nearby, and the *stench* of it, suggested he'd been here for days.

But if Magnus had been bound when the Gilded arrived, who had killed them?

Answers followed questions Mara didn't want to ask, but she kept her thoughts to herself. She had bigger problems—such as figuring out how to get the only survivor to safety. Mara was no healer, but she'd been in enough fights and had seen enough friends die to know Lazander was fighting death itself—and he was losing.

His eyes roved behind closed lids as he twitched, skin boiling to the touch. His breath, usually strong and even, came in rapid fire bursts punctuated by long pauses that made Mara's heart freeze.

Kilin, eyes red and shaking, tried to help. Gabriel ensured all his students had at least a basic understanding of the healing arts, even if they had no affinity with them, but Lazander didn't wake, no matter what Kilin did.

Holding Lazander's head carefully, Mara drip-fed him a *Stabilizer*—cradling the bottle as if it were made of gold. Knights like Lazander were trained to resist magic, which allowed them to take down even the most power-hungry mage. The cost of this, however, was that healing magic had little, if any, effect on them.

Rare as dragonscale and twice as expensive, a *Stabilizer* was a potion designed to counter this. Handcrafted by Liddy, the Ivory Keep's finest healer, it flooded a knight's body with enough magic to kill most people.

Lazander choked on the clear liquid, struggling to keep it down, but Mara persisted. Kilin expected her to wait and see if the potion had any effect, but she was on her feet the moment the bottle was empty, snapping orders.

"The potion only buys us time," she said at his questioning look. "We need to get him back to Liddy—now."

Balancing care and speed, the knights dumped the contents of their singular cart on the side of the road, tossing bedrolls, cloaks, and blankets into the back as they made a makeshift bed for Lazander. Being cold and hungry was a small price to pay if it meant giving their brother a better chance at survival.

The company traveled day and night with Mara at the head, forgoing sleep as they drove themselves and their horses to the absolute limits.

Merrin kept constant watch. She settled in at Lazander's side, her eyes locked on her childhood friend, the man who had raised her since she was a hatchling. Kilin, half dead from tiredness, would drag himself from his horse the moment Merrin landed on his shoulder, squawking loudly at the slightest change in Lazander's condition. From temperature, to chills, to a cry of pain in his sleep, she alerted Kilin to everything.

Kilin had no idea how she was able to sense such things, but he promised himself that from now on, he was going to be kinder to all birdlife. There was something about her eyes—a sharp intelligence he'd dismissed until now, that spoke of a humanity many people lacked.

He knew the spymaster's shadows had arrived at the Ivory Keep first, despite staying behind to examine and transport the bodies of the fallen, because a short, dark-skinned woman with close-cut white hair and ruddy cheeks was waiting for them at the gates.

Liddy—head of the Ivory Keep's healing house.

***

Lidia, or Liddy as she was better known, had lived in the Ivory Keep for thirty-five years and been head of the healing house for twenty-three of those—ever since Prince Valerius was born. She'd helped deliver him, guiding the queen through a pregnancy that every doctor and mage this side of the kingdom told her she was mad to go through with. Liddy turned her nose up at every single one, claiming she'd never lost a child or a mother in all her years, and she wasn't about to start now. She was an old hand, and not known to panic, but even she trembled when she saw Lazander now.

"When did the fever start?" she said, leaping onto the cart before it came to a stop.

"He was feverish when we found him," Kilin explained, shocked at how nimble the old woman was—she must have been pushing seventy. "I feared the wound had become infected so I—"

"Stupid boy," Liddy barked, forcing one of Lazander's eyes open as she wiped a finger along his sweating brow, then brought it to her tongue. She winced. "He's been poisoned—it's a miracle all your pulling and hauling didn't kill him on the way."

"What?" said Kilin, taken aback.

"*Poi. Soned,*" Liddy said with exaggerated slowness. "Nope," she said, raising a finger when Kilin opened his mouth to protest. "I don't care what little flim-flam spell you did to check for poison—you did it wrong. *Boys!*"

Two boys, twelve-years of age if that, ran through the open gate—a stretcher held between them. Liddy snapped her fingers at two knights by the cart, and they jumped to attention as if the queen herself had commanded them. The knights carried Lazander from the cart to the stretcher, Liddy supporting his head the whole time.

"The Quiet Room," she said. "Go."

The boys nodded without a word, moving at a strange shuffle that let them run at almost top speed while barely jolting Lazander.

"How about you, precious?" she said, picking up Merrin gently in her arms. The hawk chirped weakly.

"What's her disposition been like?" Liddy asked Kilin. "Has she been eating?"

"I, uh, I don't know," Kilin said. "Don't they hunt on their own?"

Liddy glared at him with a look that would crack stone.

"I know Merrin. She didn't leave his side this whole time, did she?" Liddy asked. Standing in the cart, her normally diminutive form towered over the mage. His mouth opened and closed like a skewered fish being prodded with a fork.

"Well, no," Kilin admitted.

"So tell me, genius," she said, leaning in. "*When would she have had time to hunt?*"

"Uh."

"*Mages!*" she barked, rolling her eyes. "So busy with their heads up their arses they forget to open up their eyes and *look*."

"But Liddy, you're also a mage—"

She hopped off the cart, ignoring Kilin as she gently cradled Merrin.

"Don't you worry, precious," she cooed. "We're going to get you fed and watered, and then I'm going to set you up with a lovely nest of straw right by Lazander's bed."

Merrin chirped, her eyes closing for the first time in days.

The healer sighed, trailing her index finger delicately over the hawk's head. She didn't know what had happened at the Captain's Barracks, or who was strong enough to kill the famed Gilded Knights—nor was it her business to know. As a healer, her enemies were sickness and death, and she would do everything in her power to keep Lazander's soul from the Void and Gallow's judging eyes.

She only prayed it would be enough.

Chapter Three

H'tar village, home of the molger, was forever changed. Jerome lay unconscious, one of his six legs twitching as he wheezed through a broken nose, courtesy of Lenia. What was once a barn that could house twenty animals was now a shattered wreck of broken timber and hay. One of Jerome's lackeys was trapped within while the other lay knocked out cold.

Only a handful of people had been outside when I'd first entered the barn to confront Lukas. Convenient that all of H'tar now seemed to be here, I thought bitterly. Hours earlier I thought H'tar was nothing but a quiet village of hard-working falslings, shapeshifters who loved their community, and only wished to live in peace.

Now, I knew better.

Hypocrites, I thought, surprised at the ferocity.

These people had mocked, bullied, and tormented Lukas. They'd made it their life's mission to make sure he never forgot, not for one instant, that he was born of their enemies, the predators who'd driven them from the Moonvale Mountains—the vaxion. They'd happily stood by when Jerome tried to murder Lukas in cold blood. Lukas' crime? Transforming into a "mongrel"—a hybrid monstrosity he'd no control over.

The same people who'd bullied Lukas now looked at me with a mixture of fear, awe, and suspicion that made me want to slap every one of them senseless.

All of them, that is, except for Lenia.

She stood gigantic and beautiful in her molger form. With thick, coarse fur, six legs, and short talons made for digging, she looked like a cross between an SUV and a badger. Her son Waylen, also in molger form, huddled between her legs making adorable, high-pitched cries of relief as she nuzzled him.

Lenia had chosen to protect me—a near stranger. She'd risked everything to stop Jerome so I could help Lukas. She nodded to me calmly, trusting whatever came next. My chest tightened. I fervently hoped I hadn't just ruined her and Waylen's life.

Or Lukas'.

I winced, a broken rib (or three) sending shards of pain down my side. My head throbbed as if I were deep underwater, and a tidal wave of nausea hit me—a concussion I guessed, gingerly touching the back of my head. I wanted to lie down and let the world go dark, but I couldn't. Not yet.

I looked down at Lukas, whose eyes were shut, his misshapen hybrid form, still. It was a body at war with itself, from his blind, milk-white eyes to the bone-edged jaw that stuck out at awkward angles. It was a form ruled by bloodlust and anger.

And I had no idea if I had saved him from it.

"Come on," I whispered. "*Come on.*"

It began slowly at first. His jaw shortened, his wide snout flattening to narrow slits as dark tendrils of flesh poured from his skull, cascading down his back like vipers. His paws shrank as his limbs thinned and stretched, his body elongating as into the scourge of H'tar village, the enemy of the molger—a *vaxion*.

The crowd shifted, stepping back in fear, but I stayed where I was, a smile tugging at my lips. When I first saw Lukas' vaxion form in his mind, in his *tul'gra*, I was terrified. Now I saw beauty where there was ferocity, grace where there was cruelty. A woman shrieked, and I spun on the crowd, growling—the sound as natural to me as a sigh.

"He's not done," I said.

Lukas' bones snapped, bulging with girth as he expanded. His fur thickened, becoming coarse and bristled. Once slender limbs tripled in size, becoming the tree-trunks needed to hold up his large, powerful body. Fur lightened to a dust brown, and his snout grew and widened as his eyes shrank. Two tiny ears sprang from the sides of his head.

A molger. He was a molger again.

Lukas groaned, his mind and body struggling from multiple transformations. He'd shocked the crowd by changing from vaxion to molger, but I knew there was more to him. I'd seen his mind. Seen how he'd fought the bloodlust that screamed at him to kill. To murder all those who'd bullied and tormented him. Who'd made him, on his darker days, regret being born.

I knelt down, my hand disappearing into the thick fur around his neck. "Show them," I whispered. "Show them who you really are."

He shook his head, wincing in pain. I took one of his huge paws in my hands.

"You could have killed Jerome, hell—half of H'tar. Some would even say they deserved it," I said, thinking of Zara the Fury. "But you didn't—you fought it every single step of the way. You're the bravest, kindest, strongest person here. And I won't let these *idiots* say otherwise," I continued, shocked at how angry I felt. "Screw the molger. Screw the vaxion. *You* get to decide who you are."

With a grunt, his fur receded, slipping into his flesh as he halved in size, then halved again. His skin grew pale. Curly blond hair, at odds with the dusty-brown of his molger form and the sleek darkness of his vaxion, sprang from his head—dirtied and bloodied.

I remembered the beautiful blonde woman with a thick braid I'd seen in his mind. Remembered how she had turned away from a young Lukas, walking away as he cried out for her.

He was the image of his mother.

Blue eyes, bright and human, welled with tears and I was surprised to feel my own spill over. His paw gripped my hands as it shrank, his new jaw breaking with a sharp crack as it realigned with his human skull. In the moonlight, his skin looked pale and ghostly. He'd done it. He looked half dead, but he'd *done* it.

I threw my arms around him—hugging him tightly. We'd never spoken before, but in that moment I felt like I'd known him my whole life.

He slung one arm over my shoulders, hugging me back.

"Hell of a pep talk, lady," he said weakly, his last words before he fainted in my arms. I pressed two fingers to his neck, checking his pulse as my mother had taught me. A quick but steady throb pulsed beneath my fingers.

Relief sagged my shoulders, the expelling of tension letting me feel every cut, bruise, and broken bone in my body. But I couldn't stop smiling.

Lukas was human again. No one had died. And Jerome had gotten the crap beaten out of him by Lenia.

It was a damn good night.

"Moira, I need you on the injured!" I heard Chief call. "Gowan, dig Frell out of the barn—he's half buried in there. Lenia, change back into human form. Now don't you glare at me like that…"

The noises faded as I watched the rise and fall of Lukas' chest. Confident that he wasn't going to die anytime soon I allowed myself a small luxury.

My eyes fluttered closed as I hit the dirt, the soil beneath my cheek feeling like the world's softest pillow.

Chapter Four

The Calamity System Menu appeared—its gold edged outline now as familiar to me as the shallow darkness of my closed eyes. A pop-up appeared surrounded by gaudy, golden balloons and tiny pixels I guessed were supposed to be confetti. It read:

QUEST COMPLETED: STOP AERZIN

GRADE: A+

Much like when I had failed the tutorial, a series of small pop-ups, white against black, appeared. But they were no longer a rollout of every single way I'd messed up:

No NPCs killed—Bonus

Entered Aerzin's mind—Bonus

Unlocked Aerzin's additional forms—Bonus

Sustained minimal damage—Bonus

My broken ribs disagreed with that last one.

The pop-ups continued, too quick to follow as they stacked on top of the other. One, however, was a punch in the gut:

Aerzin survived—Bonus

I thought of the quest's title, *Stop Aerzin*. It was cryptic and could have meant anything from restraining him to even…

Killing him. I could have murdered him, and I would still have, technically speaking, completed the quest. The bonuses hinted that I could solve a quest in any number of ways and still pass, but without a cheat sheet next to me, or the internet at hand, how could I figure out the best route—the "golden path"? Or even what the game *wanted* me to do?

The only reason I realized Lukas and Aerzin were the same person—one his molger name, the other his vaxion moniker—was because I went into his mind—his *tul'gra*. "Aerzin" could have died before that, either at my hand or Jerome's. Would I have finished the quest but not received any bonuses? Or would I have gotten different bonuses, ones based on killing him?

I sighed, frustrated. This world was similar to the game *Knights of Eternity*, but the system was completely new to me. In the game the objectives were simple: clear the dungeon, kill the boss, and save the "damsel," Lady Eternity, from the bad guys—mainly me, Zara the Fury. Here, in the world, I was stumbling in the dark.

My stream of thought was broken by a new pop-up, one I had only seen on an arcade screen.

QUEST REWARDS

My heart leaped. These rewards could make or break a playthrough of *Knights of Eternity*. Completely randomized, you could get mythical armor, weapons, gold, or even one-time-use spell scrolls.

The Menu darkened, and I saw the rough outline of something circular beginning to take shape. I was suddenly a kid again, watching the arcade screen with my fingers crossed, whispering, "Please, please, please."

The image solidified, and I saw a long neck attached to a circular container. A tiny stopper plugged the top, and something thick and viscous clung to the glass within. I cheered—it was a health potion!

Other games let you buy or craft potions. Not *Knights of Eternity*. Things like jinny balm, which could heal minor wounds and slow the bleeding effect of severe ones, were relatively common. Health potions, on the other hand, could only be gained from clearing a level—or in this case, a quest. The most I'd ever received in a single playthrough was three. Often, I never got a single one.

Those playthroughs were disastrous.

As the reward window closed, I saw the health potion, which was called a *Healing Void* for some reason, move to my Inventory—the only thing in an endless series of item slots. If it was in my Inventory, that meant I could use it. I just had to figure out *how*.

The Menu dimmed once more.

Stones in an array of colors, from coral pink to blood red, appeared on screen. Some were rough, others polished to an eye-catching shine. My "bonuses" vanished into the new pop-up, and the stones increased in number.

CONGRATULATIONS: ADDITIONAL ABILITY STONE UNLOCKED

A large, polished pearl and a jagged purple rock were chosen seemingly at random and deposited into my Inventory. I didn't have time to wonder what that meant before the Menu continued.

NEW QUEST AVAILABLE
WOULD YOU LIKE TO PROCEED?

Excitement and frustration played tug-of-war. If my bonuses were anything to go by, I'd knocked it out of the park with my *Stop Aerzin* quest. I wasn't just playing the game anymore, I was finally *winning*. And while the goal was still to finish the game and get home, I was surprised at the spark of competitiveness I felt—I wanted to figure out the Calamity System, and I wanted to *beat* it. With its refusal to hold my hand as a player, and its quickness to punish failure, it was like nothing I'd ever played before.

Proceed, I thought.

NEW QUEST
MAKE THE WALLOW-TAIL SHINE

"… sigh."

***

Queen Firanta Abigail Alexandria Najar the Third did not falter. She'd faced down death threats and declarations of war with a raised eyebrow. A glance from her unseeing left eye made ambassadors and kings alike squirm more effectively than torture, but her hands shook as she read her spymaster's report.

"Four dead… including Gabriel and Marito," she said quietly, the barest hint of a tremble in her voice.

Thaddeus nodded. "And Lazander is gravely injured—the poison is like nothing Liddy has ever seen. She's working day and night just to keep him alive," he said, his four claws scratching against the carpets that coated the throne room floor. The spymaster rarely left the queen's side, happy to play the role of the loyal palace dog. Right now, however, he couldn't keep still.

"My son? Where is Valerius?" the queen asked, her voice a whisper.

"Not a damn clue." Thaddeus snarled, a throaty guttural sound. He immediately bowed his head. "Forgive me, my queen, I did not mean to—"

"I know. Is it possible that Magnus took him? Perhaps cloaked their escape with magic?"

The beast hesitated, wanting desperately for his queen to be correct. "Possible, yes. But evidence suggests that Magnus was bound to a chair for some time. Unless he had some assistance…"

"Could he have had it? Another rogue mage, perhaps, or a sword-for-hire?" the queen asked, aware her heart was speaking before her mind could.

Thaddeus trotted toward the queen, heavy with the burden of his words. "We've found no indication of anyone else being present. No tracks. No sightings. Nothing."

The queen's fingers crumpled the papers in her hands. "Two Gilded, living legends lie dead, and my son appears to have vanished into the night with a known traitor. Why?"

"We only have theories, my queen. Theories I don't wish to share…" Thaddeus trailed off, his husky growl fading to a mere whisper. "… for fear they would break your heart."

The queen was glad it was just she and Thaddeus in the throne room. Her husband, the king, would arrive fresh from the Navaros and Evergarden border, and he would want answers. Answers she didn't have.

Answers she wasn't sure she wanted.

She would play her part and be stiff and impartial, as was expected of a queen. But as the report fell to the floor, and she buried her face in her hands, she wasn't a queen anymore—she was a mother. A mother whose son was missing, a boy who had drifted from her over the years. Who had been cold, and distant, maybe even in pain.

And she hadn't done a damn thing about it.

Thaddeus, taken aback by how small and frail his queen suddenly looked, rushed forward, burying his wet nose in her graying hair. It ignored all protocol—wasn't proper for a queen and a spymaster. But she allowed herself to wrap her arms around him for just a moment, squeezing him tightly.

Then she sat up and brushed her eyes dry—as if nothing had happened.

"I asked you to look into Valerius and Lazander," the queen said, her red eyes the only sign anything was amiss. "I would like a full briefing, now if you can."

Thaddeus nodded and began his report with a heavy heart.

***

Incense burned—twilight blossom, for clarity. Eternity breathed deeply, the soft floral scent as comforting as a mother's embrace. A sparse meal of grilled vegetables and fried lamb's tongue, slaughtered under a full moon as Gallow decreed, lay partially finished on a low table before four men clad in white robes trimmed with gold. They knelt on thick, feathery cushions.

Eternity knelt on the stone floor in front of them. She had not been offered a cushion or any food.

"You're certain?" one of the sages asked, looking at Eternity over ancient steepled fingers. The other sages nodded in approval at the question.

Eternity fought not to roll her eyes.

"'Calamity has returned,'" she said, almost managing a civil tone. "Those were Gallow's words. I find little, if any, room for interpretation."

A sage with a sparse, patchy beard huffed. "We've been interpreting Gallow's signs and prophecies for many years, Lady Eternity. Let us do our work."

Eternity resisted the urge to laugh at his condescending tone. She looked at the wizened old men before her, most of whom hadn't set foot outside a temple in years, a thread of bitterness pulling at her heart. Sage was the highest of Gallow's honors, second only to head disciple. But in that moment, she couldn't help but think that if being a sage was truly about wisdom, insight, and years spent serving Gallow, then she'd be the only one sitting on those feathered cushions.

"We knew this day would come," she said instead, choosing to focus on the topic at hand. "This is what I and every Eternity who has come before me has been preparing for. It is why we have spent so many years searching for Champions. The Tyrant, the evil one, *Calamity*, has returned. Who knows how long it will be before its darkness descends once more? Until it splits the world in two, destroying—"

"The Heart," Patchy beard said sharply, raising a single eyebrow. "You had this 'vision' while using the First Eternity's Heart—something you did without knowledge, permission, or safeguards in place. There is every chance that what you saw was simply a *memory*. You were likely overwhelmed by the First's power—she is the greatest of Gallow's Chosen for good reason."

Eternity had the rare, but powerful desire to slap the sage.

"We don't doubt what you saw or heard," a third, Sage Dammon, said gently. One of the others coughed, but he ignored it. "But if we raise the alarm, as you have suggested, then we'll send not only all of Navaros, but Freyley, Evergarden, and every kingdom on the continent, into a panic."

A flash of anger surged through her, and she had to fight not to get to her feet. "Three thousand, four hundred and eighty-seven," she said quietly.

Sage Dammon frowned, glancing at the other sages, who looked just as confused.

"Three thousand, four hundred and eighty-seven," Eternity repeated. "That is how many people have sought Gallow's Judgment while I have acted as his Chosen. They threw themselves at his mercy, hoping and praying they had the strength, conviction, and *will* to become one of his Champions. His holy warriors."

Her fists clenched. "Three survived."

"Lady Eternity," the sparsely bearded one began, smiling as he would at a difficult child. "We appreciate how *difficult* it can be to wield his Judgment, particularly when someone fails, but that is not what—"

"I remember every face. Every name," she said, staring the sage down, "but I have not *once* shirked from my duty."

She stood, thousands of faces flashing before her eyes, some hopeful, some terrified, others screaming at her with hate as their skin crumbled to ash beneath her palm. "This, however, I cannot allow. I won't let their sacrifices be in vain because you refuse to act!"

A heavy hand clapped on her shoulder.

Eternity turned to find Champion Imani, her eyes as dark as her midnight armor.

"The Heart," she said, looking at the temple sages while she squeezed Eternity's shoulder, urging her to be quiet. "Allow Lady Eternity to use the Heart to contact the other Champions—Malik and Vivek should be made aware, if nothing else."

Dammon smiled, nodding warmly. "An excellent suggestion, Champion Imani."

"Only if she's accompanied to the Heart," Sparse beard cut in. "She's proven she can't be trusted with Gallow's holy artifacts."

"I'll escort her myself," Imani said.

Eternity bowed her head—guilt, shame, and anger stealing her words. She was led from the temple sages with Imani at her back, feeling like a naughty child who needed tending to.

Chapter Five

Time was upside down.

Life was death.

Sound was iron nails on skin, light an inferno that burned his eyes. Lying still was agony. Moving was agony. Breathing was agony. Lazander curled into a ball, his fresh stitches straining against the force with which he gripped his chest, but he couldn't stop. If he relaxed his hands, even for an instant, he was sure he would break apart and die.

On the third day, Liddy was forced to remove Merrin. Whenever Lazander whimpered in pain, the hawk would screech and fret with distress, and Lazander would groan in return at the sound, reaching out in the throes of fever for his friend. The healer publicly claimed that separating the two was best for their individual recoveries. While this was true, she had another reason.

She didn't want Merrin to see Lazander die.

It wasn't guaranteed, of course—death was a tempestuous mistress. She could knock on the door of Liddy's patients without a word of warning. Or she could sweep into the room after many promises, her arms open—her embrace warm. After decades of service, even Liddy couldn't always tell.

But as she slathered poultices, mixed potions, and used every ounce of her magic trying to remove the poison that ravaged Lazander's body, she knew it was an uphill battle. Lazander's fever would subside, and Liddy's heart would soar. She'd order a meaty broth, cooked with the bones of the sharp-toothed grindle for strength and the heavyset koa bear for stamina. Then she'd spoon it into Lazander—by brute-force if needed. He'd improve briefly, and she'd hope and pray they'd beaten it.

Then come morning the sheets would be stained with vomit, and Lazander would lie freezing and burning hot at the same time—utterly incoherent.

Liddy had never seen anything like it. It took everything she had just to keep him alive. She was sixty-eight years old, no spring chicken by her own admission, and while attendants half her age fell to exhaustion, she insisted on staying up and watching over him.

But even she had limits.

By the fourth night, Liddy knew she'd have to sleep or risk killing Lazander from sheer clumsiness. She sent everyone but the lone night attendant home, who would do the hourly rounds, checking on not just Lazander, but all the patients of her wards. Liddy knew she was dilly-dallying, but she couldn't force herself to go to bed, her mind racing with thoughts of the young knight. His fever had broken once again that morning, and his voice—raspy from days of vomiting—whispered only two words.

"Gab… Gabriel… Marito…"

Liddy had smiled, squeezing his hand.

"They took a battering, but they'll be just fine," she lied. "They're two rooms over from you."

He nodded, sighing with relief, then collapsed into a fitful sleep.

She didn't feel bad for lying to a patient. The truth could be a tonic or a cleaver—and the truth right now would surely extinguish whatever small spark of life Lazander still clung to.

"Right," Liddy muttered to herself, dragging herself from her bed where she'd been staring at the ceiling for an hour already. She busied herself prepping for the morning's shift—dumping dirty, sweat-stained towels into the laundry basket, scrubbing work tops, and mixing poultices. The rhythm of the familiar work helped quieten her mind, and soon the wards were spick and span.

She allowed herself one last patrol of her patients.

A mother and child lay sleeping in the eastern rooms—she'd had a difficult, laborious birth, and Liddy wanted to keep an eye on them both for a few days. A stable hand had gotten a vicious kick from an unruly horse, earning three broken ribs for his trouble. A smithy. A tailor. A husband. A daughter. In Liddy's wards, it didn't matter who they were, she'd sit with them, asking how they were feeling. Often their answers didn't change the treatment plan, but being listened to set a patient's mind at ease, which was as important to the healing process as neat stitches and clean bandages.

Finally she came to the Quiet Room. A single room far from the other wards, it earned the moniker for the deathly silence that enveloped it. With only a lonely bed at its center, it was unique in that, unlike the other wards, the walls were lined top to bottom with its own supply of herbs, salves, and potions in thin vials that her attendants knew better than to touch.

Liddy always took a moment at the Quiet Room's threshold, taking in its sterile white walls, so at odds with the warmth and comfort of her other wards. The crisp white sheets were bathed in grindle-venom—diluted, of course, but capable of eradicating any foreign substance on a person's skin. Pillows stuffed with spelled feathers from the royal family's own farrow, a many-winged bird that hunted prey twice its size, were designed to bring comfort and ease to even the most fitful sleepers.

Bundled within the venomous sheets and charmed feather pillows lay a hero to Navaros. At twenty years of age, he was the youngest to ever be awarded the honor of Gilded Knight. Soldiers bowed to him, children looked up to him, knights wanted to be him. But all Liddy could see was the smoke-marked child whose family died in a caravan fire so many years ago. A child she desperately wanted to save but didn't know if she could.

Dark shadows lined Lazander's eyes, and his sun-kissed skin looked pale and ghastly. Between his complexion and the shocking amount of weight he'd lost in just days, he was almost unrecognizable. That was the thing about sickness and death. It didn't matter if you were a peasant, a king, or a brave knight who was kind to everyone, from servants to stray dogs. It broke you down, stripping away everything until all that remained was a skeletal caricature of who you once were.

Liddy shook her head, banishing the melancholic thoughts as she pressed two fingers to the inside of Lazander's wrist, methodically counting his heartbeats. She lay a hand on his forehead, frowning slightly. Spelled thermosheets could gauge his temperature accurately, but Liddy was so attuned to Lazander she found it quicker to check the old-fashioned way.

Confident that her patient was stable, she allowed herself a rare yawn, feeling every year of her age as she placed an iron bell on his bedside locker. It hung freely from a small metal stand and lit up briefly when she snapped her fingers—activating the spells within. While the bell might be plain and uninteresting, the magic within was anything but. Spells to monitor temperature were woven around others that measured sound above a certain threshold. When these levels were reached the bell would ring, alerting the attendant of the patient's distress. She was so attuned to the sound, that even on the nights she slept next door to a patient, she'd bolt upright the moment the bell sounded.

"Don't you go dying during the night, my boy, you hear?" Liddy said, her harsh tone softened by the worry that lined her face. "Or I'll be mighty upset with you." She slipped out of the room, hoping she'd still have a patient to treat in the morning.

Hours passed. Shadows lengthened as the moon rose high into the sky and a silent darkness descended on the Ivory Keep. The nightly attendant did his duty, walking the halls with a small lamp he dimmed when entering the wards. He would approach each bed, check the patient for any signs of distress, and then move on to the next.

The Quiet Room was far from the wards, and he left it until last as usual. He'd never tell Healer Liddy, but he hated the stark, sterile room. It made the hair on the back of his neck stand on end, and tonight was no exception. He performed his usual checks with messy haste before walking quickly back to his post on the far side of the wards—happy to be done for the next hour.

The attendant, in his eagerness to leave, didn't see the unusual shadow by the window. If he'd taken a moment, he might have noticed that it stood in line with the moon's glow—an impossibility for any normal darkness. The attendant's footsteps faded down the corridor, and the shadow crossed the room swiftly, coming to a rest by Lazander's bed.

A hazy gleam shimmered. Armored feet appeared at the shadow's base, followed by battered sabatons stained with blood and dirt. A cloak, once as white as the full moon, was now gray and filthy. An ivory chest plate appeared, hairline cracks along its once pristine surface. Pitch black hair, greasy and tangled, framed a marble face marked by deep purple bruises.

Valerius reached out a hand to the bell that stood by Lazander's bedside locker, gripping it in a gauntleted hand. The Operator's quest flashed before his eyes with the quest that had made him turn on his brothers-in-arms. Made him drive a sword through Gabriel's chest and cut Marito to shreds.

END THE GILDED KNIGHT NPCS

He crushed the bell to smithereens.

Chapter Six

Having eyes on me made me want to squirm on the best of days. When those eyes belonged to falslings who dogged my every step and stared at me with fear and awe, my soul wanted to leave my body.

"This is too much," I stammered as a dark-haired woman handed me a basket of lemon-shaped fruit I'd made the mistake of saying I liked. I struggled to grasp the handle with one hand, the bundle of fine cloth and the pouch of coins I held in the other threatening to fall.

"Give her space, people, come on," Lenia said, shooing away the crowd. There were some grumbles and the odd person tried to linger, but a stern look from Lenia made them shuffle away.

Lenia glanced at me and the bundle of gifts I held awkwardly in my arms. A dagger slipped from my hands, clattering to the ground. "You'll fight falslings twice your size and turn a mongrel human, but Gallow help you if you're the center of attention."

Flustered, I said nothing.

Lenia nudged me playfully. "Come on, Chief wants to speak to you—oh big scary vaxion."

It'd been two days since that fateful night. Lukas, now human, had fallen into a coma-like sleep and rested under the watchful eye of Chief. The molger leader had been nervous that someone would "kick up a fuss." (He meant Jerome), but his fears were groundless. His head resolutely kicked in by Lenia, it took Jerome a while to wake up. When he did, groggy in his gigantic molger form and itching for a fight, Chief had swatted him on the nose and told him to use his eyes.

Jerome took one look at the man he'd just tried to kill. His eyes went wide as he saw Lukas, lying still, peaceful, and very much human.

Silent, Jerome walked away. His two lackeys, unable to form a coherent thought without their leader about, followed suit.

Only Jerome's wife said anything. She appeared at the door the next day with a knitted blanket for Lukas and a freshly baked pie for me. Before I could say anything, she handed me the gifts, bowed her head, and left.

She wasn't the only one.

People didn't seem to know what to do with me. Some thanked me, others stared, but most hung back—watching me with suspicious eyes. One even spit on the ground when I approached, running only when Lenia growled at him.

Lenia, a widow who'd once been treated like an outcast, was now greeted with respectful nods and warm smiles. I guessed seeing her beat the stuffing out of Htar's three toughest molger helped her reputation.

Which reminded me.

"Your molger form?" I asked, still grappling with armfuls of gifts. "It's *gigantic*—bigger than anyone else's. What decides how *big* you get when you transform? Age seems to be a factor, Waylen's is tiny—and adorable. But I can't figure out anything beyond that."

"Short answer? We don't know," she said, taking the cloth from me and folding it—a typical mom. "Longer answer, there's lots of theories. The most popular is it has to do with our internal magic—the more we have, the bigger we get. I know one of them fancy pants mages from the Ivory Keep did a bunch of studies on falslings, mainly the vaxion, of course, but that was back when you wouldn't get your throat ripped out for setting foot in the Moonvale Mountains."

A passerby jumped to help me carry my things, but Lenia shooed her off with a wave, barely pausing. "The problem with the magic theory is that a falsling's form can change in size. It's rare, but it happens. While I'm no mage, even I know that the magic you're born with is the magic you die with. I've only seen it once, mind you."

"Where? In H'tar?"

"Yeah," she said, dodging teens on their way to the fields, worn, well-polished tools in hand. They were clutching their sides, laughing so hard at a story one of them was telling, they were crying. I smiled, feeling an odd sense of déjà vu.

Chief's house appeared, sturdy and welcoming. A curl of smoke twisted from the chimney that led to his forge. "Chief's molger form is half the size it used to be," Lenia said.

I opened my mouth to ask why but stopped at the dark look in her eyes. She smiled in apology. "Sorry, I'm so used to not talking about this stuff that I clam up. His son, Gerald was… well, what happened to Lukas happened to him. 'Blood-spiked,' we call it. *Some* people think it happens when 'bloodlines' are mixed, which is a load of pig ears."

I thought of Jerome accusing Chief's wife of infidelity, claiming she'd slept with a vaxion.

"Someone might be fine one day, and the next their scent changes. They get angry easily—Gerald threatened his dad with a hammer over doing the dishes. It gets harder and harder for them to turn molger. And then…" She snapped her fingers. "They're mindless, bloodthirsty machines that are neither vaxion nor molger—but something in-between. A mongrel." She shivered, and I imagined her watching Waylen every single day, praying she saw no sign of it.

"When we founded H'tar, we decided we didn't want to be like the vaxion. We wanted to give people a choice. When Lukas was on the brink of turning, he chose to leave. But Gerald…" She sighed, looking years older. "He was his father's son. He chose to die rather than turn. And Chief insisted on doing it himself."

I could only stare at her in horror.

"He… his own son?"

She nodded. "That's Chief—never asks of others what he wouldn't do himself. But it cost him. I've only seen him change once since, and it's… not what it used to be. He stays human these days."

"Food's on!" Chief called from the front door, rubbing an oil-splattered cloth over oil-splattered hands. "Zara, a few more gifts have been dropped in for you. Do you want…" His gray-flecked brows furrowed at us. "You two look spooked. Did Jerome give you any trouble?" His hand drifted to the hammer in his blacksmith's apron.

"We're just famished," Lenia said, recovering first. She stepped in front of me, giving me a second to compose myself as she walked into the house.

"Good," he said, gesturing to me. "In you go, Zara, before Waylen eats me out of house and home."

***

When Chief told Lenia and me we needed to have a "talk," I thought the worst. There were no police or prisons here, but the molger were still big on rules—and punishing those who broke them. Lenia and I had collapsed a barn, left three people concussed, and probably traumatized half of H'tar.

It was a big part of why I'd stuck around. I didn't tell Lenia, but I was afraid she'd get the blame once I left, and I refused to let her be exiled or sentenced to toiling fields for the rest of her life because H'tar was afraid to punish me.

I should've given Chief more credit.

"Two weeks hard labor for you and Jerome both," Chief said to Lenia. "I was sure he'd push back on it, but he just nodded and said, 'You know what's best.'" The older man laughed, rubbing a hand through his hair, which was still oil-stained even after washing up. "While I don't condone you knocking him out cold," he said to Lenia, his voice stern even as his eyes sparkled, "I can't say it wasn't effective."

He cleared his throat, solemnly asking her, "Is this fair?"

"More than, Chief," she replied. "I was sure Waylen and I would be packing up and leaving, so I'm hardly going to complain about field work."

"And me?" I blurted out, unable to keep quiet.

Chief looked surprised. "You'd allow yourself to be punished by us?"

I shrugged. "Well, I did the same as Lenia—worse, even."

Chief laughed, shaking his head. "I pray I never meet another vaxion, you've ruined me. But no. You're no molger. I've no authority over you, nor do I ask for it. Besides, Lukas is alive and... unique, because of you. It's nothing short of a miracle—one I'd wished we'd known was possible long ago." He sighed, the only hint of grief in the eyes he dropped to the table.

If Lenia hadn't told me about Gerald, I doubt I'd have noticed. "But that's not fa—"

"It's more than fair," Lenia cut me off with a nudge. "If two weeks is all I have to pay for the joy of kicking Jerome's head in, I got a bargain."

Chief coughed. "I am going to pretend I didn't hear that."

"What about..." I trailed off, eyes drifting to the sleeping form on the far side of the room.

A thin curtain split Chief's workshop in two, a tattered thing that let the light in. The shape of a sleeping man, as still as death, was silhouetted against it.

I'd checked on him this morning, and again before dinner, but nothing had changed. His pale forearms were still tucked in against his body, like a corpse at a funeral. His eyes were sunken, dark shadows marking his face. Someone, Chief I guessed, had carefully wiped him free of dirt and gore and what I'd thought was blond hair was actually closer to white-gold.

It was hard to believe the new scars that lined my forearm had come from his fangs.

"Lukas is under my protection," Chief said, his hand drifting to his hammers. "And I'll watch over him until he wakes."

"And if he doesn't?"

"I've had to discipline that kid more than any other molger," Chief began. "It was the usual stuff—skipping out on chores, running away, getting into fights, that kind of thing. Most kids, a day or two of hard labor, and I won't hear a peep out of them again. Not Lukas."

Chief nodded at Lukas. "I had that boy herding cows, cracking rocks, patrolling the town—even made him skip a meal or two, a nightmare for a falsling. He'd nod, say he was sorry, and then go right back to causing hassle." A broad smile crinkled his eyes. "He has a tongue like a whip and was quick with his fists when that didn't work—he's a fighter. He'll wake, of that I've no doubt."

He shrugged, looking uncomfortable. "Besides, it's the least I can do after how we treated him."

In Lukas' mind, I'd seen and heard what the villagers had done to him—how they'd isolated him, treated him like a sore, a *disease*. But I hadn't seen Chief in those memories. I nodded, trusting him to look after Lukas.

"What about you?" Chief said. "You're welcome to stay here for as long as you need. But I doubt a life among the molger is what you're after. Magnus is still out there, and from what you've told me, he doesn't seem like the forgiving sort."

I thought of the hate I'd seen in Magnus' eyes and of his warning as I'd flown away with Lazander and Valerius. "*You will return, Zara. And you will beg for my forgiveness,*" he'd said, every word a threat and a promise.

No—he wasn't the type to move on, but I had something else to take care of first.

"Strange question," I said, studiously examining my fingernails. "Do you have any idea what a 'wallow-tail' is?"

Chapter Seven

Valerius stared down at Lazander, his mind racing. He could hardly believe that days ago they were laughing and joking on the road as they traveled together to defeat Magnus, the "rogue mage."

He'd planned everything to the finest detail. Tracking Magnus down after Zara had burned his arm to a crisp had been child's play—the man had clearly never been on the run before. It had taken him only hours to find a "hooded man with a missing arm" in a roadside tavern a day's ride from his estate, hiding in the most lavish room like an injured animal. Carting him to the Captain's Barracks had been more difficult—he'd needed several of the spymaster's shadows, and it had taken more bribes and threats than usual. Some of them were wavering, he knew.

The mage he'd hired, a disgruntled former palace mage with a vendetta against the Ivory Keep, had cost a small fortune, but it had been worth it. The Calix Rings ensured that only a small number of the Gilded's entire company could enter the barracks.

But all that time, effort, and money had been for nothing.

Everything had gone horribly wrong. So wrong that Valerius' life, and his role as a prince and defender of the Navaros, was in jeopardy. But maybe there was a way to finish the quest, keep his reputation, *and* save Lazander's life. He looked at his brother-in-arms and the slow rise and fall of his chest.

This wasn't real, he sternly told himself, words that had become a constant mantra in the past few days. Lazander wasn't real—none of these people were real. Just kill Lazander and finish the damn quest.

"Wake up," he said instead, unable to stop himself from trying to do the right thing, one last time.

Lazander didn't move.

"Wake up!" Valerius hissed, slapping Lazander hard.

Lazander jerked awake with a groan, cradling his cheek.

"You're going to shut up and do exactly what you're told," Valerius hissed.

The red-haired knight stared up in utter shock and then, to Valerius' surprise, nodded.

"You've been poisoned with the venom of a stonebreaker, a rare beast found only in the Moonvale Mountains. No one but myself and the vaxion have access to it and its venom. Even if a knight were to ride day and night, talk their way into an audience with the vaxion, and miraculously walk away with the antidote, you will be long dead before they return. You have two days left, perhaps three, if I'm being generous."

Valerius waited for Lazander to protest—to condemn him for murdering Marito and Gabriel, but the young knight said nothing. He simply stared at Valerius, eyes alight with hatred. It stung, but Valerius forced himself to continue.

"I and I alone have the antidote," Valerius said. "So this is what's going to happen. I will show up tomorrow with Magnus in tow. I chased after him when you attacked and murdered Gabriel and Marito at the Captain's Barracks. When I arrive, you will confess to working with Magnus and conspiring to murder the Gilded Knights. And—" he said, raising a finger for emphasis. "You will publicly *resign* from the Gilded Knights. That is the most important part. Do you understand?"

Lazander's fists curled around crisp white sheets—Valerius was surprised he could even move. The hunter still had some fight in him. "That will never work—" Lazander began, but Valerius cut him off.

"In return. You'll save your life… and the queen's."

Lazander's brow furrowed. "What do you mean? What's going to happen to the queen?" He sounded panicked, scared even.

"Either confess to conspiring with Magnus, or…" Valerius gripped his sword for emphasis, proud that his hand didn't shake. "I'll drive my blade through her heart." What little blood was left in Lazander's face drained until a ghost stared back at Valerius.

"The king will follow," Valerius continued. "You, Marito, and Gabriel weren't enough to stop me and neither will a handful of decrepit knights, starry-eyed mages, and that vile beast of a dog."

"Thaddeus is more than he appears," Lazander whispered.

"I know he's the spymaster. It's obvious to the point of it being painful," replied Valerius. "Several of his shadows will back up *my* story—they've already been briefed. You simply need to play your part."

"His own shadows turned against him?"

Valerius smiled. "Coin does wonders. As does drowning a grandmother or two."

Lazander looked away, and Valerius thought he heard the faintest growl, but when the knight looked back he was calm. "I'll be executed for this."

"It's that or die from a poison that liquifies your insides as we speak. Which is more important, your reputation or the lives of the king and queen you swore to serve?"

"She's more than a queen," spat Lazander. "She's your *mother*." He looked on the brink of leaping from his bed—an impossibility, given his condition. But as he stared at Valerius with a burning rage he'd never seen, Valerius was forced to look away first.

"I'll kill everyone in this stupid, godforsaken world if I must," Valerius snapped, drawing a sharp dagger from his belt. He pressed it against Lazander's neck, who didn't so much as flinch.

"No more questions," Valerius said. "Do we have a deal?"

Lazander's eyes were narrowed slits, but his voice was steady. "Can I see it?"

"What?"

"The antidote—if you have it, I want to see it."

Valerius hesitated, glancing at the knight's thin, weak body, and his pale, shadowed eyes. He decided to risk it.

Mentally accessing his Inventory, a glow appeared in his free hand. Seconds later, the outline of a vibrant orange potion appeared, solidifying when he gripped it.

"It's the only one this side of Navaros," said Valerius. "Now do we have a deal or not?"

Lazander stared at the potion in his hands. "Curious," he said, "you can use magic—an impossibility for a knight of your caliber, *and* it's a kind I have never seen. Is this Magnus' doing, or have you tampered with sorcery beyond that traitor's ken?"

Confused, Valerius faltered, the dagger at Lazander's neck wavering. He'd seen Valerius use the Inventory before, so why…

Valerius realized his mistake a second too late.

Fangs as sharp as they were deadly burst from Lazander's mouth as he bit down on the dagger. With a lurch, he pushed himself out of the bed, throwing his full weight at Valerius as he reached for the knight—

Or more accurately, the potion bottle.

Panicked, Valerius tried to vanish the potion and summon another weapon, but they hit the ground hard right as his hand began to glow.

The bright orange bottle slipped from his fingers, clinking against the stone floor. The glass miraculously held as it rolled away, disappearing into the shadows.

Lazander's jaw lengthened, his fangs now long enough to nick Valerius' fingers as he shook the dagger in his mouth like a rabid dog. Claws burst from the red-haired knight's hands, and he swiped at Valerius' neck.

The prince raised his arm just in time, claws scratching harmlessly off Valerius' armor.

Back in the Captain's Barracks, Valerius had worn the illusion of a Freylen soldier, draining himself of his magic in the process. When he'd failed to kill his fellow knights, he'd had to rely on his weapons and armor to fight. But it had been days since then, and while Valerius was exhausted, his magic was anything but.

Fire coated his body like oil on water, erupting from his skin with a whisper. Lazander howled, leaping back, clawed fingers frantically patting down the flames that licked his skin.

Valerius leaped to his feet, his dagger vanishing in a glow of light as he summoned his sword and shield, the emblem of the royal house, the farrow, looking silver in the moonlight.

"I underestimated you, *Thaddeus*," Valerius said, projecting confidence even as his mind scrambled.

Stupid mutt, I'm screwed! Crap, crap. Crap.

"And I you, *Prince*," the spymaster hissed, his face a misshapen mess of Lazander's eyes and hair mixed with the monstrous jaw of a beast. "Why? Why betray your brothers-in-arms, your *own mother*? What could you possibly gain from working for Magnus? From kidnapping Eternity?"

"I don't *work* for Magnus—that festering toad is tied to a tree and cursing my name as we speak," he said, fighting the urge to explain everything. "I serve... someone else. Someone who doesn't take kindly to failure."

"Who?" Thaddeus asked, leaning forward, nearly drooling with the need to know.

"You'd call me insane, then hang me for treason," Valerius said, gripping his sword, furious with himself. Why hadn't he just driven his sword into "Lazander" and been done with it? Why had he hesitated?

The spymaster smiled. "True. But I'll see your head on a spike for this either way."

Fur and fang erupted from his skin as he transformed into his true and hideous form.

Chapter Eight

"I know you have to go," Lenia said, rolling her eyes. "But is sneaking out in the dead of night really necessary?"

The moon was large and full. All of H'tar lay still. The broken wood and scattered hay of the barn had been cleared, the dirt paths of the village swept clean. It was hard to imagine Lukas and I had nearly died here just days ago.

"You've seen how… weird people are around me," I said, fiddling with the straps of the pack I'd already adjusted. "Half of them still hate me, and the rest…"

Lenia's teeth flashed white in the darkness. "Treat you like some kind of godsend—the magical vaxion who saved Lukas. Yeah, fair point."

"I left notes for Chief, Waylen, and Lukas."

"I know—I'll make sure they get them."

I stood, my chest twisting as I stared at Lenia—her dark hair, her tired, bright smile. Other than Eternity, she was the first person in this world who'd been kind to me. She'd dragged me, half dead, through a forest and nursed me back to health. Had risked her life, and her son's, to help me save Lukas.

The words "thank you" didn't really cut it, but I had no idea what else to say. "Thank—"

She stepped forward, wrapping her arms around me in a fierce hug. I stood blinking like a goldfish before hugging her back, my head dropping to hers. Her skin was so hot, it felt like hugging a furnace. A warm, comfortable furnace.

"Don't get killed," she said, her words half muffled against my chest.

I laughed. "I'll do my best, and if Jerome steps a toe out of line…"

"I'll let you know," she said, stepping back with a smile. "So you can come watch me kick his ass again."

"You better."

"Go on," she said, shooing me away. "I've packed enough food to last you three or four days and some jinny balm and a few other bits too."

"Thanks, *Mom*." I smiled, raising my hand in farewell. I turned my back on the H'tar, knowing I'd probably never see her, Waylen, Chief, or Lukas ever again. Not if I wanted to do the Operator's quests and get the hell out of here.

Tears pricked my eyes at the thought.

I didn't look back as I left, but I knew Lenia watched me until I vanished into the forest.

***

Waylen stared out the window at the disappearing Zara. He thought she was a bit weird for leaving at night, but he liked her for saving Lukas so he wasn't going to complain. He was idly wondering if this meant he and his mom would move out of Chief's house and get a place in the village like she had promised when a voice interrupted him.

"And where, pray tell, does she think *she's* going?"

He froze, scared that if he looked behind him it'd turn out to be a dream. But excitement and curiosity got the better of him, and he spun to see a sleepy looking blond head peering out the window beside him. Purple shadows made sharp crescents under his eyes, and he smacked his lips like he tasted something foul, but there was no mistaking it.

"Lukas?"

A crooked smile greeted him as Lukas wrapped an arm around Waylen, ruffling his hair. "Hey big guy, what did I miss?"

***

Eternity grabbed a pillow, pushed her face into it, and screamed.

"*Short-sighted, blithering, ignorant—*" were some of the words Imani could make out from Eternity's muffled screams. They were back in the Ivory Keep's towers once more where Eternity's bedroom sat at the top of one of the tall, spindly columns of rock.

The Champion said nothing. When Gallow had ordered her back here after years in Freyley, he'd whispered only two words in her ear—Protect Eternity. And so, while Lady Eternity vented her frustrations, Imani stood to the right of the door, one hand resting on the hilt of her sword. Her eyes were trained on the singular window in the room—a security hazard she'd have bricked over but for Lady Eternity's protests. She listened hard for the creak of unwelcome footsteps on the staircase, the heavy breath of a stranger, anything that could give her an extra second against an attacker. She was so focused that she missed that Lady Eternity had calmed somewhat and raised her head from the pillow. "—think, Imani? About my vision?"

Imani glanced at Eternity out of the corner of her eye. She was Gallow's power made flesh and the closest thing this world had to a real-life god. Imani should feel only respect and reverence when she looked at her, and most of the time, that was true. But sometimes Imani yearned to reach out and *slap* the girl. Eternity, for all her years of service, had a habit of forgetting one simple fact.

She wasn't human.

Gallow demanded three things: honor, obedience, and *sacrifice*. Yet humans acted like their little shrines and meek offerings to the God of Judgment were all it took to earn his favor. In truth, they hoarded coin, drank themselves stupid, and would throw their own mothers to a horde of ripperbacks if it meant saving their skins. Humans acted like Gallow was a fanciful idea rather than the only reason any of them were even breathing. Even the temple sages, these so-called "experts" on Gallow, who waxed poetic about strict diets and endless hours of penance, didn't understand. At the end of the day, they could strip off their ridiculous robes and walk out the door without so much as a backward glance.

Imani had no such choice.

As Champion, she'd been blessed with a new life and god-like powers. But such power came at a price, one she paid with every breath. Imani was bound to Gallow's will, her duty to him more than just an obligation—to lift a hand without his blessing drew his ire, to defy him a thought so monstrous she dared not even think it. Every moment of Imani's life was defined by Gallow's orders. To the Champion, however, this was no burden. She'd happily cut out her eyes and swallow her tongue if it meant keeping this world safe from the Tyrant. In all her years of service, Gallow had never steered her wrong, proving time and again that his will was absolute, his judgment flawless.

Eternity was bound by the same rules, yet she still dared to take matters into her own hands. Using the First's Heart without permission might have seemed like a small slip up to the sages, one that merited childish admonishment, but to Imani it was akin to spitting at Gallow's feet. And while the Champion knew better than to question why Gallow himself hadn't punished Eternity, that didn't mean she was going to coddle the girl.

"You should get some rest. I'm told using the First's Heart can be strenuous," Imani said. Bright blue eyes stared into hers, and for a moment, Imani was sure the Chosen would argue. But she simply dipped her head, clutching her pillow to her stomach. Imani was at the door, preparing for another sleepless night patrolling the tower when Lady Eternity called out.

"Any word from Lazander and the other Gilded?" Lady Eternity asked suddenly. "Have they captured Magnus yet?"

Imani was silent for a long moment. The truth of what had happened to those boys who played at being knights would crush her. But then she reasoned Lady Eternity's attachment to the Gilded Knights had always been unhealthy. Perhaps this would help her focus on what was important.

"No," Imani began, "they have not. Nor will they…"

Chapter Nine

Liddy was supposed to be sleeping, but her eyes were stubbornly open. She sighed, straining her ears for the clash of swords, a cry of pain—any sign of what might be going on in the Quiet Room where "Lazander" lay unprotected. She knew it was pointless. Her wards lay on the other side of the castle, far from where she was hidden away with her patient. If the sounds of battle were loud enough to reach her here, she'd have far bigger problems.

The old healer had learned the hard way that she had a finite bank of compassion. She couldn't worry about her patients *and* Navaros politics at the same time, so she kept her nose out of the latter. The kingdom could be at war, soldiers kicking down her doors, and she'd only care long enough to make sure she had enough jinny balm and bandages in stock, but when the queen came to her for help, how could she refuse?

"Bet they're making an absolute ruin of my nice clean wards." Liddy sighed, knowing her patient couldn't answer. The red-haired knight on the bed was still breathing, but it was frighteningly shallow. Sweat gathered on his brow, yet he shook hard enough for his teeth to chatter.

"Will he live?" a voice asked, the soft sigh of steps punctuated by the clink of a cane on stone. A woman stood at the door, her gray-streaked hair unbound—a rarity. Dressed in an intricate royal blue cloak over her night clothes, she wore no socks, not even slippers, and stared at the sleeping knight with a frightening intensity.

"Firanta," Liddy said, shooting to her feet. "What in the bloody hell are you doing here?"

***

The healer looked over the queen's shoulder and hissed in fury. "You should be under lock and key in the bloody safe room! For the love of Gallow, woman, I don't need to end the night nursing you back from the brink of death too."

The queen smiled at Liddy's outburst. No one, bar her husband, dared speak to her like that, and even he watched his tone more carefully than Liddy. "How could I sleep knowing Thaddeus was risking his life to see if he was right and that my own son is a traitor?" the queen asked quietly.

Liddy opened her mouth to argue, then sighed. "Well, come in then," Liddy said, gesturing roughly to a chair. "You shouldn't be wandering about in bare feet."

"It helps me keep my balance on these floors," the queen replied, dipping her head in thanks as Liddy bustled behind her, locking the door.

Not that that would stop Valerius.

They were in a makeshift ward far from the Quiet Room where Thaddeus lay in wait for Valerius, alongside a host of soldiers and mages hidden in the corridors. The queen and Thaddeus had sat together, pouring over the reports on the Captain's Barracks and come to the conclusion that such a carefully planned attack was no act of insanity. Whoever was responsible for it, be it Valerius or an unknown enemy of Navaros, there was every chance they would return to finish the job.

And if they did, Thaddeus would be ready.

The queen appreciated that Thaddeus had entertained the idea it was someone else—as if someone powerful enough to cut down the Gilded Knights was an everyday occurrence. But she knew in her heart it was her son.

When Valerius threw Zara from Lazander's dragon, no doubt killing the falsling, he'd told the queen he suspected Zara and Magnus of carrying out several high-profile assassinations. It was a lie designed to distract the queen. It had worked—the queen's focus turned from him. For the queen's greatest weakness was that she considered every possibility.

It was also her greatest strength.

She bid her spymaster to investigate Lazander and Valerius both. The queen expected their reports to come back cleaner than Liddy's wards.

Only Lazander's did.

Reading Valerius' report felt like learning about a stranger. A man who crept out of the castle like a thief in the night. Who seemed to vanish into thin air as if by magic—an impossibility, she would have once claimed. A hand-carved toy, typical of a vaxion child, was found hidden beneath the floorboards. But what was most damning were the payments Thaddeus discovered to a rogue mage, a known enemy of Navaros. That alone would result in a trial, but that wasn't enough for her spymaster. He wanted to catch Valerius in the act, to prove beyond doubt he'd turned his back on his kingdom, his country—even his own family.

The queen agreed to his plan, hoping with all her heart that her spymaster was wrong. Something he'd never been.

It was why she'd personally asked Liddy for help. The healer had delivered Valerius, had been the first to hold him when he opened his mouth and screamed bloody murder. She'd laughed alongside Firanta when he'd taken his first steps and quietly gripped the queen's hand when Valerius donned his Gilded armor for the first time. It was only fitting she be here too, on the night when the son she knew, the son she loved, might die—in spirit, if not in body.

"Will he live?" the queen asked again, nodding at the weakened Lazander.

Liddy sighed, and that alone told the queen enough.

"The boy has no family, aye?" Liddy asked, loudly clattering about as she brewed tea (lemon piscot with a hint of honey, just as they both liked it). The methodical act of heating the inside of the pot and spooning the leaves in was a comfort to them both.

"Indeed. They died in a fire on their way to the Ivory Keep."

"Good," Liddy said, handing a cup to the queen, who was taken aback at the healer's words. "He'll go tomorrow. Maybe in the morning. And I pity any parent who lives to see their kid like this." She nodded at Lazander, who whimpered gently.

The queen looked at the knight her son had tried to kill, her mind awash with pain and possibility. And then she heard it—an unmistakable howl that made the hair on the back of her head stand on end.

"He's here," she whispered. "Valerius is here."

***

Thaddeus howled, the sound ricocheting off the stone walls, growing in rage and intensity as Valerius fought not to clamp his hands over his ears. Skeletal limbs, two a piece, shot out from either side of Thaddeus' ribs, the soft smack of flesh following as muscles and cartilage wove around the limbs anew. There was a crack as his spine snapped, elongating and growing. Flesh the color of iron-rich soil slithered over his body like oil.

Valerius knew he should attack. Knew that mid-shapeshift was the perfect chance to drive his blade through the creature's heart, but he could only stare in horror. He'd known for years Thaddeus was the queen's spymaster and a falsling in disguise, but it was one thing to know and another to see the blood-slicked flesh, to hear the crack of bone. His stomach churned in disgust. He waited for Thaddeus to drop to the ground on four paws.

He never did.

That was when Valerius realized he'd never stopped to wonder *what* the spymaster transformed into.

The creature was impossibly large, the top of its head brushing the ceiling of the ward. It was at least twice Valerius' height, its mottled skin stretched over the six arms that burst from its sides. A human torso led to two legs coated in thick fur the same color as its skin and a set of vicious hooves that looked hard enough to crush a man's skull. Ebony horns protruded from either side of the falsling's head, curving over its skull and down its back like a gazelle.

But it was the face that made Valerius' breath stop. A strong angular chin framed by cheeks sharp enough to cut marble. Large eyes, ringed by crimson, sat beneath thick furrowed brows. His face, *Valerius'* face, glared at him with unbridled hatred.

"What the hell are you?" Valerius whispered. He knew he should open the Calamity System Menu and access the Bestiary, but he didn't want to take his eyes off the monster for a *second*—he knew it would mean his death.

"You were wise to guess I was the spymaster. But you were wrong to believe me a mere 'falsling.'" Thaddeus idly flexed his fingers, his long needle-like claws piercing the fleshy tips. "I am old—older than the Ivory Keep. Older than Navaros. Older even than the Moonvale Mountains. As for the 'what'—well, that is unpronounceable to you, despite that silver-tongue."

He raised a hoof, stepping forward. Though his gait was light, and surprisingly elegant, the stone cracked where his hoof met the floor, spiraling outward.

"Why—why do you look like me?" Valerius hissed, raising his shield as his body took over, dropping automatically into a defensive stance. The monster smiled and held up his arm, twisting it in the moonlight as if showing it off. With a *squelch* of a hammer on flesh, the arm shot into his body, then burst through his stomach with a sickening crunch. The arm reached for Valerius, fingers wriggling in a "come hither" gesture. The knight bit his lip to stop himself from dry heaving.

"My flesh is clay—I can bend it to my will," Thaddeus said with a smile that revealed he knew *exactly* the effect his shapeshifting was having on Valerius. The spymaster's arm sucked back into his stomach with a *slurp*, erupting from his shoulder. "This is my *chosen* form—something no one alive today, bar the queen, has ever seen." He gestured to his face. "I thought it apt that the monster that spells your end should be none other than *yourself*."

Valerius' chin dipped, his shoulders shaking. Thaddeus stepped forward with a feral grin, but the prince didn't move. Instead he threw back his head and *laughed*. It was a harsh, raucous sound. "Oh, this is good. Well played!" Valerius yelled, voice echoing off the walls. "You haven't given me a decent boss battle in a while! Nicely done, Operator, *bravo*."

The spymaster blinked in confusion, eyes darting around the room. "But it won't work!" Valerius continued, voice thrumming with anger. "This isn't real, *none* of it is—and cheap tricks aren't going to stop me!"

"I thought you merely a traitor. I see now that was too simple." Thaddeus extended all six of his arms, haloing his body in a vicious circle of death. "You're *insane*. I planned to take you alive—the queen wanted to speak to you, one last time. But seeing you like this will only cause her pain."

Valerius laughed, nearly mad with fear and adrenaline. He bared his teeth. "I meant it—I'll kill you, my 'mother.' Hell, I'll murder everyone in this whole goddamn world. You can't stop me."

At some unseen signal, the doors to the ward burst open. Soldiers, their armor shiny and new, charged in alongside mages fresh-faced with inexperience. They stumbled when they saw Thaddeus but didn't attack—clearly they'd been warned in advance.

Valerius bared his teeth. Let them come. Let them all *come*.

Thaddeus smiled in response, the air crackling with violence. "Then die," the monster said, leaping forward, his claws aimed straight for Valerius' neck.

Chapter Ten

The Ivory Keep shook, the sound of an explosion following a split second later. It rumbled through the mighty castle's stone walls—walls that had once held armies and dragons alike at bay now trembled beneath the queen's feet.

"What in the bloody hell was that?" Liddy snapped, bracing herself over Lazander as she glanced up, watching for any sign the ceiling might collapse, but the thick wooden beams held—for now.

"Thaddeus," the queen whispered, grabbing her cane as she left the room, her uneven gait more pronounced by her rapid pace.

She ignored Liddy's confused call of, "Your *pup*?"

The queen knew it would be pointless to head to Thaddeus and Valerius. Not only would it take her an age to get there, but she'd be in the way—she fought with words, not blades. Veering sharply to the right, she gritted her teeth as she measured speed against balance and headed for the next corridor.

This hadn't been the plan. They'd chosen the Quiet Room specifically for the ambush as it was far from the other wards but close enough for reinforcements to arrive. Thaddeus had originally wanted to go in alone, where he would deal with Valerius—quick, quiet, and contained, he'd claimed. It was only on the queen's insistence had the palace mages and soldiers joined him. She'd seen Thaddeus fight, had seen the creature he could become, and while she knew no man, Gilded Knight or otherwise, would stand a chance, they had only one shot at this.

They'd discussed contingencies, had signaled the night attendant to stay away once Valerius entered, and even added extra layers of magical protection to the other wards, though they'd assured Liddy the fighting wouldn't reach that far. How could it with Thaddeus in his true form and a company of knights and mages at his back?

Yet the stone heart of Navaros now shook. What had gone wrong? What had she missed?

It was with these thoughts racing through her mind that the queen reached the end of the corridor, thanking herself for the hindsight of bare feet—shoes only slowed her down. With practiced ease she knocked her cane against the window frame, lifted the latch free, and threw the window open. At the sight of the courtyard below, all plans, all her rationale, fled, and for the first time in her life, the queen invoked the God of Judgment.

"Gallow, help us."

Thaddeus had been by the queen's side since she was a child, and in all that time she'd only seen him fight once. But she knew him in a way she knew no other, not even her husband. She'd guessed that if civilians were in danger, he'd take the fight to the courtyard—a gigantic space in Navaros' capital that was large enough to hold the guards' barracks, the Gallowed Temple, stables, a tavern, market stalls, and the king's flower garden.

She was right—the fight had spilled out to the courtyard, but it was no skillful diversion to save innocent lives. It was *carnage*.

Directly across from the queen lay the eastern side where Liddy's wards had been painstakingly built and perfected over decades of service. Half the inner wall wasn't merely destroyed—it was *gone*. A gaping hole was all that remained, a cacophony of broken stone, furniture, and bodies laid bare to the night air.

Then she heard the screams.

Her hand shook as she gripped her cane. She'd never been on a battlefield, but she knew the difference between cries of fear, pain, and pure unadulterated panic. She heard all three now, weaving together in the darkness to form a horrifying chorus.

Nestled against the ruin of the eastern wall lay the Resplendent Farrow, an ancient tavern almost as tall as the Keep's walls where generations of royalty, civilians, soldiers, and mages drank during the kingdom's highs and lows. Now a narrow, sharp line cut through its famous thatched roof, taking several rafters with it. The queen's single eye followed the trail of destruction. Several of the mage's clever lampposts were bent or even torn out of the ground, and market stalls carefully boarded up each night were reduced to broken piles of timber.

At the end of the path of destruction lay a towering statue—the heart of the Keep. The king had commissioned a sculpture of them both for her last name day, a behemoth of stone and polished glass that caught the light, changing color in tandem with the rising sun. The king stood in full armor, his sword drawn but pointed down, the sharp angles of his face a mirror-image of Valerius. At his back stood the queen, her hands resting on her cane, mimicking her husband's pose. She'd been flustered at the gift, telling him there had been no need for such expense. In private she'd been honored—especially when she'd heard he'd insisted she be depicted with her cane, despite the sculptor's suggestion otherwise.

Now the statue lay in pieces. Snapped in two, the king's head and one of the queen's arms lay splayed out on the ground some twenty feet from legs still attached to the podium. The rest was just broken stone.

And it was there, just past the statue, that the queen's eye came to a stop. A crater lay smoking as if blasted apart by one of Evergarden's war machines. At its center lay a body, impossibly small in the mess of rubble and stone. A body that had been thrown through the eastern wall, the tavern, hitting lamp posts and market stalls along the way before it shattered her husband's gift and came to a broken, aching stop.

But who was it?

The queen leaned out of the window as much as she dared, straining her single eye. Her mind and heart fought over who she wished it was—Valerius or Thaddeus. But she couldn't deny the facts. Thaddeus fought like a demon, and while she knew he'd never lay a hand on her, she'd forever fear the supernatural, inhuman way he moved. He didn't fight, he *massacred*. While her son's swordsmanship was the pride of the kingdom, he stood no chance against such a beast.

No one did.

The smoke cleared, and the queen saw the unmistakable curve of a horn, iron-rich skin, and a multitude of limbs. One of his horns was gone—snapped off at the root. Several of his arms bent at strange, unnatural angles, and a wound as thick as the queen's arm split his stomach open.

"*No.*" She gasped. Unable to look at the guts of her friend spilling out, she looked back at the eastern wall. And saw *him*. The boy she'd fall on a sword for, the man who was her pride and joy. Her son—Valerius.

Though he was too far away to tell, she could feel his eyes lock onto hers. She wanted to cry out, to tell him to stop this madness. But he took a step back, his weapons simply vanishing into thin air in a dull glow. He charged forward, running in his armor as easily as if it were made of cotton and not dragonscale.

A memory arose of the first time he'd donned the iconic royal armor, distinctive on any battlefield with its ivory sheen—he'd been twelve and had insisted on trying on his father's. It was so heavy, he'd managed three steps before falling over with a crash. They'd laughed together, helping him to his feet. The king had gripped Valerius' hand, telling him not to worry, he'd grow into it one day.

Now the queen's fingers dug into the windowsill so hard one of her nails cracked.

Valerius jumped to the fallen tavern's roof, his foot scarcely touching the surface before he leaped once more—an impossibility for someone without a plethora of magic. Magic no knight should be able to wield.

As Valerius moved closer, the details of his face sharpened, and the queen felt the cold shock of fear at the murderous look on her son's face. A look that was aimed squarely at Thaddeus.

The queen gave herself a single moment to mourn her son. The boy who had hidden in her skirts whenever his father rode out from the Keep, fighting back tears. Who feared spiders until she showed him how to carefully cup them and put them outside. Who used to greet his mother with a warm kiss and hug but hadn't touched her once in the past three years.

She mourned him.

Then she let him go.

"My queen!" A knight, a mere novice, rounded the corner. He moved stiffly, the clank of his armor sharp and unsettling. "My queen, we've been searching for you everywhere! We feared the worst when we found the safe room empty—"

"Get me every mage left in the Ivory Keep. Tell the barracks *not* to engage with Valerius until my signal," the queen said, a sketch of a plan formulating. She kept her gaze firmly on Thaddeus and Valerius as if, by sheer force of will, she could stop the execution she knew was coming. She didn't have time to wonder at her son's impossible, superhuman abilities, or to mourn the dead civilians buried in the wreckage. But this—this she could do.

"My queen, your safety is—"

"Phillip of Cassio, you hail from East Navaros, correct?"

"You know my—I mean, yes, my queen."

"Phillip, your queen just gave you a direct order. Refuse me again and I'll have you locked in the stocks for a week." She let all warmth leave her face, leaving only the queen who would kill her own son if it meant protecting her people.

The knight paled. "Yes, my queen! Forgive me, my queen."

"Meet me in the courtyard. Western side by the garden," she called, not bothering to check if he'd heard as she began the slow, laborious task of getting down three flights of stairs.

The queen walked with a cane and was blind in one eye. She was not a knight, a mage, or a soldier, but she had her mind—and that would have to be enough to stop the monster her son had become.

Chapter Eleven

Valerius stared at the ruined courtyard. The Resplendent Farrow, Marito's favorite tavern, was slowly caving in on itself. The gaping hole that was once Liddy's Quiet Room crumbled behind him as he stood. A woman screamed on the floor below him, a wretched sob in which only two words were decipherable.

"My baby!"

No, not a woman, Valerius reminded himself. An *NPC*.

He brought up the Calamity System Menu and his Character Sheet.

Current:	
Stamina	900/1000
Hit Points	970/1000
Mana	50/500

He grimaced at his mana. The *Fire Storm* he'd used to send Thaddeus flying was costly. It was why he only used it as a last resort. He instinctively glanced at the rest of his sheet.

Base Stats:	
Strength	200
Essence	90
Resistance	650
Recovery	700

Speed	120
Luck	50

Usually he felt a spike of pleasure when seeing his stats. There was a time when not even one of them cracked fifty. He'd focused on Resistance, his ability to withstand magic, and Recovery, which sped up his overall healing time. Even his Essence, a piddling five when he'd first arrived, now surpassed most mages, allowing him to wield magic unheard of for a knight.

But he felt no joy upon seeing how far he'd come. How in just three years, he'd become the strongest man in Navaros, or close to it. Instead, all he felt was anger. It wasn't enough. When would he be *enough*?

He looked back at the handful of soldiers and mages who lay scattered about the ward like discarded toys. Some moaned, barely twitching, while others lay slack-jawed and stupid in death.

He dismissed his sword and shield, summoning a *Replenish* potion from his Inventory, and knocked back the sour-smelling concoction. Valerius shivered as the potion took effect, a warm tingle spreading through him as mana flooded his body once more.

His plan couldn't have gone more wrong. It had been simple—force Lazander to take the fall for Gabriel and Marito's deaths, then be back in the Ivory Keep by morning where he'd keep playing the part of the dedicated knight. He needed to be close to Eternity, so that when the call came from the Operator, he'd be ready. Instead, any chance he had of a triumphant return from death with Magnus in hand was gone.

Movement caught Valerius' eye, and he turned to see the queen leaning out of a window on the western edge of the courtyard. Gray hair loose about her shoulders, fear naked on her face, she looked decades older than the last time he'd seen her. His heart unexpectedly pounded at the sight.

A soft clink made him look down. The stonebreaker antidote rolled against his sabaton, still miraculously intact. It was the one thing that could save Lazander's life and the reason he'd taken such a stupid risk. Teeth gritted, he summoned his sword and shield.

No more. He was *done* playing pretend. So what if he didn't follow the game's golden path? So what if he'd killed a bunch of NPCs? He just needed to *finish the damn game*.

He raised a heavy iron sabaton.

"Screw it."

He stomped on the potion bottle. It shattered instantly, the thick liquid splashing his feet.

Screw this world.

He activated *Swiftness* to increase his movement speed and cast *Levity*—his favorite spell back when he spent countless hours playing *Knights of Eternity*. He leaped, the magic tripling the distance of his jump, landed on the barely standing Resplendent Farrow, and threw himself forward.

A mage lamp wobbled—struggling to stay upright. Valerius lightly touched down on it, using it as a springboard. It toppled as he leaped, falling against the thatch roof of a market stall. The protective glass that contained the mage fire cracked, allowing the hungry flames to feast on the dried straw.

In seconds, the market stall was alight as fire spread outward. Armor clanked as soldiers rang the alarm—fire was a death knell to the Keep.

Good, Valerius thought. *Distract the NPCs, let me focus on the boss.*

Thaddeus lay in the center of the courtyard in a crater of broken stone and leaking intestines. Valerius felt no pity for the fallen spymaster—he could already see Thaddeus' skin knitting together. He aimed for the top of an upright lamppost, a single armored foot touching the cap before he leaped up.

Thaddeus groaned, and Valerius watched his own features twist in pain. The spymaster had been so sure Valerius would die, he'd taunted him. *Mocked* him with his own face.

Cocky, arrogant, prick. I'll show him. I'll show them all.

The world went white with rage, and Valerius' body glowed as his sword and shield. In one smooth motion, he sheathed his sword and gripped the top of his shield with both hands. Thaddeus groaned, eyes snapping open when he saw Valerius above him, his cloak whipping through the air like an angel of death.

Valerius shot downward, aiming the point of his shield directly for Thaddeus' neck. The falsling's flesh moved like clay at the last second, elongating and stretching around Valerius as his shield hit the ground, splitting the stone several feet deep. A hoofed foot appeared where an arm should have been and kicked Valerius in the face, knocking him back long enough for Thaddeus to slither away.

His flesh twisted and crunched as his arms reformed, his intestines sucking back into his stomach with a *slurp*. In seconds Valerius was staring into his own eyes once more, the skin of Thaddeus' monstrous form now as smooth as sea-beaten stone. It was almost as if their fight had never happened. *Almost.*

Valerius smiled at the spark of fear that now lit up the spymaster's eyes.

The knight rose from the crater he'd made, a fresh bruise the shape of Thaddeus' hoof darkening his temples. "I knew you wouldn't go down easy. Bosses always have a second health bar."

"*What are you?*" Thaddeus hissed—claws flexed. "No human can fight as you do—what foul bargain have you struck? What have you traded for the power you wield?"

Valerius thought of the voice behind his quests and that alien plane of sand and pain the Operator called home. He'd told no one who he was or where he'd come from—he'd been too afraid to break the facade. But Valerius, Prince of Navaros, leader of the Gilded Knights was gone. He didn't have to hide the truth anymore.

"The Operator," he said, shrugging, "orders me about from a desert planet—"

dO noT SPeAK oF ME to tHE ZINdor

A knife of red-hot pain drove into Valerius' skull and twisted. He gasped, sword arm pressing against his temple, the Operator's voice screaming in his head.

kILL tHE ZiNDOR

KiLL ThE ziNdOr

Ki—

"*Quest accepted*," Valerius half screamed, blood vessels exploding in his eyes. The Operator fell silent, and Valerius collapsed on one knee, gasping and shaking. His brain felt like someone had chopped the tips from a dozen needles and then slowly pressed their dulled edges into his gray matter. But he could think again.

The Operator hadn't spoken to him directly like that in almost two years. Not since he'd refused to kill the vaxion women and children. After a "talk" with the Operator, he'd finished every mission without question since.

"Zindor," Valerius said, his voice a pained whisper as he got to his feet. "You're a zindor."

It was strange seeing surprise on his own features. Valerius watched his own eyes widen as Thaddeus stared at him in unabashed shock. The prince grinned in answer, the expression spoiled by a wince, an after-shock from the Operator's visit making his head throb.

"That's a yes." Valerius didn't give Thaddeus a chance to reply. He darted forward, shifting his shield to his left arm as he drew his sword with his right, slashing at the spymaster. The monster parried the blow with his claws, sparks flying as he spun, aiming for Valerius' chest.

"How do you know that word?" Thaddeus hissed.

Valerius brought his sword up to block, then swung his shield at the spymaster's knees. The beast's right leg buckled from the force, and Valerius hooked his foot around the zindor's, knocking him backward.

Instead of falling to the ground where Valerius planned to drive his blade into Thaddeus' heart, the zindor's flesh became liquid, slithering around Valerius' incoming blade. The knight leaped back, expecting him to reform, but the clay-like flesh followed him, twisting around his body from head to toe. With a crunch of breaking bone, Thaddeus partially solidified, wrenching back Valerius' arms and neck—effectively freezing him in place.

The spymaster's head, ebony horns arching over his neck, appeared by Valerius' ear, his words a hateful whisper. *"How do you know that word?"*

Valerius forced his panic down and closed his eyes instead—touching the replenished well of magic in his chest.

Fire Wall Activated.

Flames erupted all over his body, engulfing them both. The white-hot blaze was a gentle breeze against Valerius' skin, but to Thaddeus it must have felt like being plunged into molten lava. The spymaster howled in pain, a strangely piercing cry that was daggers to Valerius' ears, but the zindor held on, tightening his grip on Valerius until stars burst in the prince's eyes. Valerius built the flames higher and higher, pouring his mana into the spell. The smell of flesh cooked to a cinder flooded his nose, but Thaddeus held on, healing himself over and over again while Valerius burned him alive.

"*How. Do you know. That word?*" Thaddeus howled, his flesh charred to the bone.

Abruptly the flames vanished. Valerius gasped, his legs turning to jelly. A line of red slid down his side. He looked down to see Thaddeus' hand buried deep in his stomach up to the wrist. Valerius' dragonscale armor, cracked by Marito's last desperate attempt to stop him, now crumpled like tin.

"Tell me, or I will yank out your intestines and tie them around your *neck*," Thaddeus spat, his breath hot on Valerius' right ear. He whirled his fingers, which were deeply embedded in Valerius' stomach, as if he were mixing dough—driving home a promise words never could.

"Operator." Tears sprang to Valerius' eyes, pain and panic overriding his fear of the Operator's punishments. "Told me to—to kill you."

The clay-like limbs that bound Valerius shook. "The world the 'Operator' hails from—the desert world. What does it look like?"

"He'll—he'll kill me—*argh*." Claws lengthened deep within flesh, shredding muscle and burrowing into his intestines. Something foul leaked from Valerius' stomach.

"Hot sand. *Two suns!*" he cried.

Thaddeus muttered either a curse or a prayer in a foreign language, Valerius couldn't tell. Distracted, the spymaster's hold slackened ever so slightly.

Valerius struck.

He dismissed his sword and shield, summoning a cylindrical object the length of a forearm from the Inventory. At its tip was a blade, sharpened to a deadly point. With a grunt, he yanked his arms up, bringing the weapon to just above his right shoulder, where Thaddeus' breath hissed in his ear.

The spymaster tensed, freezing Valerius' blade mere inches from his throat.

"You've made a deal with the devil," Thaddeus hissed. "You don't know what he is, what you've—"

His words were cut off when Valerius pressed a small button at the base of the weapon. The blade shot forward with the force of a tightly wound spring, revealing itself as a compacted spear that doubled, tripled, and then quadrupled in length.

Whatever Thaddeus had to say was lost. The spear pierced his throat, its bloodied point bursting through the back of his neck. The limbs that held Valerius slackened abruptly. With a roar the knight gripped the spear, flinging it as far from himself as he could, dragging Thaddeus' twitching body with it.

Chapter Twelve

Delirious with pain, Valerius pressed useless hands to his spilling guts as he summoned the Inventory, grasping for a *Healing Void*. Shaking, his bloodied fingers struggled with the cork of the lifesaving potion, his other hand desperately clutching his stomach.

With a curse, he popped the cork and knocked it back. As the cold liquid trickled down his throat, the squishy mound of intestines shrank. Valerius dared not look until he'd drained the bottle dry, tears of pain and fear blurring his vision.

His ivory dragonscale armor, the pride and joy of the royal family and the most powerful armor in the game, now sported a large, fist-sized hole. Valerius' pale stomach was visible through it. He touched it with frantic fingers, not trusting that his intestines were once more inside him.

Stupid, stupid! You may as well have bared your throat to him and said "kill me please." The Operator is going to be furious.

He thought of that grating, echoing voice as it took away his sight, stripped him of his weapons, and ripped him apart piece by piece until he begged for mercy.

No, I killed him—I killed the zindor. It's fine. I'm fine.

A high-pitched whine cut through the night air, like iron nails on a chalkboard. It was punctuated by a gurgling, choking sound that made Valerius' mouth twist in disgust.

The spear, still lodged in Thaddeus' throat, was pointed upward like an exclamation point, buried where Valerius had thrown it. A long coil of flesh, bones, and muscle half formed curled around the blade like a puddle. Only Thaddeus' head was complete, Valerius' own face staring back at him as the spymaster gulped, slowly drowning in his own blood.

"How in the hell are you still *alive*?" Valerius spat. From his Inventory he summoned a wicked metallic green blade, the edges thrumming with power as he stalked toward Thaddeus.

I can fix this. Kill the zindor, grab Eternity, and pray I've done enough to trigger the endgame.

His world narrowed in focus as he repeated these thoughts over and over. If he allowed himself to think the game was ruined, that he was trapped in this world, in this body, for all time, he would lose his mind. The courtyard was a wall of noise as flames spread from one market stall to another. Smoke, thick and black, caused chaos as soldiers frantically passed water buckets.

"Is that… Lord Valerius?" a guard called, emerging from the smoke soot-stained and wide-eyed. He clutched a bucket of water in his hands, not a single piece of his leather armor out of place despite the hurried awakening he must have had. "My lord—you've returned! The courtyard isn't safe, we must—"

Valerius' blade snaked out, his stride barely breaking as he cut the guard's head off.

Just an NPC.

He ignored the cry of outrage from his left, followed by the thud of a dropped bucket. The sound caused a domino effect as one guard called out to another, and someone barked a familiar order. It was an order he himself had roared while riding into battle with Lazander, Gabriel, Marito.

"To arms!"

But this time, he wasn't the Ivory Keep's stalwart defender. This time, he was its enemy.

A spear appeared, a glimmer of silver in the moonlight. Instinctively Valerius activated *Swiftness* again, dodging around the blow in a flash of white. The woman blinked, Valerius too quick for her eyes.

"Wha—"

He drove the longsword through her stomach and out her back, severing her spinal cord. She gasped, an ugly, throaty sound that was all pain.

"*Fester*," Valerius whispered.

His blade reacted, drawing from his mana as it lit up. In a flash, tendrils of malachite etched down the weapon, flooding the woman's body.

"Necrotic damage," he said as she twitched, a rasping sound for help. "Don't bother—you'll be dead in seconds."

With a yank, he pulled the blade free, turning away as she fell. Veins of forest green crept up her cheeks, a yellow foam bubbling from her mouth.

Just an NPC.

Something moved out of the corner of his eye, and he dismissed the deadly blade, his trusted sword and shield returning to his hands. When the axe flew at him from the dark, he moved as if in a dance, stepping forward smoothly as he brought his shield up, activating *Rebound*. The axe bounced harmlessly off the dragonscale and then hovered there for a moment before shooting backward into the dark. He heard the thud of flesh as the axe returned to its owner, burying itself in a skull.

Just an NPC.

Two men and a woman approached, shaking but determined. Their eyes were alight with fear and determination. Valerius raised his sword. "Just an—"

His nose crunched against something large and solid, forcing him back. Annoyed, he strode forward, but he couldn't move more than a step before he collided with an invisible, immovable force. He backed up but was blocked again.

"Enough."

Fire and screams for water should have drowned her out, but her voice easily cut through the noise.

"That's enough, Valerius."

The queen emerged from the darkness barefoot, hair streaming. She was dressed no differently from the scared woman he'd locked eyes with from across the courtyard, but gone was her shock and fear. Now she gripped her cane, back straight, eyes defiant as she stared him down.

"Lay down your weapons."

It was only then that Valerius spotted the purple cloaks.

There was one hidden in the shadows of two stalls to his right. Another on the roof of the building to his left. Three more behind him. And one on either side of his mother, their hands raised, a dull glow emanating from mana-infused fingers.

"I'm surprised you were able to summon so many palace mages at this hour. I know they like their beauty sleep," Valerius said, raising a carefree eyebrow for good measure.

"You can come quietly and live to see the dawn, or I will order the palace mages to burn you to ash—it is your choice."

Her voice was level and emotionless, as if she were commenting on the weather. Only Valerius noticed the tremble in her hands.

"Speaking of mages, I have a question for them," Valerius said, vanishing his sword and shield to their open-mouthed gazes. "Have you heard of a 'zindor'? And did you know my mother has been keeping one on a leash?" He pointed at Thaddeus, whose gurgling had quietened down to a pathetic whine. "What other secrets are you keeping, Mother? Who else have you chained to your service?"

The change in the air was palpable as the mages strained for a better look. One even gasped.

Valerius had drawn attention to Thaddeus for a reason. The barrier that encased him was similar to *The Cage* he'd used back at the Captain's Barracks. It needed a constant stream of mana. With the mages as a focal point, if he moved quick enough, he—

"Thaddeus!" the queen cried, her stoic veneer vanishing as she dropped her cane and frantically limped toward the broken, bleeding pile of limbs that was her canine companion.

Valerius lost all thoughts of escape as the queen knelt down, trembling fingers cupping the zindor's face. The tenderness as she stroked the creature's forehead was utterly alien to Valerius.

The sight broke something inside him.

There was a cracking sound, and a mage cried out, clutching his head as he fell to one knee, the magic vanishing from his fingers.

Another crack, and a second mage fell. Valerius hefted the huge hammer he'd summoned, struggling even with *Iron Strength* activated. It was a huge, vicious-looking weapon, the silver head embedded with jagged dragonscale fragments. He slammed it into the invisible shield again, feeling a fury and hatred he couldn't name.

"Valerius! Valerius, stop, please!" the queen cried, cradling Thaddeus' head in her lap, his blood leaking onto her nightdress in pulsating streams.

With a roar, Valerius shattered the barrier, sparks of broken mana falling about him like rain as the last mage collapsed, unconscious.

"Why are you doing this?" the queen said, her voice shaking. "What did we— what did *I* do to you to make you like this?"

"Three years ago, when I was… 'sick,' I woke up confused and terrified. I told you I didn't know who or where I was. I told you I needed *help*. And as I lay there crying, do you remember what you said to me?"

The queen blinked, brow furrowing in confusion. "I don't know what you're—"

"You said." Valerius strode toward her, hefting the hammer over his shoulder with a grunt. "'You are the Royal Prince of Navaros. You are the leader of the Gilded. Stop blubbering like a child and act like it.'"

The queen opened her mouth to protest but couldn't—she knew it was true. He could tell by the look on her face.

"And I did just that. For three years I broke my back on pointless errands for you and Navaros because I wanted so badly to be Valerius. To be a hero. And in all that time, not once did you look at me the way you're looking at your *dog*."

He lifted his hammer above his head.

The queen raised her chin—defiant until the end. "You are no *hero*."

Valerius brought his hammer down, aiming straight for the queen's skull.

Chapter Thirteen

Eternity had spent most of her life confined—usually in the Gallowed Temple of whatever kingdom held dominion over her, and now in one of the Ivory Keep's towers. She was the link, the tie between this world and the God of Judgment. If she died, they had no way of knowing when the next Eternity would be born, not to mention the long and arduous task of finding those worthy of becoming Champions.

It was why neither she nor the Champions could raise a finger without Gallow's blessing—no matter the cost. In her time as Chosen, she'd been held for ransom, marooned on an island, trapped on a mountain of ice, burned, stabbed, and held at knifepoint—not to mention her recent imprisonment at Magnus' hands. Sometimes Gallow sent his Champions to save her. Sometimes he didn't. It wasn't her role to ask why, she knew that.

That didn't mean she always liked it. Or that it didn't *hurt*.

She gripped the windowsill, her nails denting wood softened by weather and age. Fire raged in the courtyard beneath her. Valerius, stone-faced, imperious Valerius, cut down soldiers he'd once led into battle. She watched, heart in her throat, unable to believe the man who'd once stood by her side in a parade, the very image of a stalwart knight, was now butchering people like they were cattle. She waited for Gallow to say something. All it would take was one word, and they could stop this. But the God of Judgment was silent.

She felt her sense of duty stretch and fray. Imani pressed a hand to her shoulder, gripping it tightly enough that Eternity wasn't sure if it was a comfort or deterrent.

"Can't we do something?" Eternity whispered.

Valerius spun, driving his sword through a woman's spine. Her mouth froze in horror.

"My orders are to protect you, and you alone. Unless your life is in danger, I cannot lift my blade to help," the Champion replied, stepping back to her customary position by the door. "I suggest you close the window and return to your bed, Lady Eternity."

Eternity fought very hard not to tell Imani that only a callous wretch would be able to sleep right now. "Why is he doing this?" she asked instead, staring in horror as another died at Valerius' hand.

"Greed, power, madness—who knows?" Imani's shoulder rose and fell in an elegant shrug. "What humans do to each other isn't my concern."

Eternity glanced back, shocked at the coldness of Imani's words. "We may serve Gallow, but we're still *human*, Imani."

Imani smiled. "We're not, my lady. You know that better than anyone."

Eternity frowned, turning back to the fight—unwilling to argue semantics with the Champions. Valerius had finally been contained within a *Fortified Entrapment*. Eternity eyed it for cracks, breathing a sigh of relief when she saw how expertly it was cast. Her worries had been for naught, she chided herself.

Still, the treacherous part of her mind wondered why any of this had happened. If Gallow had intervened, if he'd just stopped Valerius from killing the Gilded Knights in the first place… her eyes welled at the thought of Marito and Gabriel. How they'd drunk and laughed with her, welcoming her to the Ivory Keep. The wonder in Lazander's voice as he sat with her beneath the night sky, shyly pointing out constellations. The thought of the young knight lying half dead, betrayed by his own prince, made her chest constrict.

Why hadn't Gallow saved them? Surely the Gilded Knights were worthy?

The queen cried out, pulling Eternity back to the present. A strange glow appeared in Valerius' hands, and he slammed a gigantic rune-etched hammer into the boundaries of the *Fortified Entrapment*.

"No. Valerius, *stop!*" Eternity cried, knowing he couldn't hear her.

She winced, feeling the mana bridge the palace mages had spun between them shatter. With growing horror, she watched them fall with each crack of Valerius' hammer—something no mortal weapon should have been able to accomplish.

"My lady, get away from the window," Imani said, not bothering to hide her irritation.

Imani was the epitome of a Champion—someone who put aside her humanity and followed Gallow's teachings to the letter. Eternity admired her for it. But even after all these years as Gallow's Chosen, she couldn't do it. Because first and foremost, she was *human*.

"*Eternity*!" Imani cried in a rare display of emotion. The Champion moved at supernatural speed, but it was too late—Eternity already had one foot on the windowsill.

"Imani," she said without looking back. "Protect me."

She threw herself out of the tower.

***

All Valerius saw was a flash of blonde hair land in the path of his hammer before he was flying backward.

He didn't even know who hit him. All he felt was a crushing blow to the chest before his body hit the ground and kept going—skipping like a flat stone. Instinct took over, and he dug an armored hand into the cobblestones. The sheer force was so great, his fingernails split inside his gauntlet, but he slowed to a stop—his hammer still miraculously in one hand.

Breathing hard, he raised his head to see Imani. Her dull black armor blended into shadows, drawing a silhouette of the Champion with her right arm extended from where she'd driven her fist into his chest. *A punch? She sent me flying with a single punch*? Valerius thought, horrified.

"My lady, that was *unwise*," Imani said through gritted teeth, not taking her eyes off Valerius. "We should go."

Eternity ignored her, her hands glowing as she pressed them against the ruined flesh that was Thaddeus' body. Imani rolled her eyes before raising her fists.

Smoke clogged the night air; the crackle of flames was punctuated by shouts as the guards finally began to contain the fire. Valerius touched his chest, feeling the cracks along his dragonscale armor from where her fist connected. He should run. He'd never seen Imani fight, or any of the Champions for that matter, but that punch was all he needed to know that she was stronger than him—stronger even than Marito.

But all he could think of was Imani's impervious expression. How she strode about the castle as if being in her very presence was a gift. *She's a lapdog of a god*, he thought, *a brainwashed idiot incapable of a single original thought*. How dare *she look down on me*.

"You can't win." Imani smiled, as if sensing his thoughts. "But it would make my *night* to see you try."

There were groans off to his side. The palace mages the queen had managed to scramble together were getting to their feet, nursing splitting headaches from the mana backlash, he imagined, but very much alive. As the soldiers contained the fire and the smoke died down, the cover he'd made use of would vanish—and then he'd have to contend with mages, soldiers, and a Champion of Gallow.

No. As much as he wanted to, he couldn't kill Imani right now. But that didn't mean he couldn't finish the Operator's quests. Without the antidote, Lazander would be dead in hours, and as for Thaddeus…

He cast *Whispering Darkness*—vanishing from sight.

***

Sweat beaded Eternity's brow, but she refused to look up, refused to do anything but pour her magic into the strange, broken body of the creature before her. She didn't know what he was, or where he had come from, but she didn't need to. The queen cradled his head in her lap, refusing to let go even as Eternity frantically worked to save his life.

He was important to the queen. That was enough for her.

"Thaddeus, wake up," the queen whispered, voice steady despite the tears in her eyes. "You wake up this instant. That's an order."

Eternity had no affinity for healing magic, a rare branch that was notoriously difficult. The body was a complex system where a single change could have catastrophic effects. But she'd seen the creature fight and knew it had healing abilities of its own, so instead of panicking at the gaping wound in his throat, she decided to let his own body do the work by boosting his magic with her own tidal wave of power.

The broken charcoal of his skin began to break off, revealing new skin, fresh and pink. His throat was slower to follow, the winding muscles of his vocal cords struggling to intertwine. The creature, who bore a striking, bloodied resemblance to Valerius that Eternity did not have the time to ponder, heaved a sigh. His eyelids fluttered.

"Thaddeus. Thaddeus, that's it. Stay with me. You're safe now," the queen whispered, lovingly stroking his broken horn.

"My queen…" he croaked, eyes fluttering open.

"Shh, don't speak," she commanded, even as she smiled in relief.

"No, listen…" he rasped. "Valerius isn't working… with Magnus."

The queen narrowed her eyes. "Then who?"

"The… Tyrant, he has—"

Imani appeared at Eternity's back, her hands gripping the Chosen's shoulders, and yanked her sharply back. Her hands broke contact with Thaddeus, and she nearly cried out in frustration. She could save him, she could! All she needed was another— but the thought vanished when Thaddeus' head split from his body in a bloodied fountain. A sword, blinding white in the darkness, drove through his neck and into the queen's leg where it rested.

The queen didn't scream. No one did. It happened too quickly. Instead Eternity's world narrowed in on Thaddeus' head as it rolled, mouth agape, the courtyard awash with blood.

Chapter Fourteen

The forest clearing was dominated by an ancient tree that curled in on itself, its sparse leaves doing little to block the piercing moonlight. I took a breath, letting my hearing and sense of smell expand.

Tithe of Beasts Activated.

Once so overwhelming my head spun, using *Tithe of Beasts* now felt like slipping into a hot bath. My shoulders dropped as I listened to the claws and paws that padded into the night and breathed in the smell of damp soil, fresh grass, and sweet flowers. It wasn't all sunshine and rainbows—there was the stink of animal droppings and the metallic burn of urine-marked trees, but each note added to the symphony of life that was the forest.

I smiled. I had a feeling that outside beneath a starlit sky was where I—where Zara—was always meant to be.

My bare feet took me to the base of the twisted tree. Lenia had tried to give me shoes, a beautiful leather pair would have torn apart the moment I used *Partial Transformation*. I'd fumbled an excuse, and she'd side-eyed me but let it go. It was easy to forget that not everyone had to deal with clawed feet that doubled in size, not even other falslings.

The tree's bark was graying in parts—a large split, possibly from lightning, separated part of the trunk from its body. But the tree wasn't what drew me, it was the near-fluorescent green moss at its base. I pressed my hand into it, expecting dampness but finding only crinkling dryness. As I pulled away, the imprint of my fingers stayed, springing back seconds later.

Creepy foreboding tree, surrounded by pillow-like moss. This feels oddly appropriate.

Dropping my pack, I flopped down in the moss, relishing the sensation—I'd insisted on taking the floor at Chief's (Lenia and Waylen took one bed, Lukas and the Chief the other two), and while I didn't regret it, my back was fervently thanking me as I wiggled into a more comfortable position.

It had been two days since I'd left H'tar. I'd picked the deepest part of the forest and walked into it pretending I knew where I was going. Lying down, eyes closed, aches and pains from days of labor and the near frantic pace I'd set since leaving H'tar, wormed their way into my muscles. To the surprise and/or fear of some of H'tar, but mainly Chief's amusement, I'd thrown myself into daily life—clearing the debris of the broken barn, harvesting a wheat-like substance called "grax," and helping Chief deliver orders. I'd initially tried to help him with his blacksmithing but wasn't allowed near the forge after an incident involving Chief's eyebrows and an open flame. Before I left, I'd driven myself to near exhaustion. Lenia thought it was because I "wanted to leave a good impression," but it was far simpler.

I needed to be able to fall asleep, and the more tired I was, the quieter my mind got.

I'd still put it off, snatching only brief naps in the sun as I got as far away from H'tar as possible. On cue, my mind began to whir with the potential idiocy of my plan, playing a greatest hits edition of how stupid and useless I was. *Remember that one time three years ago you did something embarrassing? Let's analyze that in* great *detail*. But as I relaxed, my aching muscles released a delicious day of tension, and exhaustion began to beat out anxiety.

It was pure dumb luck I'd stumbled into the solution for my last quest. If I was to survive here, finish the Operator's quests and *Summon Eternity* (whatever that meant), then I couldn't wander around blindly and hope for the best. I'd asked Chief and the others if they knew what a "wallow-tail" was, and they'd stared at me like I had two heads. I needed answers. And I knew only one person who could help me…

Question was, would she talk to me?

The telltale golden outline of the Calamity System Menu appeared, and I knew I'd finally drifted off. I scrolled to the Origin tab, trying to mentally prepare myself.

ORIGIN OF PLAYER CHARACTER: ZARA THE FURY. STATUS: AVAILABLE.

WOULD YOU LIKE TO SPEAK TO ZARA THE FURY?

The little I remembered of Zara when she'd taken over my body scared the crap out of me. Speaking to her was the absolute last thing I wanted to do, but if I didn't do it now, I'd be scared of her for the rest of my life. And damn it, I was scared of so many things already, I *refused* to add something else to the list.

I mentally clicked on "Yes," and was instantly transported.

***

I blinked, the darkness blinding me. I was lying on the ground on my right side, curled up into a ball. I frantically patted myself down, thinking of the Operator, its strange alien plane and the inky-black symbols that sank into my skin every second I was there. With relief, I realized I was both fully clothed and sigil-free. Flopping onto my back, I sighed—being naked was an extra layer of vulnerability I didn't need right now.

As my eyes adjusted to the darkness, I became aware of a dim light coming from behind me. Turning my head, I looked for the source and shot up—my jaw hanging open.

A creature built like a panther stood before me, long tendrils of flesh undulating like vipers around her ice-blue eyes. A vaxion twice the size of Lukas glared at me—the naked flame of pure hatred in her eyes. I instinctively knew the vaxion was female. The curve of her jaw and the flat plane of her nose were details I'd have missed before. Now they seemed as obvious as if she'd had two heads instead of one. But that wasn't what made me freeze.

Unlike Lukas' ink-black fur, this vaxion was a pure, startling white, glowing like a moon in a dark sky. She was a vision of light and dark, beauty and death. I'd never seen anything as beautiful or as terrifying.

"Zara?" I whispered, my voice loud and echoing.

Whatever spell woven around her by my arrival broke, and she leaped forward, fangs bared, jaw unhinged, ready to crush my skull like an egg.

I skittered back, but I was too slow, and she was fast. Impossibly fast.

Zara abruptly jerked back, yanked like a puppet on too-tight strings. Her growl became a hacking, choking sound. It was only then that I saw the chains.

A manacle as thick as I was wide wrapped around her throat, looping under the coils of flesh that fanned out from her head like sentient dreadlocks. Links as long as my forearm led into the darkness, trailing deep into the shadows. She snapped her jaws, ice-blue eyes wide and manic as she shook her chains like a dog.

I hadn't known what to expect—I thought she'd be an ephemeral voice like the Operator or maybe sitting here in human form. I'd prepared an endless list of arguments, tackling how I knew she hated me but if we worked together I could give her body back. I'd spent literally days and nights running through every version of our imaginary discussions, working up the courage to speak to her.

But I'd never imagined this.

"Stop it! Zara, stop, you're hurting yourself!"

She growled, pulling against her collar with a *hrrk*. Her breath was a horrible rasping sound, but she kept lunging for me. Choking. *Furious.*

"Zara, I'm sorry. I didn't—I didn't know you were stuck here in your vaxion form. I know you hate it, but—"

"*Lies.*"

Her voice, my voice, the voice I heard every time I opened my mouth to speak in this world, echoed in my mind. She shouldn't have been able to speak while transformed, but I could hear her as clear as day. "You did this. You cage me as Magnus did! As they all did."

"Zara, I swear, if I could leave right now and give you back your body, I would!"

"*Lies. Lies.* Lies!" Her head snapped left and right with every word, near rabid. Panic rose in my chest as welcome as a knife in the eye.

"I just need to know who, or what a wallow-tail is!" I shouted, prepared for another onslaught of rage, but Zara simply froze, eyes widening.

"Will Magnus stop at nothing?" she hissed, but it lacked the anger she'd wielded seconds ago. "He pushes my mind to the brink of madness until I scarcely know my own name. Will I ever… will I ever be rid of him?"

Abruptly she collapsed on the ground, curling up into a ball. Her lithe body halved in size as she burrowed into her side. Her curling tendrils followed suit, wrapping around her body like a curtain of flesh—hiding her from the world. A soft sound came from her. I leaned forward, straining to hear.

She was whimpering.

"I'm sorry," I said, tying my fingers in useless knots. To my surprise, tears sprang to my eyes. The last time Zara and I had "met," she'd dominated my mind with her rage, her very presence a tornado. I could never have imagined her looking so… lost and vulnerable. "But with your help, I can finish these quests quicker and—"

"Leave."

After the booming echo of her anger, her voice was painfully small. Almost childlike.

"Please."

My mind flashed with a memory… *her* memory. Magnus had locked her alone in a cell for days on end until the mere *smell* of water made her body shudder with want.

"Say it," he said, gray eyes colder than the stone she lay curled up on. He held a cup of water high above her head, the sound of it sloshing within like a tidal wave. Her lips split, blood trickling down her cheeks as he smiled.

"*Say it.*"

Zara was in human form, her skin shades of yellow and purple with healing bruises while a layer of grime was all that covered her bare shoulders. Shaking, she lifted her head, red-rimmed eyes locked on the water in Magnus' hands.

"Please," she whispered.

Then I was back. Back with Zara. Back in the dark chambers of my mind where once again Zara was a prisoner. And I was her warden.

I left without another word.

Chapter Fifteen

The sun was high in the sky when I woke. Wincing, I unlocked my fingers from their white-knuckled grip around my knees, pinpricks of pain shooting down my limbs as blood rushed to starving nerves. I rolled onto my back, the once inviting bed of moss feeling like rocks beneath me.

Zara.

She'd plunge a hand into my chest and rip my heart out in an instant to get her body back. The thought carried the usual shiver of fear, but it was overridden by something I never expected to feel for a woman known as the Fury.

Pity.

Called a traitor by her own people, she'd been battered, abused, and outright tortured by Magnus—her "betrothed," a man she was desperate to be free of. Zara's aunt and her aloof, imperious expression flashed in my mind. I'd seen only fragments of Zara's memories, but I knew her aunt was the reason she was condemned to serve Magnus.

To Zara, I was just another person in a long line who'd hurt her. Tormented her, even. I fought not to lie down and fall asleep again so I could speak to her. To explain I didn't choose this.

"Not. About. You!" I yelled, slapping my forehead with every word.

Still, I allowed myself another few minutes of self-pity. The forest that was once a restful Eden now felt silent and judgmental. Seeing Zara hit home the feeling that had been so easy to ignore while shifting hay back in H'tar—that I was a stranger from another world. And I had no idea what the hell I was doing.

I sighed, weighing my options.

I could wander around blindly and hope I'd figure out my quest, *Make the Wallowtail Shine*. Pros: It had worked with *Stop Aerzin*. Cons: It was pure dumb luck I wasn't dead.

Or… I could head for Eternity and the Ivory Keep. Pros: I knew the endgame had *something* to do with her—the endgame was called *Summon Eternity*, so that much was obvious. She'd been nothing but kind to me, even when she had no reason to trust me. Hell, she was the only reason I'd escaped my prison cell back at Magnus' castle. I thought of her soft smile and the care she took when bandaging the wound in my back. How tightly she'd held my hand on the castle roof. On the worst night of my life, she'd made me feel safe.

Cons: Valerius. Well, all of the Gilded. Who knew how they'd react if I, Zara the Fury, came strolling through the gates of the Ivory Keep. I might be decapitated and stuck on a spike before I could say, "Hey, guys!"

My choices boiled down to wandering around like a clueless idiot or getting my head cut off by the Gilded.

"I don't even know what a wallow-tail is!" I said, throwing my hands up to the sky.

Think—this is a game, which means you need to treat it like one. If this was a level in *Knights of Eternity*, what would you do? What would my nephew do? What would…

I stopped. My nephew.

The one I gamed with every Friday in the arcade. Who liked chocolate and banana sandwiches but hated carrots. Who was better at racing games than me even though I would never admit it. Who watched me get shot in the chest.

What was his *name*?

Not just his. What was my mom's name? And my sister's?

"Oh, god."

I shot up, heart battering my ribcage. My hand gripped my chest, tightening as claws peeked through my fingertips. "You knew you'd forgotten your own name, but that's okay. You remember everyone else's, *you do*. You just need a second." I pressed my hands against my face, dimly aware I'd nicked the skin of my forehead. Droplets of blood crested my eyebrow, trickling down to my nose. I barely felt it in my panic. "Your P.E. teacher is Mr. Gord. Then there's Principal May. And my mom…"

A blank void occupied the space where my mom's name should have been. I tried to circumnavigate it, grabbing at random information. "My mom is a nurse. She works in the ICU. She likes poached eggs, even though they stink, and can't function without two cups of coffee in the morning. Her name is... her name is..."

My palms tingled, static clinging to them like a dying storm. The sun darkened as clouds, black and furious, swam above me.

"My sister... my sister loves medical dramas and had her first child at twenty-two. She's Cl-Claudia? No." The feeling in my palms grew, the air becoming thick and heavy. The wind picked up, whipping my hair around me. "Her son... her son is..."

Dark hair and serious expression. Hopping from foot to foot as he did battle with Zara the Fury. Valerius' shield coming up just in time to block a pixelated fireball. Crying out in the dead of night—another nightmare. Another wet bed. Changing the sheets and lying down with him until he fell asleep. Tears in his eyes as he held my dying hand. Held my dying hand. Held my—

"*Noah!*" I yelled at the top of my voice—something small and hard cracking in my left hand as lightning erupted from my fingertips. It struck a nearby tree, snapping it in two. But I wasn't done—a sharp pain pierced my skull, threatening to drag Noah's name away from me.

"Noah," I roared, snapping my hand out, fingers splayed. A coiled spiral of electricity burst from my palm, singing the grass as it struck a rock, splitting it in two.

"Noah. Noah. *Noah.*" Lightning followed every word—a spell, a prayer, a lifeline as I turned the forest around me into a charred, lifeless husk of charcoal.

I had a brief memory of a boy I thought I loved, his brown hair and gentle smile—an offer of ice-cream once I passed my exams. Then he was gone—his face and name vanishing along with my mother's. My sister's. My own.

God, what did I look like? Was I tall? Short? What color was my hair? My eyes?

"Noah," I hissed, digging my hands into my hair. Minutes ago, the sky had been blue, the sun high and warm. Now it was as cold as the dead of night. Clouds sparked with lightning, but I didn't duck for cover. Instead I looked up as the heavens opened, a sheet of rain hitting me like a waterfall.

I flung my arms wide.

"**Strike me in fury,**" I yelled, the words coming to me like a familiar prayer. "**Strike me in death!**"

A bolt of lightning struck me, and my world turned white.

ABILITY STONE ACTIVATED.

WRATH'S STORM UNLOCKED.

***

The night was clear, the moon heavy and full but for a small patch of sky deep within the forest. Lightning and thunder erupted from pitch black clouds as Zara the Fury laughed, her own lightning striking her.

A shadowed figure watched the legendary falsling from afar. This was more than the usual vaxion bloodlust or their desperate urge to dominate—that he could handle. No, there was no doubt about it, Zara the Fury was simply *insane*.

He was about to run when his right forearm burned, forcing him to stop. One hand gripping the strange wound, he looked back, weighing the balance of his fate. Then his eyes narrowed, and he nearly stepped out of the shadows in surprise.

Zara the Fury wasn't laughing. She was *crying*.

The storm clouds above vanished as quickly as they had appeared, the sun returning as if it had never left as Zara collapsed to her knees. The earth around her was scorched and burned but for the tidy circle of moss she knelt in.

The figure hesitated, but his forearm burned. Teeth gritted, he settled back into the shadows once more.

Chapter Sixteen

The moss beneath my cheek was warm and made me feel toasty and safe—like I was curled up in bed beneath my favorite blanket. I groaned, knowing I should open my eyes, get up, and figure out the Operator's stupid quest. But I didn't want to move. Every time I drifted off last night, I'd picture Zara's face, and jolt awake—until the hatred in her golden eyes was burned onto the inside of my lids.

"So, did you mean to barbeque half the forest, or was this a warning for me to stop following you?" called a male voice. "Because if it was, consider me *gone*."

My eyes shot open to see a curly blond head staring down at me.

"Ahh!" was my dignified response. I rolled over, claws peeking through my fingers at the foreign scent that hit me. I felt Zara's bloodlust spike.

He dare… show his face… to me! Her thoughts echoed in my head, muffled at times, then booming on the final word—as if she were trying to push through.

I froze. She'd never been able to speak to me outside of Lukas' mind.

"Right, so this is the *opposite* of what I was going for," the man said, raising his hands in surrender. He was tall, with blond hair that curled around his ears. Startling blue eyes sat in tanned and freckled skin.

"Kindly don't cut me into teeny-tiny pieces. Thanks ever so much." He smiled, taking a cautious step back. His face was sharp and angled, with a full mouth that looked best when he smiled.

He was also painfully familiar.

"I don't even have my claws out," he said, wiggling human fingers. "It'd be almost *too* easy to kill me, right?"

The last time I'd seen him he'd been covered in dirt and blood and was, well, completely naked.

"*Lukas?*" I said, my claws disappearing into my fingers.

"The very one! I clean up nicely, don't I?" he said, gesturing to his dark brown shirt, simple gray trousers, and black boots. He wore a single worn leather bracer on his right forearm. "I woke up clean and fresh as a twilight blossom in the moonlight. Chief must have given me a sponge bath. Or Lenia, which is a horrifying thought—that woman is as prickly as a spike-hog in heat."

"But what... where... how..." I said stupidly, staring at him like a gaping fish. I'd seen inside his mind, seen his memories, but I was quickly realizing that didn't mean I knew *him*.

I'd had no idea he was so... so...

"Take your time," he said, eyeing the ground for a patch of grass I hadn't burned to a cinder. "I tend to have this effect on people." He sat down with a plop, crossing his arms behind his back and stretching out as if he were on a sunbed by the sea.

"How are you *awake*? And *here*?" I finally spluttered.

"I simply woke up—bright-eyed and bushy-tailed," he said, closing his eyes with a contented sigh. "And hungry enough to eat H'tar out of house and home—even Jerome chipped in with a big meat stew. Of course he got his missus to deliver it, but we all know she does the baking, and he does the dinner, so it was *definitely* from him. Not much of an apology for trying to kill me, but hey—it was delicious, so I'll take it."

He spoke rapidly, his voice a rhythmic sing-song. He cracked an eye to see me staring at him in utter confusion and snapped his fingers. "Ah yes, sorry—why am I *here*. Apologies, I tend to ramble."

"I noticed."

"Well, I'm *here* because of you. Lenia told me a smidge—about Magnus and the whole treating you like a torture puppet. Oh, and that Valerius tossed you from a dragon after you rescued Eternity, not very knightly of him, I might add. Sorry, I'm getting distracted. The long and short of it, my dear, is that you saved me from a life as a deranged murder-machine, so I decided to tag along with you. I knew you wouldn't mind."

"What do you mean, you 'knew I wouldn't mind'?"

"Oh—did you think the mind-peeking went one way?" he said, raising an eyebrow. "You went traipsing about my mind, but I caught a glimpse of yours too. Not much," he hurriedly clarified at my panicked expression, "but enough to know you are as in over your head as a koa cub in water."

He leaped to his feet, hands wide. "So here I am, Lukas Van Fyodin, at your service." He bowed low and dramatically but made sure, I noticed, to always keep one eye on me. I smiled. He might be over-the-top, but he wasn't stupid. Zara would approve—even if she hated him.

"I appreciate the offer, really. But you don't owe me anything."

He rolled his eyes. "I'm not suggesting you put a leash on me, that costs extra." He winked. "But I'm doing this for myself as much as you. You see, I can either tag along with you or stay in H'tar where everyone keeps looking at me like I have three heads." His veneer cracked for a split second, his smile faltering. "I almost miss when they hated me—at least I knew how to deal with that."

My heart constricted. "Lukas, I—"

"Mushrooms!" he exclaimed, cutting me off. "That's a good start—sit tight." He turned on his heel and marched into the forest while I stared after him—unsure of what to make of the chaotic falsling.

***

I smacked two rocks together at opposing angles. They made a short, sharp crack. Annoyed, I tried again, harder this time…

… and immediately dropped them.

"Don't take this the wrong way," Lukas said, sitting opposite me with his arms crossed, an eyebrow cocked. "But how are you *alive*?"

"That's rich," I snapped, rooting for the rock I'd dropped in the bundle of twigs and moss that should now be a fire, "coming from the guy who came this close to chewing his own leg off a few days ago."

I stopped, immediately regretting my words. Lukas looked at me with open surprise and threw his head back, laughing. It was a loud, booming sound that shook his whole body. I laughed in return, the sound infectious.

"A parry to my riposte! Well played. Well, now you have me—and every hero needs a sidekick, right?" he said, grabbing the two rocks from me and cracking them against each other. They sparked immediately, a precious ember catching a piece of dried moss. Lukas knelt, blowing on it gently as he coaxed the fire to life.

It had been a strange day.

After Lukas returned with an armful of mushrooms, he announced he knew a far better place to camp and promptly strode back into the forest, cheerfully telling me to keep up. We walked for hours, and he spoke a mile a minute the entire time—pointing out the names of trees (the red and yellow leaved-ones were called "scarlet sunders" while the blue ones I'd seen were "twilight blossoms"), flowers (I'd forgotten most of them already, but I noticed he didn't point out the "salily"—the flower H'tar used to make their scent blocking soap from) and the occasional animal (something with six-legs the size of a squirrel was a tree-topper mouse.)

I kept waiting for my heart to start beating like a drum and for my mind to start listing all the ways I was messing up or how this was all a trick, and he was going to turn on me. My school once ran some "ice-breaker" games in a vain attempt to prevent "cliques" from forming. I'd gotten so overwhelmed, I'd forgotten my name then hid in the bathroom until the janitor had to tell me it was nighttime and he had to lock up. Yet here I was, striding through the forest with a near-stranger, my mind quiet, comfortable even.

I looked down at Zara's body, *my* body. I was so different here to the person I was back home. How much of it was the game, and how much of it was Zara? And if, no, *when* I made it back home, would I go back to who I was? Did I even *want* to?

I was so distracted by these thoughts that Lukas had to elbow me when we reached the "camp site." I finally looked up, and my jaw dropped.

"I know, right?" he said, grinning smugly. "Not too shabby."

We stood on the precipice of a cascading waterfall. I'd heard it long before I saw it—I'd taken to using *Tithe of Beasts* sporadically as we walked, the sounds and smells of the forest a comforting backdrop against Lukas' ramblings. But hearing something and seeing it were two very different things.

The waterfall crashed, monotonous and soothing against rocks so deeply purple they looked black. This close to water, the grass was a rich, vibrant green, and we were surrounded by scarlet sunders that huddled together in a protective ring. Lukas, for once silent, beckoned me forward with a mischievous grin. We got closer to the edge, my toes instinctively gripping the craggy rock for purchase. Leaning over, I realized the waterfall ended in a deep pool before returning to the rushing river. I had the overwhelming urge to jump into the water below.

When I'd asked him how he'd found it, it was at least a three day walk from H'tar, he'd shrugged. "I ran off once and stumbled on it. Wasn't the first or the last time I did a runner, but I'd always end up here until I calmed down."

It was evening now, and the sun had finally set in the south (another crumb of knowledge courtesy of Lukas). Content with flames that eagerly ate the dried moss, Lukas produced a frying pan from his pack, cooking the mushrooms and other pokey-looking vegetables he'd picked along the way. He pulled several leather pouches from his pack, sprinkling their contents on the meal. The smell of spice in the air was intoxicating, and I had to fight not to grab the pan and tip the contents into my mouth. My stomach growled.

Lukas laughed at the sound. I felt my cheeks turn red.

He doled out the food, and I barely managed a thank you before I was shoveling it into my mouth with a spoon (provided, of course, by Lukas). The mushrooms were heavy and woody while a fat green vegetable he pulled from the ground provided a salty kick. I cleared the plate and was about to lick it when I caught myself, ready to apologize, until I spotted Lukas dragging his own tongue over his.

I eagerly did the same, licking it clean.

"H'tar's soap might hide our scent and let us live among humans, but if there's one thing that gives us away," he belched, "it's our table manners."

He stood, reaching for my plate.

"I'll do it," I said hurriedly, standing up.

"I'm already—"

"Nope!" I said, snatching his plate with a smile. "After a meal like that, you're going to sit right there and do *nothing*."

His eyes widened with fear, and he sat down so hard, the fallen tree truck he'd been using as a stool cracked. I moved to help him up, worried he'd hurt himself, but he simply laughed. "As Chief would tell you, I *love* getting out of chores. Off you pop, those plates won't wash themselves!"

I left the circle of firelight, the frying pan, plates, and spoons balanced precariously in my arms. Something tugged at me, and I glanced back to see Lukas with his head in his hands. Feeling uneasy, I headed to the river, wondering what I had gotten myself into.

Chapter Seventeen

Every year, the King of Navaros promised he would spend more time at the Ivory Keep with his wife and son, and every year he broke that promise.

It wasn't on purpose. But there was always a land dispute to settle, a noble who needed their ego soothed, an ambassador who demanded a personal tour of the kingdom. He would swear he would do better the following year, and then time would fall from his fingers like grains of sand.

He had never regretted breaking his promises, however, as much as he did right now.

Things at the border had been tense—Evergarden circled them like hawks with their banners of green and gold, pushing a little closer every day. The rattle of enemy armor seemed unbearably loud as soldiers' minds turned darker. The pressure of waiting with no news of Eternity's whereabouts grew like a storm cloud, effecting even the king, who was normally stoic and unflappable.

Where was Eternity? Who had taken her? How much blood would be shed before she's found? were questions the king asked himself every night before he fell asleep, his sword within arm's reach.

When Eternity was discovered in Magnus' castle, thankfully safe and sound, and returned to the Ivory Keep, both sides stood down. Yet the king's gut remained twisted. His retinue itched to return home after weeks of restless nights, but he stayed behind, waiting until every regiment had cleared up and left. He couldn't shake the feeling something was wrong.

Clutching his wife's small hand now, feeling how cold and clammy it was, he realized his gut had been right—something was wrong, but the enemy wasn't on the battlefield. The enemy was in his own home where the man he once called son threatened to destroy everything the king loved.

Firanta lay still in the bed, her graying hair sticking to her forehead that blossomed with fever. Her dark brows, usually pinched in a perpetual frown, were still and peaceful, which only made the king worry more. Even sleeping the queen frowned, tossing and turning throughout the night. Early in their marriage, the king used to grumpily grab a pillow and sleep on the floor. Now he desperately wished he could curl up next to her, only to get a swift kick in the knee when Firanta jerked in her sleep.

The door was flung open, and Liddy bustled in without so much as a curtsy. He forced his irritation down as she dumped a basket of bandages, bottles, and herbs onto the bedside table.

"I'm going to check her leg," she said by way of greeting. "Best leave the room."

"I'll leave when I'm damn well ready," he snapped. He could only imagine the dark look his wife would give him at his tone, but he refused to apologize—Liddy may be close to Firanta but that gave her no right to order him about.

Liddy simply shrugged, gripping the bed sheet where she gently, almost reverently, rolled it down Firanta's body—what remained of it, at least.

The smell hit the king first. A foul, stomach-flipping stench. His eyes moved of their own accord to the ragged chunk of meat that was once his wife's right leg.

Liddy carefully removed the bandages. Cut off at mid-thigh, what was left of her leg was a swollen, blistered mass, the skin ridged and angry from where Eternity had frantically and inexpertly burned the flesh, stemming the bleeding. Firanta's right hand had suffered the same fate—cut off at the wrist from where it had cradled the spymaster's head, or so Eternity claimed.

The king knew he should be grateful—he'd seen men bleed out in minutes from such a blow, and it was only thanks to Eternity that his wife was alive. But as he looked at the deep, angry burn wounds he couldn't help but think of his own battle mages—how they'd have cauterized the wound without leaving half the flesh scarred. How they'd have taken care of possible infection then and there, instead of her blood only being checked once she was carted back to the makeshift ward Liddy threw together. By then, of course, it was too late, and now his wife lay in the throes of a deadly infection. If Eternity, or any of the palace mages for that matter, had spent more time on the battlefield and less prancing about in the Ivory Keep, his wife wouldn't be suffering right now.

"Stop it," Liddy said as she coated Firanta's wounds in a thick yellow paste. "You're doing it again—running through every possible scenario. Every 'mistake.' I know you are. I can tell by your eyebrows."

"My wife is half dead because not a single one of you so-called *mages* thought to cleanse the wound."

"Your wife is half dead because your son had the fine idea to cut off the spymaster's head," Liddy snapped.

"Valerius is *no son* of mine," he spat, standing now, the anger he kept locked down and contained threatened to explode.

"I must have put the wrong name down on the birth certificate then," Liddy snapped, getting to her feet. She was comically small in comparison to him, barely reaching his elbow, but her words towered over him. "You know, instead of getting arsey with me, maybe you should point that finger at yourself, Your *Highness*. While you were taking your sweet time at the border, Firanta was here *alone*, and I've a fine mind to—"

"Shut… up," whispered a voice, every word a struggle. "Both of… you." Firanta sighed as her eyes rolled back in her head, falling unconscious once more.

Shame burned hot and heavy in the king's chest. He pressed a hand against Firanta's brow, wiping away her hair. "Liddy," he began. "Forgive my—"

"Now look what you've bloody done," the healer snapped, pushing the king's hand away as she checked Firanta's temperature, fussing over her patient.

The king forced himself to take slow, stilling breaths. It was a practice he usually reserved for the battlefield, but being around Liddy had a similar effect on him. Hand on his weapon, he moved to the window—the warmth from the noonday sun doing little to lift his mood.

Below him, the Ivory Keep's courtyard was a disaster. His soldiers, exhausted from traveling through the night once they received a frantic visit from one of the spymaster's shadows, had refused to return to their dorms for a well-deserved rest. Instead they worked tirelessly to clear the rubble, debris, and bodies that littered the capital's heart. The swell of pride in his heart was tainted by the anger he felt when he saw the ruin that was the eastern wall.

He'd had soldiers desert, a right-hand commander turn traitor, and even a lover once stab him in the back (quite literally). These things had left a crater in his heart, one those loyal to him had slowly filled. He was older now, his eyes sharper as he kept watch for anything that might prove a threat to him, his family, and the country he would die for. But such betrayals were a flickering candle compared to the inferno of hurt, pain and fury he now felt.

Liddy was right. The leader of the Gilded, the Prince of Navaros, his *son* had done this—and the sooner he dealt with it, the better.

He forced his anger into a ball, then flattened it, honing it like the blade he imagined swinging at Valerius' neck. The image made him go cold, but he pictured it over and over again until he was calm.

A low groan came from the other side of the room where a low, rickety bed faced his wife's.

"Can't you put him somewhere else?" the king asked, not even turning around.

"Thirty-five dead, including a babe just born," Liddy said, her voice a sad lilt at odds with her usual sharp tone. "He'll be next. And he deserves to have someone with him when he goes."

The king fixed his blue eyes, so like Valerius', on the twitching form of Lazander. Firanta had always said how important it was for Navaros to have "symbols," something that would inspire people. The Gilded were perfect, she'd argued—valiant knights who embodied everything they strived for as a kingdom: Honor. Justice. Strength.

The king preferred having a trained regiment of soldiers at his back, but he saw her point. And every single Gilded had proven themselves a hundred times over.

The problem with a symbol, however, was that it could be broken. Corrupted. And what would his enemies make of Navaros, now that their "stalwart" defenders were dead, crippled, or deserted? The king frowned, crossing the room at a quickened pace. Biting down on the fingers of his leather glove, he ripped his hand free of it, then pressed two fingers to Lazander's neck.

"Leon? What's wrong?" Liddy said, irritated once more. She watched him with one eye as she finished binding the queen's wrist. The king ignored her use of his given name, a privilege reserved for only those closest to him, and instead dropped his ear to Lazander's mouth.

"Too late," he said, straightening up. He looked down at the cracked lips and blue-tinged face of the young knight. His eyes were open, pupils dilated. There was a cold stillness to him that the king knew all too well.

"The boy is dead."

Chapter Eighteen

QUEST COMPLETED: END THE GILDED KNIGHT NPCS

The words flashed in front of Valerius' eyes. He was dead. Lazander was dead.

Valerius' ivory armor lay in the dirt next to him, broken beyond repair. He had stripped down to his trousers, his bare chest stained by blood and sweat that he dabbed at with a filthy rag.

The fire before him crackled and burned too high, threatening to burn him, but he grabbed a log and threw it on. And another. And another. The flames lapped greedily at the kindling, burning through it with a vicious hunger.

"Can I speak now, or are you going to hit me again?" Magnus asked, trying and failing not to recoil from the flames like a scared rat.

The once proud mage sat in the dirt. The unlikely pair were sheltered in a cave whose walls were damp with mildew, but the mage pressed his back up against the stone as far from the fire as he could get. His legs were bound, and his one remaining hand was chained to a spike Valerius had driven into the stone. An iron collar was clamped around his neck, the deep black stone at its center glowing a dull white every time Magnus' mana replenished, draining him dry.

If a filthy and disheveled Valerius was a mockery of his once resplendent self, then Magnus was a caricature. Gone was his snide arrogance, lustrous blond hair, and marble grin. In its place remained a dirtied, cringing creature. When Valerius had first taken him captive, the mage had bitten, kicked, and cursed every step of the way. Upon his return from his disastrous mission at the Ivory Keep, Valerius had expected much of the same. Instead, Magnus had sat up with a smile, babbling at Valerius like an excitable child.

Valerius had struck him in the head with the pommel of his sword in reply. Now Valerius ignored Magnus, who kept staring at him with wide, wondrous eyes, and focused on the Menu.

GRADE D+

He thought of Gabriel's eyes as he drove a sword through the mage's chest. Of Lazander, bleeding and broken at his feet. Of Marito's last words as he gripped Valerius and threw them both from the Captain's Barracks.

"Come back, Valerius," he'd said. *"Come back."*

The Calamity System flashed, pulling him from the memory. While he had succeeded in his mission, it still outlined his failures in bold: he'd outed himself as a traitor, become an enemy of Navaros, and now had nothing to show for himself but a set of broken armor and whatever resources he had left in his Inventory.

He received only one bonus for the whole thing.

Destroy people's faith in the Gilded Knights—Bonus

He could almost hear the whispers about the fallen prince. Of the treachery of the Gilded's finest. He wondered what his father, what the *king*, would do when he returned to find the Ivory Keep a shambles. To find his wife cut to ribbons.

No, not his father, *Valerius'* father, he told himself, dismissing the quest reward without looking at it. He stared at the wall of the cave, imagining how it would feel to drive his head into the wall over and over until his brains leaked from his ears. He grabbed a log instead, throwing it onto the fire. Then he grabbed another, and another, not stopping even when the fire grew dangerously high.

"Valerius? *Valerius!*" Magnus called, cowering from the flames. "Please, the fire—if you would just—"

The mage's words were cut off by the hand Valerius slapped over Magnus' mouth.

"Don't speak to me. Don't even *look* at me," Valerius hissed, his nails digging into Magnus' cheeks. "The only reason I haven't killed you is because *it* needs you."

The mage nodded eagerly, his eyes alight with a delight Valerius didn't understand.

"Trying… tell… you," he mumbled.

Frowning, Valerius took his hand away.

"Don't you see?" Magnus asked, smiling with yellow-stained teeth. "All this time, we thought ourselves enemies, when in truth we dance to the same tune. I know you can hear him. I know you've been to his prison—that plane of sand with its twin suns and the symbols that burn into our flesh."

Valerius froze. He immediately thought the mage's collar was malfunctioning, and that Magus had somehow read his mind, but the collar lit up as it drained his captive once more.

How could Magnus know about the Operator? The Calamity System had told him days ago that a new player had entered the game, but he'd already guessed who it was. It couldn't be Magnus—he still spoke and acted the same. No, he wasn't the new player, unless…

Magnus burst out laughing, a high-pitched hysterical sound. "I thought myself alone. Thought Zara's betrayal was a punishment for failing him. But it was all part of his plan! He led me to you, and you to me."

Valerius' world tilted, and the fire burned higher.

"You're a *player*? But if he dragged you here before me, that means you've been here for…" Valerius started, his words failing him. "… Years. Five? Six? More?"

"What does time mean when we serve the Void-star, the ruler of time, the speaker of truth? Calamity is all we need." Magnus reached for Valerius as if to embrace him, forgetting the chains that bound him. He was abruptly jerked back while Valerius recoiled at the look of manic joy in the mage's eyes.

Magnus shook his manacles in irritation, almost tripping over his words. "We've wasted so much time hating each other when we seek the same thing! We seek—"

"—to *Summon Eternity*," Valerius said in time with Magnus.

"You don't have to hide anymore, Valerius." The mage smiled. "Not from me."

***

"… careless, reckless, outlandish behavior befitting a *child*, not a Chosen of Gallow!" the Head Disciple spat, pacing the opening hall of the Gallowed Temple. It was a wide, open space—the dark marble walls making a perfect echo chamber for his fury, his voice amplifying and reverberating across the sparsely furnished room.

Eternity stood with her head bowed, trying to look suitably chastised.

Head Disciple Harrow was one of the oldest sages in the temple, and his acidic tongue was as legendary as his dedication to Gallow. His strict diet of rice and beans and hours-long daily penance had earned him some renown. But it was the black eye patch he wore that had made him the prime choice for Head Disciple. He'd driven a blade into his left eye, claiming the loss was nothing in comparison to what the Gallow's First Chosen, the original Lady Eternity, had suffered.

The head of the Ivory Keep's Gallowed Temple was rarely seen. He spent his days, and most of his nights, pouring over visions recorded by previous Chosen. When Eternity had first arrived, he'd eagerly invited her to the library where he sat primed and ready to record her experiences. He wanted to know everything, he'd said, hold nothing back. She'd spoken to his predecessor about the same thing almost a decade past and his predecessor before that. She knew her words were recorded somewhere already, but she humored the Head Disciple, knowing he was eager to prove his worth.

She spoke of the Void from when Gallow and the Tyrant came, the dimension where the First Eternity had locked the evil god away. How rare it was that Gallow spoke to her directly, yet how frequently it seemed to occur with the other Champions. How opening the door to his power hurt every single time, and it took all her effort to force her body to accept it.

Initially Harrow took detailed notes. But as the conversation progressed, his quill moved less and less until he ended the interview with the words, "While previous Chosen have reported ill effects when channeling the God of Judgment, your account suggest you suffer most severely. This is a sign that you need to dedicate yourself more thoroughly to Gallow, Lady Eternity. I suggest you spend your time here focusing on penance—you are clearly in desperate need of it."

They'd barely spoken since.

Now he stood before her, patches of red bursting along his pale cheeks. His usual pristine black robes were rumpled, and Eternity doubted he'd slept at all. Not that anyone had after Valerius carved both the capital and the queen into pieces. Disciples and novices alike crowded the temple floor, huddling as they stared openly at Gallow's Chosen being lectured. The whispers began.

Eternity's fists clenched.

"Perhaps we could retire to the library," she began, keeping her tone civil. "Or maybe the sages' meditation hall, instead of—"

"No!" he spat, a finger raised. "That is a privilege I would grant a Chosen! You, however, have proven you are little more than a careless child, who cares not for either Gallow or his Champions!"

He strode back and forth, hands moving through the air furiously. "You may be the hand who shall find this world's saviors, but you're also the key to their destruction. How could you defy Gallow like this?"

"I didn't *defy* Gallow. Did he order me to intervene? No, but Harrow—"

"*Head Disciple* Harrow," he barked, coming to a halt in front of her.

"Head Disciple Harrow," Eternity said, unable to keep the bite out of her words. "The queen was about to be *murdered*, by her own son no less. I knew Imani would be able to stop Valerius, and *she did*. With great ease, I might add."

"Of course she did, she's a Champion. Gallow is generous to those who follow his tenets. Tenets *you* have spurned with your misuse of the Heart and last night's ludicrous attempt at *heroics*. Tell me, if bandits were to kick down these doors right this instant and begin murdering your fellow disciples, what should you do?" he asked, his face inches from Eternity's. He had a small mole on his left cheek she realized, with two little hairs popping out of it. She focused on these, straining for politeness.

"Well?"

"… nothing. I should do nothing."

"Precisely. Gallow's word is law, and if he meant for you to save the queen, he would have ordered you to do so!"

"But Valerius serves the *Tyrant*!"

"So you claim," he said, chin raised, daring her to argue.

Today, she dared. "The spymaster himself said so, right before Valerius *cut off his head*."

"You mean the zindor? The falsling creature who fought alongside the Tyrant's lieutenants?"

"What?" she said, confusion replacing her anger. "What are you talking about?"

Harrow sighed, shaking his head. "This is why we ask you to leave the interpretation to us, Lady Eternity. We have precious few records from the First's time, but there exists an account from about a hundred years after her death. It tells of a horned creature that could take the face of its enemies. A creature that sounds exactly like the one Valerius fought last night. A creature who was an *enemy* of Gallow."

"I don't understand," she said, her confusion briefly overriding her frustration. "You think it's the spymaster who serves the Tyrant, not Valerius?"

"That's what the records suggest," Harrow said, looking every one of his eighty years. "But for all we know, the queen might have fallen prey to the Tyrant's promises."

He held up a hand at Eternity's outraged expression. "I believe she was deceived, as all of the Ivory Keep was," he conceded. "But only Gallow knows. Which is *precisely* why we don't interfere."

"But look at the Ivory Keep!" Eternity argued. "The eastern wall is in ruins from a *single man*. A man who killed two of the Gilded and gravely injured a third—knights who have faced down armies and not flinched! He *must* have made a bargain with the Tyrant, how else could he have done this?" She wanted to pull her hair out in frustration. Everyone was so busy arguing about ancient records and pointing their righteous fingers at her, they were skimming over Valerius as if he were a footnote on the page.

Harrow shook his head. "You act as if the Tyrant is the only evil in this world. Perhaps he serves the Tyrant. Perhaps not. But if you were meant to know, then the God of Judgment would have revealed it to you. All any of us can do is kneel and pray Gallow deems us worthy enough to save. And I think it's past time you were reminded of that."

He turned, his black robes snapping. "Lady Eternity is to be confined to the tower. Two meals a day of rice and beans. And no less than six weeks of sublimation."

A flurry of whispers sounded as Harrow left, not even glancing behind him. Eternity looked up, meeting Yolana's eyes, the young novice who usually followed her like a shadow at every opportunity. The novice stood with a huddle of other new recruits, their heads bent as they gossiped. Yolana turned away, refusing to meet Eternity's eyes.

Eternity's cheeks burned.

Half the world was afraid of her and the other half tiptoed around her like she was Gallow himself. Other than the Gilded Knights, her fellow disciples were the only people she could talk to. Now they looked at her with shame and judgment while whispering to one another.

She almost regretted what she had done. Almost.

"Come," Imani said, appearing like a shadow at her side. The Champion had barely spoken since the fight, but it was obvious she was as happy with her as Harrow was. Eternity sighed. She had forced Imani into a difficult position, and for that she owed the Champion an apology.

"I'm sorry—"

Eternity's words were cut off as her vision shattered, an explosive pain in her skull rendering her deaf and blind. Her head shot back, body nearly folding in half.

When Eternity channeled the God of Judgment, she cracked the door a few inches, then carefully opened it wide enough to borrow his power. It had taken her years to learn how to carry out his will without being crushed by the tidal wave that was his presence. This time, the door between her and Gallow wasn't carefully opened. It was shattered into a million pieces, her skin bubbling from the onslaught of power. She couldn't scream. Couldn't even breathe, so great was the pain. She could only watch, as if outside her body, as her spine bent at impossible angles.

Her eyes shot open, dark as the Void from which Gallow came. Symbols, those of his word, his Judgment, scurried across her body like spiders.

Novices and disciples alike threw themselves to the floor, heads bowed. Their prayers: the fifth sublimation and the eighth mercy fluttered about her like lights in the dark—a welcome distraction in the face of searing pain. Shadows trembled when she lifted from the floor, body twitching as she focused the inch of her soul that remained on keeping her skin and muscle still attached to her bones.

Only Imani still stood. The Champion didn't pray. Didn't bow. Instead her face split into a wide grin, her eyes wide and joyous.

Eternity would later learn that at that precise moment another person in the Ivory Keep was suffering the same fate. His back was arched in a makeshift hospital bed, body hovering above the sweat-soaked sheets. A hand reached out from the Void beyond and gripped his cold, still heart, squeezing it tightly.

Forcing it to beat with life anew.

Chapter Nineteen

"So, he sits in a dark space and 'judges' people?" I asked. The hour was late, and the fire was just an ember, but I couldn't bring myself to go to sleep just yet.

"The 'Void,' actually. With a capital 'V'—so we know it's *important*," Lukas replied.

Once I'd washed up, I expected us to settle down for the night, but dinner was only the beginning. Lukas perched on a log and asked if I wanted to hear a story, then immediately launched into an hour-long tale without waiting for an answer. He told me about the Gilded Knights and the time they bested a xandi, some type of horned beast. There were duels to the death, a corrupt noble, even a damsel to rescue—the works. I doubted a word of it was true, but listening to Lukas as he mimicked the knights' voices, leaped about pretending to swordfight, and finally fell to the ground, clutching his chest as the xandi died was the most fun I'd had in ages.

While Valerius hadn't been the hero I thought he was, hearing stories like this made me wish I could meet the other Gilded Knights. I'd only met Lazander once, but he'd been nothing but kind and fair to me. He'd even leapt to my defense, quite literally. Maybe Marito and Gabriel would be the same.

Lost in the daydream of meeting arcade game knights, I almost missed when Lukas mentioned he'd take a Gilded over a Champion any day. At my confused look, he bitterly explained that a Champion of Gallow had actually passed through the town as a xandi rampaged, people screaming for help.

And kept walking.

Thus Lukas launched into a new tale—this time of Gallow and his eternal foe, an evil god known simply as the Tyrant. It was even more dramatic than the last. The Tyrant descended, murdering, pillaging, and enslaving his way across the world until a single woman stood up to him—a woman called Eternity. I sat up straighter at the mention of her name, and Lukas noticed, rubbing his hands together as he described how Eternity's family was slaughtered in front of her, her tongue cut out, her eyes popped like melons, but still, she refused to bow.

I grimaced, trying to imagine going through that. I'd nearly lost my mind when Noah ended up in the emergency room once, and all because he'd... he'd... the thought vanished into dull fog as quickly as it had appeared, and I shook my head, trying to pick up the threads of Lukas' story.

"And so Gallow, the God of Judgment—a guy who is clearly the life of the party, decided to reach out and bring Eternity *back* to life. Then she found a bunch of people, called them Champions or whatever, and together they pushed the Tyrant back. She gave up her blessed, god-like life to bind him to the Void from whence he came." Lukas waved his fingers dramatically but couldn't hide the look of disdain in his face. "Every one of Gallow's Chosen have taken the name Eternity since, all in honor of the First."

I thought of Eternity, *my* Eternity, though the thought made me blush. I couldn't imagine anyone else having her name. Or her smile. Or—

"Now, Gallow saved us from a tyrannical god, thanks ever so much, and so on," Lukas said, interrupting my thoughts. "But his followers are the *driest* bunch you'll ever meet. They spend the whole time whining about the Tyrant's return and how Champions can save us, but these so-called 'saviors' would use our corpses for kindling if Gallow said so. And don't get me started on Eternity."

"What's wrong with Eternity?" I said sharply, surprised at how defensive I felt.

"Zara, her entire job is frying people from the inside out in the hopes she'll find a 'Champion.' That's thousands of people she's *killed*, and for what—three superpowered sweat-stains who don't give a damn about us?"

"Eternity *saved* me," I snapped, suddenly angry.

Lukas raised his hands in surrender. "I'm sure she's absolutely lovely, but I wouldn't let her touch me for all the coin in Navaros."

"Sorry," I said. "That just doesn't sound like the Eternity I know. I'd still be trapped in Magnus' dungeon if it wasn't for her."

The falsling shrugged, pointedly yawning. "Look, I've only got the stories— you're the one who met her, and I'll happily take your word over that of a drunk, Gallow-obsessed human I met in a tavern."

I nodded, taking his hint as I stretched out on a bedroll provided, of course, by Lukas. The man could have scaled Mount Everest with how prepared he was. "Night," he mumbled. He was asleep in seconds while I stared up at the star-filled sky, jealous of his snores.

My mind was filled with Lukas' stories of Gallow and the Tyrant. I'd heard Lenia mention the name "Gallow" in passing, but I had no idea who or what he was until now. I shivered. Nothing like that had been in *Knights of Eternity*. While Lukas' tale of the Gilded Knights felt, at best, like a highly entertaining exaggeration, nothing about Gallow and the Tyrant rang false. I'd kept my questions light, but my heart was pounding the whole time, and I'd had to force my claws to stay hidden.

Was I getting worked up over this because of Eternity? The girl who'd ripped up her own dress and used it to bandage my back. Who'd looked at me with tear-filled eyes, praying I'd save her. None of that matched with the Eternity who wielded the power of a god and burned through innocent people in the hopes of finding a Champion.

So why did Lukas' stories feel true?

I shook the thought off. Eternity hadn't mentally reached out to me since I'd woken up in Lenia's. I barely knew her, and worrying about her, gods, Gilded, and Champions, wouldn't help me figure out my quest or how the Calamity System actually *worked*. After seeing what a lifesaver Lukas and his endless supplies were, I was more determined than ever to figure the Inventory out. Only one thing sat in it now—one of the ability stones I'd received as a quest reward.

I'd accidentally activated one ability stone already, unlocking *Wrath's Storm*, but I'd no idea how I did it or what this other one did. When I fell asleep tonight, I'd try to figure out how to summon the other—

I blinked as a soft glow emanated from my right hand. Warm and comforting, the tips of my fingers tingled, becoming heavy. The glow vanished as quickly as it had appeared, leaving a jagged amethyst in its place. Tiny lines of white snaked through it, pulsating at my touch. I stared, mouth agape at the thrum of power, of *potential* that coursed through the stone.

Afraid this was dumb luck, I pictured the nearly endless empty slots of the Calamity System Inventory. The warm glow captured my hand once more, but I kept my eyes closed, opening them only once my fingers felt light as a feather—the stone was gone.

Biting back a whoop of joy, I scrambled out of my bedroll like an angry cat caught in a blanket. Grabbing pebbles, sticks, and even an entire log, I practiced adding them to my Inventory and then making them reappear once more in my hands. Unlike when I used my abilities and magic, it didn't tire me out. However I quickly discovered the Inventory had some limitations.

If I entered a rock and a pebble *together* into the Inventory, then I had to remove them both at the same time. I couldn't take out one and then the other. I also couldn't enter more than four things at any one time—not without a splinter of ice stabbing me in the brain. Even with these arguably very small restrictions, my mind raced with the possibilities. I could hold a near endless supply of food and water, but how long would it last in the Inventory? Would it slow down the rate of decay, or would it remain frozen in time until I used it? Could something *living* be kept in the Inventory? I recoiled at the thought of testing that one. As eager as I was, I didn't want to trap an adorable tree-topper mouse and then kill it by sticking it in a free slot. But there was something *else* I could test.

In minutes, I was looking over the edge of the waterfall, which was even more breathtaking at night. I smiled at how comfortable I felt beneath the night stars. Back in my old body, I'd always been nervous at night. When walking home, every kicked bottle, phlegmy cough, and tread of a stranger made me look over my shoulder and grip my keys tighter between my fingers. Here I felt sharper at night. More alive.

More at home.

It didn't take long to find what I was looking for.

The boulder was at least half my size. A deep purple like the rocks at the depths of the waterfall, moss and weeds clung to its base. It looked like it hadn't been moved for decades. I could just press my hands on it, send it to the Inventory in order to test the effects of size and weight. But where was the fun in that?

Cracking one of my shoulders, I gripped the rock. **"If the world will not yield— then I will break it."**

Monstrous Strength Activated.

I bent my knees, gripping the boulder at its base with both hands. I braced myself, but the boulder nearly shot up into the air, and I held it high above my head. Biting back a laugh, I closed my eyes, picturing the empty Inventory slot.

I stumbled when the boulder vanished.

"*Amazing,*" I said, wiggling empty hands with glee. I eyed an even bigger boulder, one twice the size of the last and even taller than me. Abandoning caution, I grabbed it with both hands and lifted.

I struggled, thighs burning, but that only made me more determined. With a whoop of joy, I raised the gigantic stone above my head, laughing in the cold night hair. Eyes closed, I focused on an empty Inventory slot.

> ERROR. ERROR. LIMITS EXCEEDED.

The Calamity System message flashed before my eyes, and I sighed, disappointed. Guess there was a weight and size limit after all. The boulder still above my head, I was about to place it back down when I spied the waterfall.

What's the point in being this strong if I can't have a little fun with it?

I drew my arms back, straining at the weight, and threw the boulder as hard as I could.

It went flying, careening through the air like a pebble. It hit the water so hard it created a huge wave that blasted outward. I laughed aloud, the rush from using my abilities making me heady. There was a joy, an *exhilaration* to my powers that was almost intoxicating.

"Just what, exactly," came Lukas' voice behind me, "are you doing?"

Chapter Twenty

Lazander stood in darkness. At any other time, in any other place, this wouldn't bother the knight. He was a hunter by trade and at home in the shadows. But this was no ordinary darkness. He couldn't move. Couldn't see. A complete and total void pressed in on him from all sides, threatening to crush his body to bone dust. It was hard to breathe, hard to *think*.

A scratching began in his palms and eyes as long, broken fingernails raked along his skin. He tried to tell them to stop, but opening his mouth was a mistake. The fingernails jammed down his throat, clawing and tearing his insides apart.

"PREPARE YOUR HEART."

Lazander's mind exploded with the bloodied pages of his life, his every mistake and every regret laid bare.

"FOR YOU FACE JUDGMENT."

***

Much like the queen, the king had never been a particularly devout follower of Gallow. He believed, of course—how could he not? He'd seen the scars the Tyrant had left behind and knew the Champions wielded supernatural powers of their own. He'd witnessed it for himself once when Champion Imani split the earth in two in a terrifying feat of strength.

Afterward, he'd paced the castle late at night, his mind refusing to grant him sleep. Did all the Champions possess such power? Did their abilities vary? Had they ever turned on a kingdom? Yes, yes, and no, were the answers he wrangled from a very annoyed Head Disciple Harrow at midnight. The castle's librarian and historian, an owlish woman who was only too pleased to be awoken for such questions, answered in the same vein.

Still, the king couldn't sleep. Not until he'd sketched out a strategy to trap and contain a Champion, though he hoped he'd never need it. It involved boiling black tar, fifty soldiers, and two days of preparation, but it was a plan. The king would never risk Gallow's wrath by attacking a Champion, not unless the situation was dire, but he told himself he was prepared for the worst. It was a comfort, a measure of control in an unpredictable world.

Now a voice in his mind whispered that he was a fool. When it came to gods, he was powerless. *Useless.*

Lazander's body rose from the hospital bed, his limbs jerking as if yanked by an inexperienced puppeteer. The king stepped back, his body moving on instinct as he drew his sword and shifted into a defensive stance.

"Get away, you old fool!" Liddy yelled, her diminutive frame trying to shield the unconscious queen. "It's him—it's Gallow!"

The room shrank as the invisible presence grew. Powerful. *Endless.* The king struggled to breathe, and his hands shook, but he gripped the hilt of his sword, unwilling to let it drop even an inch. A god. A literal god was in the room. And it took all he had just to stand. What use was black tar and soldiers against such power?

"BEHOLD."

That single word made the king's insides curdle, his teeth rattle. He knew if he spent too long before Gallow, his insides would turn to liquid from the sheer *force*.

"THE LAST IS BORN."

Blood dripped from the king's nose, but he planted himself squarely between Lazander's jerking body before him and Liddy and his wife at his back. He didn't dare take his eyes off the boy and the soul-shaking power emanating from him.

Lazander opened his mouth. The king braced himself. But the boy didn't speak. He *screamed*.

It was a scream the king knew well—that of someone dying in unending, agonizing pain. A scream he'd inflicted on others when the choice was between protecting his kingdom or sparing another's life. But Lazander didn't stop, not even to take a breath. He simply screamed, and screamed, while ink-black symbols crawled all over his skin.

The door to the ward kicked open, a figure in black armor bursting into the room at supernatural speed. Champion Imani managed two steps before she grimaced, slowing to a halt as she was forced back.

"The queen… get…" the king managed, but the words were trapped in his throat. He fell to one knee, driving his sword into the wooden floor as he forced himself to stay upright.

Get up! Your queen is half dead and helpless at your back. Get up!

Imani appeared at his side. He held out a hand, gesturing for her to grab the queen and run, but the Champion ignored him. Eyes set with rock hard determination, she gripped his shoulder and shoved him, using the momentum to push herself forward. He stumbled, his death grip on his sword the only thing that kept him upright. Fat red droplets fell from his nose and ears. He wouldn't last much longer.

Imani was chanting, a low guttural mantra that dimmed Lazander's screaming.

Ears bloody, the king could only catch snatches of it.

"Knife-hand… bloodbound… submit…" she hissed, power answering power in kind. At last she reached Lazander, and the king waited for her to pray to Gallow, cast a spell, or do *something* to contain the screaming knight.

Instead, Imani punched Lazander square in the face.

His body hit the bed with a crash. The overwhelming force vanished, and the king hit the floor. Bloodied and gasping, he forced himself to his feet in an instant.

"Liddy?" he barked, not taking his eyes off Lazander's prone form.

"Head is pounding something fierce, but I'm fine. As is Firanta." Liddy huffed. "She was out like a light the whole time—think she fared better than us."

"Imani!" the king spat. The Champion stood by Lazander's bed where she stared at him with wide, glowing eyes. "What in the Gallow-damned Void was that?" he swore.

The Champion's head snapped in the king's direction, and he took a step back at the look on her face. Imani was known for her stony expressions and clipped tone. In all his years, he'd never even seen a whisper of a grin. Now her mouth split in a wide, gleaming smile. "He was here," she said, breathless and reverent. "Gallow was here! Did you not feel him? Was he not *astonishing?*"

Unnerved, the king fumbled. "*Imani*," he said, his voice sharp and commanding. "What bloody happened?"

"Something that hasn't occurred in over a thousand years." The Champion took a steadying breath, and the king saw her stern facade slowly settling in once more—but the childlike spark of wonder remained. "Not since the First Eternity has Gallow himself reached out his hand and intervened like this." Imani placed a reverent hand on Lazander's naked chest. She closed her eyes, head tilting to one side as if listening to a silent voice. Then she nodded.

"A *Blessing of the Righteous* was placed on this boy by Lady Eternity," she said. "I can feel her touch, her earnest wish that he be protected. Her hope that Gallow would find him worthy." A flicker of sadness crossed her eyes, but then it was gone. "Gallow named her his Chosen for good reason."

"Champion, I am one word away from having you thrown in the stocks if you do not tell me why a *dead* knight floated off his bed and screamed loud enough for all of Navaros to hear."

"Eternity did what she was born to do," Imani said, gesturing to the dead knight. The king frowned, his breath catching when he saw Lazander's chest slowly rising and falling.

"She found a Champion."

Chapter Twenty-One

Lukas' blond hair was stuck up so straight, it looked like he'd been fighting it in his sleep. His arms were crossed, his body tense and stiff. He looked *angry*. An intense reaction, considering all I'd been doing was throwing rocks off a waterfall in the middle of the night.

"I... um. Couldn't sleep?" I said, shrugging awkwardly.

Lukas shook his head, then smiled. It was a thin painful smile. "You can drop the naive do-gooder act. We're not in H'tar anymore."

"What are you talking about?" I said, instinctively stepping back, his shift in tone making me tense. My feet gripped the stone, and I became keenly aware of the massive drop behind me.

"You saw my mind—parts of it, at least," Lukas said, edging closer. "The vaxion kept to themselves on the Moonvale Mountains, even when the molger were still welcome there. And while everyone and their mother has *heard* of Zara and Ashira, almost no one has met them."

At the name *Ashira* something unlocked in my mind—a memory of a tall, powerfully built woman with arms like tree trunks and a smile sharper than a dagger. I'd "met" her twice—once in a memory Zara had shown me and another time in Lukas' own mind where she taunted him, telling him he would return one day to the Moonvale Mountains.

Ashira was Zara's aunt—and leader of the vaxion.

"No one has met them, that is, except little old me. The glory of being a vaxion-molger bastard." He shook his head. "I met Zara when we were kids. She was eleven years old and burned half of the Moonvale Mountains for *kicks*. The Zara I know isn't some quiet tree-topper mouse who has never heard of Gallow and looks like a puppy died whenever I talk about the Gilded Knights. Now in your defense," he raised a single finger, "your look is perfect—the eyes, the scar, everything. But your acting would get you thrown out of a children's play."

Crap. Crap! He's actually met Zara? I have so many questions—no, that doesn't matter. Should I tell him the truth? But it sounds insane. I could lie, but I have the poker face of a toddler who is terrible at, well, poker. That doesn't matter—just say something, anything! Stop—

He leaned in close, making a show of looking around him. "What I can't figure out is what you're after. At first I thought this was an elaborate con. Travel to H'tar, scam the molger, and go about your merry way—with my blessing, I might add, but you left most of their gifts behind, and no one who didn't understand the vaxion *intimately* would have been able to... save me like you did. So," he clapped his hands together, "what's the play here?"

Every step back I took, he took another forward until I was inches from the waterfall. The Lukas I'd met, the jovial, excited, rambling falsling who always had a story on the tip of his tongue was gone. A muscle twitched in his cheek. I realized I'd been wrong. Lukas wasn't angry—he was *scared*. He was just better at hiding it than most.

"There's no 'play,'" I began, wanting to assure him. "I'm just trying to get back... home."

"To the Moonvale Mountains?"

"Not exactly." I held up my hands, the thunder of the water at my back near deafening.

"Woman, talking to you is like eating soup with a fork," he said, exasperated. "Who are you, and what are you after? And don't say 'nothing.' You don't risk your life for a stranger unless you want something."

I fumbled for an explanation that wouldn't make me sound insane—that I was a girl from another planet? A player in a game world? The prison warden of the real Zara the Fury, who was trapped in my mind? But then something cut through the haze, something that wouldn't have occurred to me back when every thought was cloaked in anxious energy.

Why was I letting this guy push me around?

"I saved you because I could. Because it was the right thing to do. And what do I get for my trouble? Yelled at in the middle of the night!" He blinked in surprise, and just like that the conversation shifted. I drew myself up to my full height, fists clenched. "*You* followed me. *You* said you wanted to help. But if you're going to stand around, accusing me of being a scam artist, then—then you can just leave." I felt Zara's presence grow in the back of my mind, but instead of being a threat, it was a comfort. I shoved past Lukas, my heart pounding.

I can't believe I did that! Even Zara would be proud.

"The, ah, campsite is that way," Lukas called out, pointing in the opposite direction.

I froze, mortification burning my cheeks. I ducked my head, mumbling a "thanks" as I slinked back to the camp, unable to look him in the eye.

Lukas didn't follow.

***

A pop-up appeared, framed by golden balloons. I blinked, amazed I'd fallen asleep. I'd lain awake for hours, fueled by nervous energy as I waited for Lukas to return to camp.

He didn't.

I sighed—maybe it was for the best. *Knights of Eternity* was a solo player game after all. I focused on the pop-up, and my heart leaped.

CHARACTER SHEET UNLOCKED.

Well, *that* was new.

Knights of Eternity had no "Character Sheet"—the armor, weapons, and potions you earned along the way were all that mattered. Curious, I clicked the new tab.

Current:	
Stamina	75/300
Hit Points	300/300

| Mana | 500/500 |

My jaw dropped. I'd known Zara was a powerful character, but I had no idea she was *this* strong. I returned to the sheet.

Base Stats:	
Strength	80* (note, *Monstrous Strength* triples this stat.)
Essence	100
Resistance	50
Recovery	70
Speed	80
Luck	15

I wondered what "Essence" meant as a new pop-up appeared.

> *Essence refers to the magic that naturally occurs in every living creature. Essence can influence spellcasting time, frequency, and the ability to cast in non-affinity branches of magic. Falslings have a particularly high level of essence due to their inherent shapeshifting abilities.*

Impressed, I brought up the "Resistance" stat.

> *Resistance refers to the body's ability to withstand magical attacks. Falslings have a lower level than non-magic-based players such as knights.*

I grimaced, thinking of Valerius. It wasn't just his armor and shield that had let him go toe-to-toe with Magnus. If my Resistance was considered "low," what was his? He could probably get hit with Zara the Fury's ultimate *Inferno* and just walk it off.

I paused on my "Luck" stat, surprised at how low it was in comparison to everything else, but then I realized it made sense. Zara wasn't someone who would ever rely on luck for anything—she'd just get the job done. Often brutally.

I almost missed the final column of my Character Sheet.

Racial Bonus:	
Refusal in Death	*Vaxion culture demands complete defiance in the face of death. This bonus grants the player a one-time use skill that prevents their HP from dropping below zero.* *Uses left: zero*

I gasped.

Valerius. When Valerius had thrown me from the dragon, I'd gone crashing through a forest and woken up staring at the sky, wondering how I'd survived.

I hadn't—*Refusal in Death* had saved me. I'd lost the one life I had, and I hadn't even known it. The next time I died, it would be permanent. The thought shook me to my core, but I pushed it to one side. It was no different to *Knights of Eternity* where there were no bonus lives. This was just a game I had to figure out, I told myself.

I ran over my stats once more. While *Knights of Eternity* hadn't had Character Sheets, they weren't new to me. But that wasn't what made me uneasy. It hadn't escaped my notice that figuring out the Inventory had unlocked the Character Sheet. Every time I mastered one aspect of the Calamity System, a new one appeared.

The edges of the Menu started to fade as dawn broke.

What else could the System do, and would I spend my entire time in this world just trying to understand it?

***

"Morning!" came a sing-song voice. "I caught a spike-hog—prickly bastard. But they go *excellently* with the eggs I snatched from a sparrow-wick's nest."

My eyes snapped open to see Lukas perched on a log. He was cheerfully spooning what looked like scrambled eggs onto a wide leaf. "I was a bit stingy with the salt I'm afraid," he said, handing me the leaf.

I hurried to take it, and he spooned out another serving for himself.

"I thought you'd left," I finally managed.

"I almost did," he said. "But then I realized you were right. I was so convinced you were trying to screw me over I didn't think about what you'd actually asked of me—which was a big fat nothing." He shrugged, the motion spoiled by the egg he shoveled into his mouth. "Maybe you're Zara. Maybe you're not. It doesn't change the fact that you saved my life. Which means I'm going to spend more time helping and less time throwing around accusations." He smiled, warmth and ease in every crease. He meant every word. I had yelled at him, and he wasn't even annoyed. Tears pricked behind my eyes.

"Oh no!" he said, looking panicked. "Are the eggs bad? I thought they tasted fine, but I'd lick moss off a stone, so—"

"No," I said, shaking my head. "The eggs are great." I tipped the food back into my mouth, and he chuckled, doing the same.

We sat in companionable silence. I cleaned up afterward, washing out the pan in water nearby. When I returned, Lukas was stretched out in the sun like a cat, his back arched, hands behind his head. "What's next, boss?" he asked cheerfully, his eyes still closed. "If the plan is to never move from this spot again, I'm absolutely fine with that."

I wanted to ask him again why he was fine with all of this—no sane person would be. But then I wasn't exactly being honest with him either.

"Well, we need…" I said, watching his face carefully. "… to make the wallow-tail shine."

Chapter Twenty-Two

Eternity stared in wonder at the rise and fall of Lazander's chest. Behind her, the king and Head Disciple Harrow stood arguing—as they had been for the last hour.

"... I *know* what I heard," the king said icily. He'd arrived hours after Valerius' attack, nearly two days ago now, and he still looked like he'd just stepped off the battlefield. His once ivory-colored armor was dirty and bloodied, and his cloak was tattered and gray. Eternity doubted he'd slept since he got here, but the king's eyes were sharp, his words even sharper.

"You're *sure* those were his precise words? Few mortals are fortunate to witness the power of Gallow, let alone be in his presence. Perhaps you were simply overwhelmed?" Harrow asked, his hands in the sleeve of his robe, the quill and parchment he'd brought to take notes abandoned with barely a scribble on them.

Eternity sighed. Unlike the sages, she'd spent time in the royal court, as well as around other... well, *people*. Harrow, on the other hand, had spent most of his life cloistered in a temple where people tiptoed around him. He wasn't used to speaking to kings—a fact that was becoming painfully obvious.

"'Behold,'" the king said, audibly grinding his teeth. "'The last is born.' And if you ask me to 'repeat,' 'clarify,' or 'recall' again I will order the Gallowed Temple stripped of stone and used for the Ivory Keep repairs."

Harrow's infamous splotches of red appeared on his cheeks. Eternity muttered a quick prayer to Gallow that the Head Disciple would hold his temper. A small part of her, however, was enjoying listening to Harrow fumble so badly. Not that she would ever admit that, of course.

"You would *dare*?" Harrow spat, drawing himself up to his very inconsiderable height. "Gallow owes no allegiance to king or country, as you well know! You have no right-"

"Unless Gallow wishes to return the coin we spent building that ridiculous behemoth of a temple you *claimed* to need, I can do whatever I damn well please," the king said, dismissing the sage with a flick of his fingers.

Harrow turned the shade of an overripe tomato.

"Leave—now. Before I make good on my threat."

"I will *not* be spoken to—" Harrow began, but Eternity stepped up beside him with a smile on her face.

"I've stabilized Lazander," she said brightly. She hadn't wanted to intervene, but at this rate Harrow was going to leave her and two hundred other disciples without a roof over their heads. "Champion Imani's method of… ceasing the flow of magic was unorthodox, but effective—without our intervention, Lazander's body wouldn't have been able to contain Gallow's power. The resulting explosion would have taken out at least part of the Ivory Keep."

She smiled at the king, noting the surprise in his eyes. While it was good Harrow had been put in his place, there was nothing wrong with reminding the king that having Gallow's Chosen in his capital, along with his temple, was a benefit worth keeping.

"Liddy!" the king barked.

Silence.

The walls of the makeshift ward were cracked in places while chunks of the floor were missing. Once Imani had "knocked the boy's lights out," as Liddy put it, Imani had made no attempt to hide her supernatural abilities. She'd half run, half flown to the Gallowed Temple, grabbed Eternity, who was only getting to her feet, her head splitting, and then sprinted back to Lazander without a word. Eternity scarcely had time to take in what had happened before her hands were on Lazander's, and she was fighting to calm the magic that still raged inside his body.

It didn't take long for Head Disciple Harrow to join them, snapping his fingers at Liddy for a quill and parchment. The healer had announced she was going to "take a nap" and left—ignoring Harrow entirely.

"*Liddy!*" the king roared, making Eternity jump.

There was a scuffle from the hallway. The healer appeared in the doorway, her gray hair sticking up, eyes red from lack of sleep. "Leon, your arm better be bloody hanging off."

"Move the queen."

"I *have* moved her," Liddy said. "Three doors over—at your specific and insistent request."

"Move her again," the king said. "I want her on the other side of the castle, as far from the boy as possible."

Liddy's mouth formed a thin line. "I've more than your dear wife to look after, and if I'm tearing from one side of the castle to the other—"

"Liddy—"

"—then I'll end up killing someone in my stupor," she said, talking over the king. "Firanta is staying put, and you're going to let me *sleep* for the first time in *days*."

Eternity hid a smile with a cough as the healer slammed the door. The king sighed, running a tired hand over his eyes.

"Your majesty," Eternity began, dipping her head. "The danger has passed. Champion Imani saw to that. Lazander will need time to recover, but he is no threat to anyone in the Ivory Keep. You have my most solemn vow."

The king took a breath, his eyes flickering from Lazander's prone form to Eternity's earnest smile.

"Very well," he said. "You'll stay with the boy until he's up and about."

"I'm afraid that won't be possible," Harrow said, looking smug. "Lady Eternity is to be confined to the tower for the misuse of the First's—"

"Get this man out of here before I break his neck," the king announced.

Eternity looked around, unsure who he was speaking to, until two shapes formed from the shadows that lined the northern wall. Clad in black, the spymaster's aptly named "shadows" bore cloaks imbued with the Gilded Knight Gabriel's own magic, which allowed them to mold and shape the darkness.

To Eternity's shame, she recoiled from the shadows—remembering Harrow's claim that the spymaster served the Tyrant. Judging by the rage in Harrow's eyes, he did too.

"I will *not* be manhandled by traitors," he snapped when one of the shadows, someone tall with arms the size of Eternity's head, moved to grab the Head Disciple. "They serve the *zindor*—the Tyrant's lapdog!"

"Who served my wife—a better judge of character than anyone I know. And if they were good enough for her, then they're good enough for me," the king replied, eyes flashing with a warning.

With an undignified snort, Harrow strode out of the room. The shadows stepped back into the darkness, vanishing once again. Eternity sighed, knowing an hours long lecture awaited her when she returned to the temple.

"If he gives you any trouble, tell me. I'll have him banished from the Keep," the king said.

Eternity chuckled, thinking he was joking. Then she saw his expression. "Oh! There's no need for that. Though I appreciate the offer," she hastened to add.

"This has never happened before, correct?" the king said, nodding at Lazander.

She noticed he made a point to never call him by his name. "Not like this, no," she said, moving toward the Gilded Knight. He sighed in his sleep, his brow furrowed as his eyes roved behind his lids—lost in a dream. Or a nightmare. Instinctively she brushed back his hair, and he softened at her touch. A blush tinged her cheeks when she realized the king was watching them intently.

"When someone offers themselves up for Judgment, I act as a conduit," she explained, eager to divert his attention. "Gallow has a Chosen for good reason—this plane, this *dimension* isn't meant for gods. It's why when the Tyrant first set foot here, he nearly tore the world in two."

The king looked unconvinced. "I've heard the bedtime stories. The force from 'a single step' formed our mountains and valleys."

"You might have heard it, but I've seen it. *Felt* it," Eternity said, more sharply than she'd intended. "When I open the door to Gallow, it takes every ounce of my own magic to keep myself from being torn asunder. It's why Gallow uses me to create his Champions. He grants them power, and I ensure it doesn't kill them. At least until they're strong enough to withstand it on their own."

"Hard to kill someone who's already dead."

"When the First was Chosen, my namesake, she was dead too. Or so our records say," she said, unwilling to be like Harrow who quoted eye-witness accounts as if he were there himself. "What I'm more concerned about is what Gallow said. 'The last is born.'"

"Why concerned? Sounds like your duty is done. One I don't think you enjoy very much," the king replied.

Eternity schooled her face into a smile, unsettled at how easily he was able to read her. "We don't have to enjoy our duties to carry them out—as I'm sure a king understands," she countered.

The king chuckled. "A fair point." The richness of his laugh caught her by surprise, as did his blue eyes, so like Valerius'. He was a handsome man, she had to admit, one who loved his wife and kingdom proudly and openly. A tinge of loneliness twisted in her heart.

"That doesn't explain what your god meant though," he said, bringing her back to the present.

"That's for Head Disciple Harrow to figure out." She smiled, side-stepping the question. "I'm merely Gallow's conduit."

The king narrowed his eyes but didn't press her further. "Then I'll be sure to follow up with him—whether he likes it or not."

He turned on his heel, his armor barely rustling as he left. She wondered what else he had gleaned from the conversation, more than she had revealed she guessed, but there was little she could do about it now.

Glancing around to make sure she was alone, she gently closed the door after the king…

… and collapsed on the floor.

Chapter Twenty-Three

"The wallow-tail?" Lukas asked, sitting up with a smile. "*That's* what you're after? Why didn't you say so!" He leaped up, rolling up bedrolls and tidying away supplies with a smile.

"You know what it is?" I asked.

He frowned, pausing with a spoon in one hand and a frying pan in the other. "Zara, haven't you learned by now? There's *very little* I don't know. The benefit of being nosey." He tied the frying pan to the outside of his pack. "Why do you want to—nope. I'm here to help, not ask questions." With a devilish grin, he leaped up, slipping his arms through the straps and striding into the woods without a word.

"Wait—what is the wallow-tail?" I asked, running after him.

"I said I wouldn't ask questions, not that I'd give any answers." He winked. "Knees to chest, Zara. We've got a hike ahead of us!"

He sped up, dodging through trees and leaping over rocks with ease as he tore ahead. I shook my head, trying and failing to be annoyed. I'd finally met someone who knew what the wallow-tail was, and it hadn't escaped my notice that the answer to my next quest lay in the solution to the last. I must be doing what the Operator wanted—this must be "the golden path."

So why not have some fun along the way?

"I am death's mistress—bow before me." Claws burst from my fingers. My feet grew in size, and I felt the whisper of the beast I could be, the *vaxion*, run through my body.

Fury's Claw Activated.

"Hey, Zara!" Lukas called from up ahead. "Do I need to get you a walking stick, or are you—"

"You're it!" I cried, playfully slapping the back of his head as I zipped past. I focused on the balls of my feet and leaped straight up. The air rushed past me as I landed on scarlet sunder, lightly touching down before jumping to the next. I felt happy. I felt *alive*.

"Oh, it is *on*." Lukas laughed.

I was so busy having the time of my life, I didn't even glance behind me, believing there was no way Lukas could catch up.

Something heavy gave a staccato growl, a mimicry of a laugh, and then a dark shape shouldered me *mid-air*. Knocked sideways, my body spun as I twisted, one hand slapping off a passing tree to correct my direction. I hit the dirt with a huff, landing on the balls of my feet.

I looked up, my breath vanishing at the creature in the trees above me.

Long coils of flesh circled his skull like Medusa's snakes, the tendrils moving in a hypnotic pattern. Shaped like a panther, but twice the size, it crouched in the trees, all muscle and darkness. A vaxion, beautiful, dark, and deadly, stared down at me. It carried a pack in its mouth, a long fang threatening to puncture the frying pan strapped to the back.

"How—you changed in seconds!" I cried, half in outrage, half in wonder.

Lukas growled again, the same staccato laugh. The vaxion closed one eyelid, then opened it—the movement awkward in his beastly form.

"Do not *wink* at me—hey!" But he was already gone, leaping from tree to tree at twice his previous speed.

I stared after him, my cheeks hurting from how hard I was smiling. Only a week ago he was trapped in the body of a monster, fighting night and day not to kill his neighbors. Now he was *willingly* transforming into the beast H'tar hated him for being. It was silly. I barely knew him. But as I watched him tear off into the forest, my heart swelled with pride.

I still wasn't going to let him win though.

I knelt in the dirt, letting the soil under my fingers ground me. I couldn't transform into a vaxion—nor would I, knowing how much Zara hated that form. But I could get close.

"**Untethered—the beast screams.**"

Partial Transformation Activated.

The words flashed as my ankles broke, elongating and snapping backward with a sickening crunch. My fangs grew longer, my skin rippling like a pebble dropped in a moonlit lake. I felt no pain, only an electrifying numbness that made the hair on the back of my arms stand up straight.

Standing, I took a step on my new legs. Dark fur began at my mid-thigh, and my ankles bent back like a cat's. I balanced on dainty paws—paws built for *speed*.

Grinning, I ran after Lukas, determined to catch up.

***

"That was… insane… damn…" Lukas panted. His words were muffled from either exhaustion or the dirt he was lying face down in.

"That's—that's what… you get for showing off," I said, trying and failing not to sound as dead as I felt. We'd run for *hours*, the sun reaching its zenith and then fading to a dull orange, and kept running. Lukas had dropped to the ground when I'd sprinted past him, tearing up the dirt as he chased after me. Despite the fact he was in his full vaxion form, I'd kept up with him the whole way. Unfortunately I was paying for that now.

I groaned, every muscle in my body screaming as it burned. It hurt to move. Hurt to *breathe*. I didn't care though.

"Beat… your ass," I managed to say, half collapsed on a log. I'd been trying to sit on it, had missed, and was now simply sprawled on it.

"Did not!" he said indignantly. With a groan, he rolled onto his side. "I had to carry… a pack in my mouth!"

"I know," I said. "The silence was glorious."

He laughed, then winced. "Don't be funny," he groaned. "One, that's my job. And two, *ow*."

"Your job is to be funny? Weird. I hadn't noticed." I ducked to avoid the twig he threw.

"Right." He grimaced, forcing himself to sit up. "We've enough leftovers from this morning for dinner. Do you want a fire or…?"

"Lukas, I'm hungry enough to eat that stick you threw."

"That was the right answer!"

We polished off "dinner" in seconds, including the fruit he had in his pack for emergencies. Licking my fingers clean, my stomach gurgled—still hungry.

"That's what we get for staying changed for so long." Getting to his feet, he winced. "Let me see if I can't find us something else."

"Are you joking? It's the middle of the night—stay right where you are," I said.

Lukas froze mid-step, his eyes wide. Then he sat down with a smile, but I hadn't missed the look of terror on his face. "I hate being hungry," he explained at my questioning look. "But you're right—let's wait until morning."

"Are you all right?" I asked, concerned. Why had he looked so scared?

"Absolutely." He nodded. "Just eager to get to bed." But he made no move to get up. When the silence dragged on, I grabbed our bedrolls, rolling them out for us both. We had no fire, but we didn't need one. The night air was warm on my skin, and I was already looking forward to falling asleep beneath the stars.

I lay down with a pleased sigh, but Lukas still sat up straight, eyes on me.

"Go to bed, Lukas," I said, frowning. "Or are you still sore over losing?"

"Nope!" he said, springing up. "Night!" He rolled over onto his side without another word.

I shrugged, too tired to push him further. Closing my eyes, I held the image of my nephew, Noah, in mind. I pictured his frown as he glared at a plate of broccoli. His laugh as he overtook me in a racing game. How tightly he squeezed my hand at his dad's funeral.

"*Noah*," I whispered to myself as I drifted off. "Noah…"

In seconds the Calamity System Menu, bright and golden, hovered before my eyes.

I hesitated. While running, I'd been lost in my own world, and a glorious rush of endorphins, but the moment we started setting up camp, all I could think about was Zara. Yes, she was trapped. And yes, she blamed me for it, but ignoring her while I ran around in her body wasn't the answer. She deserved more than that.

I mentally brought up the Origin tab.

ORIGIN OF PLAYER CHARACTER: ZARA THE FURY. STATUS: AVAILABLE.

WOULD YOU LIKE TO SPEAK TO ZARA THE FURY?

Yes, I thought, knowing I was probably going to get my head bitten off.

***

"… in the end, I managed to beat him. Not that Lukas will admit it," I finished. I sat with my legs crossed, my elbows on my knees.

Zara still lay with her back to me, the luminous white glow of her vaxion form a beacon in the darkness.

My eyes strayed, as they had countless times that night, to the chains around her neck.

"We should reach the wallow-tail tomorrow," I said, looking away. "But I still don't know what it is, or how to 'make it shine.'"

Zara said nothing. When I arrived, she hadn't even growled. The only sign she was alive was the methodical rise and fall of her shoulders as she breathed. She looked like she hadn't moved a muscle since we last spoke.

At first I didn't know what to talk about. I'd almost told her about my old life—what little I remembered of it anyway. But then I decided against it. I didn't even know how I'd describe an arcade game to her, let alone that I came from a different world.

So I started from the last time Zara and I had met—when we'd fought one another for control in Lukas' mind. I told her how I'd returned to discover Lenia had beaten the crap out of her brother-in-law. How Lukas lay half dead on the ground, surrounded by all of H'tar. How he'd done the impossible and transformed from his vaxion to his molger form, then back to human. Her entire body had stiffened at that, muscles coiled. I thought she was going to speak, but she simply took a long, deep sigh.

She was listening, at least.

I ended with Lukas' and my silly race. Other than the tension that rocked her body at the mention of Lukas' transformation, she stayed as still as a lake's surface. Feeling stupid, I sighed in the sudden quiet. I didn't expect us to become buddy-buddy or anything, but I thought she'd at least say something.

Light flickered in the distance, and Zara's white form grew soft around the edges—the darkness slowly giving way to dawn. "I'm waking up," I said, standing awkwardly. "But I'll be back again. I just… thought you should know what's happening out there."

She vanished, and suddenly I was awake and on my back, dawn's light tickling my cheeks. It was a new day, but the memory of Zara, alone in the dark, was burned into my mind's eye.

Chapter Twenty-Four

Lazander wasn't awake yet, not fully, but he could feel that something was wrong. His limbs felt slow and strange. Even twitching his fingers took a supreme amount of effort. He remembered Gabriel collapsed on the ground, Valerius' sword through his chest. Marito falling, his arms wrapped around their former leader. Merrin shrieking.

What happened after?

At once he was struck by the memory of a voice—one that called for his Judgment. He remembered his darkest thoughts and desires being stripped from him like pieces of flesh until he lay boneless and empty. He was dead. He must be. There was no other explanation.

"Lazander," came a voice, warm as honey. It was a voice he'd dreamed of on lonely nights. "Lazander, I'm here—you're safe."

"Eternity...?" came a raspy voice he belatedly recognized as his own. He cracked an eyelid to see Eternity, her usually pristine blonde hair limp and dry. Deep shadows marked her eyes, and he caught a smudge of dried blood beneath her nose. Without thinking, he raised a hand to wipe it away.

His calloused fingers brushed her skin, and she blinked in surprise. "Are you all right?" he managed. He didn't know what had happened, or where he was, but Eternity was bleeding—this was important. This was something he had to fix.

"Oh! Oh, I'm sorry," she said, flustered. She grabbed a rag, wiping it away.

"Are you hurt?" he asked, distracted by a small scar on her bottom lip he'd never noticed, translucent with age. Her eyes, blue to his memory, contained tiny flecks of silver that shone in the morning light. How had he never noticed that before?

"No, I'm fine. As are you, I think." She smiled. "I was afraid we'd lost you to the process—I don't think it's ever been interrupted like this before. But if the first thing you ask is if I'm hurt, well, I think I have my answer."

Her warm fingers gripped his. "I'm so glad you're all right, Lazander."

"What happened?" Words, both his and hers, were treacle, each one a struggle. He caught snatches of what Eternity was saying, but the world was overwhelming.

The woolen blanket he lay under felt unbearably rough while the sun that shone through the open windows hurt his eyes, making him wince. Had the world always been so sharp and bright?

"Shh," she said gently. "The first few days are the hardest, Lazander. Or so the other Champions say. I know this might not be the life you chose, but fate isn't always up to us. Gallow *saw* something in you, and he's given you another chance—another life." She squeezed his hand, and Lazander felt his own squeezing back in return.

"I will not pretend I know what this means," she continued, blue eyes shining.

She was upset? No—he had to fix it. Eternity shouldn't be upset. But then she smiled, brilliant and open. Lazander's heart skipped a beat.

"When I cast *Blessing of the Righteous* on you, I had no idea it would do, well, this. But I… I'm happy it happened. Selfishly so. You'll be an amazing Champion. I just *know* it."

Releasing his hand, she pulled his covers farther up. The wool felt like nails against his bare skin, but he said nothing. He was in a strange bed, in a room he didn't recognize, but his sharpened eyes noticed the gray stone walls, and he knew he was in the western wing of the Ivory Keep.

"Rest, my Champion," she said, pressing a cold cloth to his brow. The cool water felt electric against his skin, but his lids grew heavy at her words. As he drifted off, he couldn't help but feel someone else was in the room.

Someone who stared straight into his soul, laying every inch of him bare.

***

Later, he was told he had slept for three days. After he died, that is.

Lazander tried saying it aloud in the rare moments he was alone. "I died." But the words felt distant, like it had happened in a long-forgotten storybook. Still, he knew it was true. He felt it in every shaking step he took from his bed to his window. Felt it in the simple act of clenching his fist. Even half wasted from sickness and death, he could tell he was stronger than he'd ever been as a Gilded Knight.

He was different. His body alien and strange. These things he could handle—he was a Gilded, after all. What he couldn't handle, and what he dared not say aloud for fear it would make it real, was the boy in the room with him.

The boy was small, perhaps seven or eight years of age. At least he thought it was a boy—the shape and outline of the child was blurred around the edges while only darkness lay at his center. When he looked directly at the boy, he seemed to fade into the background, and so Lazander could only watch him from the corner of his eye where the boy would quietly stand. Watching. Waiting.

He once made the mistake of mentioning it to Eternity but hurriedly backtracked at her panicked look. He fumbled a lie—it was a trick of the light. At her look of relief, his stomach tightened.

Was he going mad?

Champion Imani only came to see him once. Eternity still hadn't left his side, and was feeding him warm grindle-broth made by Liddy every morning, when the black-armored Champion swept into the room.

Eternity stood ramrod straight, moving closer to Lazander's bed.

"How's your head? I hit you pretty hard, Champion," Imani said, her dark eyes roving over Lazander, cold and clinical.

"He'll be fine," Eternity answered for him. "He's transitioning well. He should be up and about in ten days, I think."

"You have three," Imani said, not taking her eyes off Lazander.

He raised his chin to meet her eyes head on. They'd "met" several times, if you could call it that, but had never spoken. He didn't carry Valerius' obvious disdain for followers of Gallow, but he didn't exactly trust them either. No one ever knew what they were doing, where they were going, or when they would appear. They answered only to Gallow—or so they claimed.

It had always made him uneasy. No one should be above the law—not even a "god."

"Three days?" Eternity exclaimed. "Imani, you took a full fourteen to recover! How can you expect—"

"The sages have passed their ruling," the Champion interrupted. "You'll be pleased to learn they agreed with you—the Tyrant has returned." She pointed an armored finger at Lazander. "Which means war is upon us, and Gallow will need every Champion he can muster." She smiled. It was not a smile Lazander cared for.

"You should be happy, Lady Eternity. 'The last is born,' Gallow decreed. That means there will be no more Judgment. No more failures. All you need do is stay alive until the final reckoning."

Lazander frowned at her turn of phrase. "Eternity?" he began. "What—"

A blink, and Imani was at his side. She lightly slapped him in the face, but it sent him careening to the side of the bed from the force. Not even Marito, who could crush dragonscale armor with his bare hands, had ever hit him so hard before.

"First rule, *Champion*," she said. "Don't address Lady Eternity so casually. She is the conduit of Gallow's power and the reason you and I exist."

"*Imani!*" Eternity snapped, looking angrier than Lazander had ever seen. Head ringing from the blow, he was struggling to sit up when Eternity marched up to Imani, and pointed at the door. "If you want him up in three days, you will stop *beating him senseless*. Out!"

Eyebrows arched in surprise, Imani inclined her head, a mockery of a bow, and headed for the door.

"Three days, Champion," she called without looking back.

Eternity hurried to close the door, wringing her hands nervously. "You've only just woken up," she said, pacing the room. "Imani could barely make it down the stairs after ten days. Malik was quicker, mind you, but he became a Champion in the heart of Evergarden, right as the vaxion invaded, so it wasn't like he had much choice."

Lazander's mind, fogged from the blow, frowned at her words. The vaxion hadn't left the Moonvale Mountains in over seventy years, what was she—

"And Vivek! Vivek, well he couldn't even stand after a week. How are you supposed to walk, let alone *train* with Imani? This is ridiculous!"

"Eter—Lady Eternity," Lazander said.

She paused mid-stride, moving to his side. "Please don't, Lazander," she said, sitting down with a sigh. "So few people speak to me as a friend. I don't want to lose that. Not with you."

"Eternity," he began again, a flush of pleasure at her words. He had to be careful, he knew, he'd never seen Eternity so frazzled. The idea of being a Champion was something he hadn't even begun to wrap his head around, but it had something in common with the Gilded Knights—a duty to protect Eternity. He focused on that.

"If I'm needed in three days, then I'll be up in three days. I know that's not ideal," he continued at her worried look, "but I once fought a xandi with my arm in a sling, and a killer hangover—courtesy of Marito. If I survived that, I'm sure I'll survive this."

Instead of smiling at his joke, as he'd intended, Eternity looked sadder.

"I still can't believe they're gone," she said quietly.

Lazander didn't need to ask who she meant. "Have they had their last rites?" he asked instead.

She nodded. "The mages lit up the sky with all manner of beasts: dragons, pyrions, xandi. People came from all over Navaros. With the Ivory Keep still in ruin, we could barely fit them in. But people didn't care—they stood on top of each other to see. To speak. To sing about Gabriel and Marito."

Her breath caught, and Lazander knew her voice had been one of the loudest.

"The other knights insisted on building their tombs by hand," she continued. "The king let them use white marble from the southern isles, something usually reserved for royalty."

"Three days," he said quietly. "In three days, I'll go to their graves to pay my respects. Afterward, Imani can do whatever she wants to me."

Chapter Twenty-Five

"This is it?" I asked, frowning.

"Yep," Lukas replied.

"You're sure?"

"Positive."

"There isn't... another wallow-tail you could have mixed it up with?" I asked, grasping at straws.

We'd been hiking all day—in human form, this time. Lukas had, shockingly, spent the entire time talking. He'd pluck something from a tree or bush, eat it, and not even take a breath with his mouth full. He had a particularly horrifying story about an eighty-seven-year-old grandmother in H'tar who'd rob booze and fall asleep naked in the village square. After he went into great detail about a cluster of moles on her backside that kind of looked like Chief, I began to tune out.

Lukas got the fire going behind me while I stood, staring dumbly at the structure before us.

"If there is another wallow-tail, I've never heard of it. Food will be ready in abouuuuuut twenty? Give or take," he said, distracted by the endless ingredients he was taking out of his pocket, sniffing, then tossing into the frying pan with a shrug. While I loved Lukas' cooking, I had a feeling it wouldn't pass the health and safety standards back home.

Sighing, I considered the crystal in front of me.

I'd seen crystals before, usually on the wrist of an aunt who'd tried to convince me apple cider vinegar cured everything from acne to the common cold. But this wasn't a tiny piece of amethyst on a string. Wide at the base, the wallow-tail's shards exploded from the ground like daggers. The "daggers" varied in size from that of my fist to the length and breadth of me, like angry frozen stalagmites. The area around it was empty of life, the earth dry and barren. Evening light bent within its crystalline teeth, turning the transparent crystal a hazardous orange.

It was also over two stories tall.

I should get closer, I knew, but I couldn't bring myself to move. The second I'd seen it, every hair on the back of my neck stood up. A shadow in my mind warned me to fight or flee, kill or be killed. I felt like a cat with its claws out, hissing at an unseen enemy.

"Lukas…" I called without turning. "Does this thing make you feel…"

"Inspired? Awestruck? Dumb enough to use it as a toothpick?"

"Never mind." I'd wondered if the unease I felt was a falsling thing, but if Lukas felt fine, it must be something else. Something connected to my quest, or the Operator.

Make the Wallow-tail Shine.

I'd found the "wallow-tail." At least, I was pretty sure I had. Now what the hell was I supposed to do with it?

"Dinner!" Lukas called.

I retreated into the copse of trees we'd made our base from, grateful to no longer be looking at the thing.

Dinner was delicious, as always—a stew made out of a goober-pig (I didn't ask what it was, or how he got it), that was salty enough to make my eyes water. Lukas assured me he'd added no salt to it, it was simply the goober's natural flavor.

"Why is it called the wallow-tail?" I asked, licking my plate clean as had become our gross, nightly custom.

"Back when the Tyrant came down from the sky and was busy stomping us mere mortals into dirt, there was a… spirit. A creature made of pure mana." He leaned forward, dropping his voice low, and I couldn't help but smile. If there was one thing Lukas loved, it was a good story. "It flew on wings of flame and never touched the ground—for fear it would set the whole world on fire." He wiggled his fingers for effect. "It appeared in this world only once, on the day the Tyrant made the vaxion kneel. But, and here's where it gets interesting, I've heard two *different* versions of this story."

I leaned forward in turn, the fire casting dramatic shadows on his face. "In one, the wallow-tail bursts through the clouds, diving into the heart of the Tyrant. *Whoosh.*" He waved his hands over fire, which leaped for his fingers. "The Tyrant stumbles, light piercing the impenetrable darkness for just a moment. But alas, the wallow-tail's sacrifice was in vain. The Tyrant plunges a hand into its chest, and with a mighty pull yanks out its *own heart*—freezing it solid. And that right there..." He pointed a finger over my shoulder, to where I knew the crystal lay.

I didn't look. "Is the wallow-tail, trapped inside the Tyrant's heart," I finished. "And in the other version?"

"Well, that one I heard in a human village. The *other* during my... vaxion education." His mouth twisted, and he looked away. "According to our clawed brethren, the wallow-tail wasn't a magical being sent from the skies—it was a servant of the Tyrant who burned half the vaxion to death."

I whistled. "Only slightly different then."

"Oh, it gets better. In the vaxion version, a *shi'ara* bound her soul to the wallow-tail, forcing it to land. There she clung to it as it melted the flesh from her bones, using the last of her magic to form a crystal prison—where the two would burn together for all of eternity."

The word *shi'ara* summoned an image of a woman naked beneath the sky, a vicious wound splitting her face in two from temple to chin. By her side fangs and fur burst from her fellow vaxion. I didn't understand what I saw, but it sent a shiver up my spine.

"I know stories and legends tend to change depending on who's telling them, but that seems... a bit much," I said.

"Hardly. The vaxion can't *stand* the thought of needing help—even if it did come from a magic bird in the sky. I wouldn't be shocked if some very liberal *editing* happened over the years to make them the heroes." He yawned, crossing his legs as he settled against a log. "So—what are we doing out here? If you want to answer, that is."

He added the last bit so hurriedly, I felt guilty. I couldn't leave him in the dark, that wasn't fair to him. But I couldn't tell him the truth either. I settled for something in-between.

"I'm... working for someone. I can't say who," I added. "But they asked me to come out here and..." I winced, trying to figure out a way to say this that didn't sound insane. Finding none, I decided just to be blunt. "... 'make the wallow-tail shine.'"

Lukas, to his credit, didn't get up and walk into the forest with his pack on and a cheery wave goodbye—arguably, the sane thing to do. He did, however, look at me like I was crazy.

"I know." I raised my hands. "I don't know what it means either. But based on your stories, I think I have to break that crystal open. Unless you have a better idea?"

"I do. Don't work for people who give such terrible instructions."

I laughed, and he smiled in return, scratching his chin. Stubble had begun growing in over his chin, the color several shades darker than the shocking blond on the top of his head. "If that's bothering you, I can help you shave," I said without thinking.

"Used to keeping your own trim, is it?" he joked, gesturing to my chin.

"No, I used to help a friend of mine shave… I think?" I frowned, a memory just grasping out of reach. I remembered a white shirt, a big-bellied laugh, and a hand on my shoulder. But that was it.

"You *think*? Well, while that's a startling proclamation of your handiness with a blade, I'm good," Lukas joked, trying to cover his wince at my offer. He'd run through the trees with me, laughing and joking, and in the next breath he'd tensed up, unwilling to trust me with a blade at his neck.

I was hurt, but I couldn't blame him.

He made a point of yawning, and I took the hint, rolling onto my side. I began my whispered chant, my new nightly routine. I started with Noah, as I always did, and tried to picture as many details as I could. I remembered the arcade, and the games we used to play, but my mind struggled to remember who else would be there. The image of the white shirt returned, and I jolted awake.

Uncle Jacobi. I used to shave Uncle Jacobi's beard whenever we had a BBQ. Tears filled my eyes at the memory of him calling for a burger, and how the last time I'd seen him he'd been lying bleeding on the floor of his arcade.

Chapter Twenty-Six

The queen wished she were dead.

She lay in a room she didn't recognize, but she wasn't afraid. The twilight blossoms on the nightstand told her that her husband was here—she was safe. She raised her right hand to reach for the glass of water on her bedside, freezing when a bandaged stump greeted her. Struggling into a sitting position, she yanked back her covers with her remaining hand, staring in horror at the jagged hunk of meat that was her right leg.

Her lost limbs burned. A deep searing pain that began in the marrow of bones that no longer existed. Tears spilled from her eyes as she looked at her bandaged body, a vessel that had grown steadily more frail and more breakable over the years. Her grief was dwarfed by the memory of Thaddeus' decapitated head.

Her spymaster, her friend, was *dead*.

Bones poking through the thin blue-veined flesh of her back, she folded in on herself and sobbed.

***

The king had taken to visiting the queen every morning before his seemingly endless duties—the continued repair of the Keep, the nobles and ambassadors who clamored at his door demanding "answers" about Valerius, the veiled threats from Evergarden, the bards and criers that circled his home like carrion. He'd already heard some of the new ballads being composed. The "traitor prince, and the queen's horn-lover!" was the current crowd favorite.

He'd tried to stop them spreading, but he might as well have tried to catch moonlight.

When he opened the door, he stopped at the sight of his wife sitting up in bed, her face turned away from him. Silhouetted against the morning sun, she looked closer to a spirit than his wife of thirty years.

"Morning, Leon," she said without looking at him. "How badly was the Keep damaged? I can't see from here."

"Don't let anyone in—not even Liddy," he said to the guards at his back. "If she argues, tell her I gave you permission to stab her."

"But, sir," said the younger of the pair, looking terrified. "Liddy—"

The king shut the door behind him, cutting the guard off.

"I can only imagine the chaos you've had to deal with. Has Yati contacted you yet? She was Thaddeus' choice as spymaster should he… well, she was dealing with an uprising in the southern isles, so it may take her some time to get here." The queen remained still, her back ramrod straight, her voice bereft of emotion.

As she spoke, the king removed his helmet. He'd taken to donning a full suit of armor every morning, meetings tended to end quicker when he did.

"What was the death toll? I imagine it was in the thirties at least. We should see to it that the families are compensated," the queen continued, cracks beginning to form in her voice.

He removed his cloak, a beautiful ermine his wife had given him on his last name day, and his sword, a gift from his father on his deathbed.

"Has there been any sign of—of Valerius…" Her voice faltered as the king knelt on the bed behind her, wrapping his strong arms around her.

He gently pulled her close, aware of how small and thin she felt. "Forgive me," he whispered in her ear. "I should have been here."

He said nothing when her tears fell on his gauntlets, the pale fingers of her left hand gripping his. He did his best to ignore the bandaged stump of her right.

"What did you do with Thaddeus' body?" she asked quietly, head bowed, refusing to look at him.

"We hid your spymaster's corpse beneath the Keep. Though it will do little good—any hope we had of keeping his monstrous form a secret is gone." He sighed, trying and failing not to sound angry. "The mages and palace guards ran about like smacked toddlers for hours after Valerius fled. They left the body on show for all to see." He was proud that his voice didn't waver at the mention of his son's name.

"The Gallow Temple knows of him? That's a problem." Her voice grew stronger with every word—more confident.

"Already dealt with," the king replied. "Head Disciple Harrow has come to the conclusion that the creature who fought Valerius could not possibly be the zindor who served the Tyrant. A generous donation to the Gallowed Temple may or may not have helped."

The queen laughed, and the king couldn't help but smile at the flutter in his heart at the sound. "As subtle as ever, my lord." She sighed. "We'll have to see new replacements chosen for the Gilded Knights. The sooner they can start, the better."

Bracing himself, the king knew he could put it off no longer. "I disbanded the Gilded Knights."

"You *what?*" The queen spun to face him for the first time, nearly falling out of the bed.

The king tried to cradle her against him, but she slapped his ivory breastplate. "How dare you make such a decision without me! The Gilded Knights are a *symbol* of peace, our champions of justice! They're heroes to the people and have done wonders to—"

"—make us appear weak. Corrupt. *Dangerous*," the king finished. "People have lost faith in them because of Valerius. They've lost faith in *us*."

The queen flinched as if struck, but the king plowed on. "When Marito's father died, the Keep and the hills beyond were full of people singing their heart's truth. At his son's last rites, the courtyard was barely full. Valerius' betrayal has tainted the Gilded, the Keep, *Navaros*. Our enemies watch us—waiting for us to crumble."

"No, this can be fixed. For Gabriel's last rites, we should—"

"I held their last rites together," the king said. "I know it's not protocol, but with my soldiers stretched so thin, I couldn't justify two days away from Keep repairs."

"Disbanding the Gilded Knights is a *mistake*," the queen said with a glare that had made grown men stammer. The king, however, was made of sterner stuff. "It makes us look like we can't trust our own knights."

Arguments died on the king's lips when he looked Firanta over. Dark purple crescents framed her eyes while her bandages, freshly changed the night before, were already dark and stained.

"You need rest," he said, stepping away from the bed. In seconds his helmet was on, his cloak tied, and his sword buckled. "I'll let Liddy know you're awake."

Instead of lying back however, Firanta pulled her covers off. "I am your *queen*, not some doe-eyed maiden who needs coddling. We need to discuss Valerius. Thaddeus said he served the Tyrant—"

"I said the Head Disciple is now happy to claim that Thaddeus and the Tyrant's zindor are two different beasts," the king said, his hand on the door, eyes locked on his queen. "I never said I was."

"Leon," she said, eyes wide in shock. "Thaddeus has a dark past, I won't lie to you about that. But he doesn't... didn't serve the Tyrant. He was loyal to me, to *Navaros*."

"You told me you saved Thaddeus' life when you were a child, and that he'd been bound to you since. When I wanted to know what he was, and where he'd come from, you said you were sworn never to reveal it. I haven't asked since—not once. But now I return home to find your 'dog' nearly leveled the Ivory Keep and left you *half dead*." He opened the door more forcefully than he intended.

"Thaddeus was *trying* to catch Valerius in the act and save Lazander—"

"Gallow's new pet needed no help from you. If you had simply let things be, we could have caught Valerius *quietly* afterward. Instead, nobles now meet in secret where they discuss ways to force us to abdicate." He sighed, his breath sounding more like a hiss. "You will *rest*. *I* will handle this."

He slammed the door shut behind him.

The guards snapped to attention at either side of him, from where they'd clearly been listening to every word. The king sighed, trying to ignore the queen's sobs behind him. This was exactly why he had little time for palace guards and mages—they had no discipline.

"You breathe a word of what you heard and I'll have you stripped naked and flayed," he said.

"Yes, sir!" they squeaked.

The king strode away, knowing he had been harsh with Firanta. She'd done what she thought best, and her instincts had proven right time-and-time again. But he knew all too well that one wrong move could mean the collapse of an entire kingdom, and Navaros now stood on the brink. Only one thing could fix this.

"Rhys!" he called. A split second later, a dark-cloaked man appeared at his side, his silver armor polished to perfection—as expected of his second-in-command. "Contact Breaker. I have a job for her."

"She'll want payment up front," Rhys said, lip curling in disgust. He'd never had time for the assassin.

"Then pay her. Tell her I'll empty the damn vaults if she brings me Valerius. *Alive.*"

"My lord." Rhys dipped his head, but not before the king caught the surprise in his eyes.

The king had chastised the queen for not handling things quietly, and he was a man who practiced what he preached. He had little time for the public heroics of the Gilded Knights and would normally have dealt with a traitor quickly and without fuss. But this was no ordinary traitor. This was the Prince of Navaros, leader of the Gilded. This was his *son*. And he needed to prove to every noble and civilian, doubter and accuser, that he was in control. That he was still *king*. And what better way to do that, than to make the entire kingdom watch as he swung his sword and cleaved Valerius head from his shoulders?

The king's soul fractured at the thought, but then he pictured his wife's broken body. He would do it—he would kill his only child, even if it meant he'd never sleep again.

It was what duty demanded.

Chapter Twenty-Seven

Lazander hit the dirt, breath leaving his body in a spit-soaked gasp. A booted heel stomped on his back. "Weak as a kitten." Imani sighed. "I expected more from a *Gilded*."

Lazander rolled to his side, kicking out at Imani's knee. His foot connected and simply glanced off, his bones vibrating from the force.

She raised an eyebrow. "Your goal is to beat me, Champion. Not send me to sleep."

Jumping to his feet he backed up, instinctively raising his arms. It was the only thing that saved him from the fist Imani swung at him like a hammer. Another came for his stomach, and he tensed up, absorbing a blow that made his eyes water. Frustrated, he drove an elbow into her face.

Her head knocked back an inch. He dropped his guard, opening his mouth to apologize…

… but the Champion drove her head forward, slamming her skull into his nose with a sickening crunch.

When next he opened his eyes, he was in the dirt once more, black spots dotting his vision. He reached up a hand to touch his nose, finding blood on his fingers. But when he prodded the flesh, expecting it to be tender and sore, there was no pain.

"Courtesy is for the weak," Imani said, staring down at him. She made no move to help him up. "There are no rules, no 'honor' in a fight. Fight hard, and fight dirty. Again."

"Surely Gallow's *Champions* have better things to do than brawl like thugs in a bar fight," Lazander said.

Imani raised a single amused eyebrow, crossing her arms at his show of petulance.

Dressed in loose clothes, it was the first time Lazander had seen Imani out of her customary black armor. He wasn't surprised to see that her usual full-plate barely added to her bulk. Corded muscle lined her shoulders, and her back was nearly as wide as Marito's.

At the thought of Marito, his mind flashed to the tombs he'd visited that morning with Eternity—to the dying flowers that lined the marble, their petals already mulch, and the scattering of coppers left as an offering, barely enough for a pint at the Resplendent Farrow. Even the white marble that housed his friends, his *brothers*, wasn't the sign of respect he'd assumed. Instead it was an excuse for why Gabriel and Marito were hidden in the bowels of the Gallowed Temple, far from prying eyes. Without Eternity to guide him, Lazander would never have found them.

His fists clenched in anger. His friends had dedicated their entire lives to Navaros, and in return they'd been locked away like an embarrassing secret.

"We're brawling for two reasons," Imani said, jerking him back to the present. "One: you're as steady as a newborn fawn. The quicker you get used to your new body the better." She tapped his nose, and he flinched. "See? Healed already."

"And the second?" he asked, fighting to calm himself. He rolled his shoulders, wincing when he heard the fabric strain. The last time he'd worn his sparring gear, it had hung loose and comfortable on him. Now it pulled against his back while the tops of his trousers barely scraped his ankles. Days ago, he'd been mere skin and bone.

"You fight like you've got gloves on and a ref watching your every move," Imani said, eyeing him critically. "How you Gilded survived this long is beyond me."

"We didn't, in case you'd forgotten," he said, anger sparking his words.

"I hadn't." She smirked.

Lazander had the violent urge to press his knee to her throat.

"Valerius' betrayal didn't come out of nowhere," she continued. "You'd guessed he'd turned on you. Submitted your little reports to the queen and her dog, hoping she'd see what you saw—how he treated Eternity when she was taken by Magnus. How quick he was to kill Zara the Fury when his plan went awry. How his thirst for mercy waned until all that remained was the blade."

"How do you know that?" Lazander said, scrambling at her words.

"Gallow knows all, Lazander. And he knows that if you'd had the courage to kill Valerius then and there, none of this would have happened. Instead you chose to rope your fellow Gilded into your childish plan to gather 'evidence' against Valerius. You gave him the benefit of the doubt, and what did you get? *Murdered*. By your own leader, no less. Champions on the other hand?" She smiled. "We don't hesitate. We don't question. We get the job done. And if you'd done the same, Marito and Gabriel would still be alive." Her last words were cold and matter-of-fact—like she was commenting on the weather.

An anger Lazander had only felt once before, when fighting Valerius, raged in his chest. "Why would you say such a thing to me?" he managed.

"Because it's the truth. You got your friends killed because you followed lofty ideals of 'justice' and 'truth.' Ideals that fall apart the second your enemy doesn't play by the same rules. Champions," she dropped into a fighting stance, her fists raised, "live in the real world."

Lazander let his fists answer. He swung at Imani with a right hook, blocking her answering left. When she tried to step past his guard, he feigned a jab that she swiftly dodged—as he knew she would.

Snapping a leg out, he caught her in the knee. When he heard her knee crack, sharper than a whip, he didn't stop. Didn't apologize. Instead he gripped her head in both hands and drove her face into his knee.

Or would have if she hadn't stopped his leg with the barest touch of her palm, kicking him squarely between the legs.

Spittle flying from his lips, he fell to the ground—vomiting.

"Good. You made me try a little," she said. "*Again.*"

***

Exhausted, bruised, and broken, Lazander felt unbearably lonely. Ten more bouts they fought, and ten more times she'd left his head spinning, his vision dark, the meager contents of his stomach on the ground.

"Practice is over," she said, eyeing the sun that had turned heavy and orange. They were outside the Ivory Keep, partially hidden from the white towers by a line of trees. There were private rooms for sparring in the Keep, as well as the barracks, but Imani had insisted on this precise spot. While he'd been confused before, he was grateful now.

He didn't want anyone to see him like this. Well, no one but *him* anyway. The boy watched from beneath a tree. He stood still and silent, his darkened outline the only hint that someone was there. Lazander looked away.

"Up," Imani said. "We have more to do."

"*Imani*, I haven't eaten or had so much as a drop of water since this morning. I can't—"

"Are you hungry?" she asked. "Thirsty?"

He was about to snap that of course he was when he realized that was a lie. Despite throwing up his breakfast in their second bout, his stomach felt full and satisfied. He touched a finger to his lips to find them wet, as if he'd just downed a pitcher of water.

"Gallow sustains you now," she said, beckoning him with one finger as she strode into the forest. "But you must earn his grace."

Lazander found his feet following Imani, despite his growing unease. The God of Judgment was an all-seeing eye who had been part of Lazander's life since he was a child. His mother would warn him to behave, for Gallow was watching. His teachers would hang up maps, showing where the Tyrant had first descended to the world, the evil god's steps forming craters that would become the lakes of Freyley, his home country. Birds' skulls, bleached and empty, hung everywhere, from tanneries to royal courts. And the Gallowed Temples themselves were revered, sacred places, where everyone dipped their heads and whispered.

Gallow watched. He judged. And more often than not, he found you wanting. This was the Gallow Lazander had grown up with. But as he walked with Imani through the forest, he realized that for all the influence Gallow had on everyday life, he knew very little about the god and his Champions.

"Here," Imani said, coming to such a sudden stop, Lazander almost barreled into her.

"Where are we? What are we doing here?" Lazander asked, irritation hiding the fear that coiled in his chest like a viper. The shadowed figure of the boy, who normally kept his distance, now hovered at his side. He raised his head, his face as blank as parchment as he stared into Lazander's soul.

The knight looked away, closing his eyes.

"I don't know," Imani replied.

They stood on the precipice of a ravine, the air cooling sharply as the sun sank lower. Beneath them a shallow river gurgled gently while tufts of a vivid green herb burst from the rockface—river moss, Lazander knew. It was a common ingredient in poultices used to bring down a fever. He remembered his mother rubbing the foul-smelling ointment as he loudly complained.

"What do you mean you 'don't know'?" Lazander snapped, sore and exhausted despite the ease with which he could still move. "You brought us here!"

"No, I didn't," she said. "*He* did." She bowed at the waist to Lazander, lower than she ever had for the Queen of Navaros. Lazander frowned, about to ask what she was doing when he froze. A hand, small and icy, pressed to his back. He turned to see the shadowy form of the boy behind him.

He leaped back, fists raised in fear. "You can see him too?"

"For as long as he allows me. Curious. He appears as a young boy to you. He's a tall, powerfully built man for me. Malik sees a teenager. And Vivek... well, he's never said. But that's Vivek."

"Don't tell me that's…"

Imani's hand gripped the back of his neck as she forced him to bow.

"The breaker of tyrants, the savior of the world, and your new lord and master: Gallow—the God of Judgment."

Chapter Twenty-Eight

"Step back," I said, cracking my knuckles.

Lukas grimaced, taking a single step back.

"Do you not remember the night you found me?" I asked, pointing at the sky.

He sighed and backed up as far as our campsite. "For what it's worth," he called. "I think this is a *terrible* idea."

"We tried yours, and it turns out that *punching* the impenetrable crystal hurts. *A lot*," I said, holding up my poorly bandaged hands. Lukas, for all his talents, couldn't tie a bandage to save his life, and neither could I when shards of crystal were buried inches deep in my knuckles.

So far that day I had spent hours circling the wallow-tail, trying to find a way into its center. I'd used *Partial Transformation* on both my arms but hadn't so much as scratched the crystal's surface. Lukas then suggested I "punch it real hard," and I'd been frustrated enough to try it.

Turns out it works. Kind of. *Monstrous Strength* was enough to dent it, even if my knuckles didn't appreciate it. But I was still no closer to making it "shine."

"Yes, but trying to blow it up with lightning is hardly a better idea." He threw his hands up in surrender. "I'll be making lunch. Let me know when you're done trying to kill yourself."

I ignored him, spreading my legs slightly as I took a steadying breath. I remembered the night I'd called down the storm—how lost and broken I'd felt. A thrum of electricity began in my fingers, and I focused on it. The wind picked up, the air crackling as the temperature dropped. Static raised the hair on the back of my arms.

I am fury. I am loss. I am grief. I am death. The words were a mantra, a promise, that made my claws yearn to burst from my fingertips.

"Ah… Zara?" Lukas called from somewhere behind me, but the words faded away, lost in the storm of my mind.

I opened my eyes to see the bright light of day gone—the wind whistled through my hair as clouds darker than night circled overhead. A thousand needles of pure lightning ran over my skin with a pain that bordered on pleasure. I raised my hand, pointing a single finger at the towering form of the crystal.

"**Strike me in fury,**" I roared. "**Strike me in death!**"

Wrath's Storm Activated.

A bolt of lightning struck the crystal, turning everything a blinding white. I closed my eyes too late, wincing as the world vanished. Spots danced in my vision, and I cracked open an eye to see the wallow-tail crystal now glowed softly—a warm, cozy lantern against the stormy sky.

"Lukas, I did it! I made it shine!" I said, turning to see him tearing toward me in a frantic sprint, his eyes wide.

"Lukas? What's—"

He hit me full force, tackling me to the ground. Something whipped through the air, striking where I'd been a split second before.

"What the hell was *that*?" I said, struggling to sit up, but Lukas refused to let me go.

"Look," he said, pointing to where I'd stood. Embers of icy blue fire lit up the grass, which didn't burn so much as simply vanish at the strange fire's touch. It was like nothing I'd ever seen.

"It's... beautiful," I said, my words a whisper.

"And *deadly*. Did you forget the deadly bit?" Lukas asked, frowning when I shrugged him off. "Careful!"

I didn't have my fire abilities anymore, the Calamity System had removed them as a penalty for failing the tutorial, but I still felt a kinship to it. In my old life, I wasn't afraid of fire—I'd found it comforting at best, something to be wary of at worst. But in this world, sitting by a fire beneath the stars was where I felt safest.

This fire, however, didn't feel safe. A whisper of something powerful and alien called out from the flames, begging to be touched. *Understood.* I brushed against a dying ember with the tip of my finger, determined to figure out this strange flame.

Fire shot through my veins. My blood screamed as it boiled inside me.

I fell back, screaming as I kicked wildly. I rolled around in useless circles, frantically trying to put out the flames that burned inside me.

"Zara? *Zara*! Where is it, where's it burning?" Lukas yelled, yanking my hands from my chest. I could only shriek and flail, choking on my words.

Strong arms gripped me, and suddenly I was cradled against Lukas' chest as he sprinted. Every jolt sent stabs of pain through me. Dark spots clouded my vision. I must have blacked out from the pain because next I knew we were falling. We hit the water with a slap, Lukas absorbing most of the blow as the icy cold river washed over us. Like a raging inferno in a monsoon, the fire within me was smothered—cooling in the freezing water. I could think again.

But I couldn't breathe.

Instinctively I tried to kick out, but Lukas had me in a death grip. He kicked hard, bursting through the surface. "Is it out? Are you all right?" he asked, panicked eyes roving over me.

I tried to speak but coughed up half the river instead. Gasping, I managed to nod. He closed his eyes in relief, releasing me a fraction, but still kept one arm around my back, the other under the crook of my legs. "Show me the burn."

Wincing, I held up my right index finger. At the very tip was a burn the size of a pin.

"Are you *joking*?" he said, glaring at it—a glare he swiftly turned on me. "Why did you *touch the crystal fire*?"

"I—I was trying to—" A coughing fit left me gasping. Holding me close, he kicked toward the shore. As it got shallower, I waved a hand to put me down, but he refused, carrying me all the way out of the water while I still struggled to take a full breath.

Later, I would be glad I was still coughing up a lung and not able to speak without sounding like a choking frog. If I'd had a brain cell to spare, I'd have curled up in embarrassment. Not only did Lukas have to save my idiot self, but he'd also had to carry me out of the water like a damsel in distress.

"Lukas, I—I'm fine. Put me down."

With a grunt of pain, he practically dropped me, making me stumble. I was about to ask if he was all right when he rounded on me.

"What were you *thinking?*" he snapped, his anger dampened only by the fact he was, well, sopping wet. His clothes clung to every inch of his body, and I had to concentrate very hard on meeting his eyes.

Bad brain, I chided myself. *Now is not the time.*

"Well?" he said.

"I—I was trying to… understand the fire," I said, wincing at my words.

Lukas stared at me like I'd just said the sky was pink.

"How did that go, exactly? I take it you and the wallow-tail are best friends now?"

"I heard someone. Or something," I said, ignoring his sarcasm. The split second I touched the fire, I heard a voice calling out, but it was so quick, I didn't hear what they said. "I think they were crying."

"So you nearly died, but now we know the crystal is *sad*. Great. Fantastic!" He said, kicking off his sopping wet boots. His shirt followed, and he wrung it out as he stomped toward the camp.

"Why are you so angry?" I said, following him.

"I'm *not* angry," he barked. He went to remove his soaking bracer on his right arm, then changed his mind, grabbing a bundle of firewood. He threw it roughly into the ring of stones I'd set up, then took out the flint, slamming two pieces together. One of them broke instantly, and he hissed with a rage I didn't understand.

"Lukas, stop. Give me those," I said. Eyes wide with fear, he roughly shoved the flint into my hands, then sat down—his head in his hands. Frowning, I said nothing as I started the fire. Lukas had saved my life, then nearly dropped me in the dirt in the next breath. He went from laughing with me to looking at me like he expected me to slit his throat. *Something* was going on, but I'd no idea what.

I bided my time, thinking how best to ask while I added dried leaves to the wood, blowing gently on the spark as Lukas had taught me. He didn't say a word. Every time I thought I had him figured out, he'd pull back, or we'd have a fight. Like now. I couldn't figure him out. Nor could I find it in me to be angry at him. He sat, head down, his hands digging into his hair, muscles vibrating with anger, worry, or something else entirely.

"Thank you for saving me Lukas," I began. "But I can't help but feel like something else is wrong."

"It's fine," he said, his head still in his hands. "Let's just dry off."

"It's not fine," I said, my heart pounding. *You said you'd stand up for yourself more*, I told myself. *That means not being such a chicken.* "You're clearly upset."

"I'm not."

"You are. Tell—"

"Zara, don't!"

"—me *why*," I finished.

He grimaced, slapping a hand over his mouth. His eyes bulged, veins popping along his cheeks. Words, muffled and unintelligible, burst through his fingers.

I gripped his shoulder, afraid he was having a seizure. "Lukas, what is it? What's—"

"If you die, I die!" he gasped.

Chapter Twenty-Nine

Lazander didn't know what he was supposed to feel when standing before a real-life god—awe. Joy, maybe. Right now, however, he only felt the cold plunge of fear as it sunk its icy tendrils into his heart.

"The fear is normal," Imani said as if reading his mind. "I nearly passed out the first time he spoke to me. By using me to bring you here, he's showing great patience for your state—you should be grateful."

"Thank… you," Lazander managed. Gratitude was the last thing he felt, but Imani's hand still gripped the back of his neck, forcing him into a bow before the childlike form of Gallow. Abruptly she released him and he backed up, staring at the boy with new eyes.

When he focused on him, he grew more blurred and shadowed around the edges. Lazander turned his head slightly to look at him out of the corner of his eye.

"To remind us that he is always present, always watching," Imani said, watching him turn his face away. "In time, his presence will be a comfort to you. It's been that way for me, for many years now."

Lazander doubted that he'd ever feel the same.

Imani cocked her head to the side, her eyes sliding to the left—and Lazander knew she was listening to her own shadowed form of Gallow. "Understood." She pointed a finger at a patch of grass. "One of the hardest lessons a new Champion must learn is this—we do not lift a hand in aid without Gallow's blessing. You will wait. You will watch. And you will *not* move."

The red-haired knight did as she ordered, making sure to keep the boy in the corner of his eye. Now that Lazander knew who it was, it felt painfully obvious. There was an air to him as he stared at Lazander, as if his new Champion's every move was being watched, weighed, and measured. Fitting for the God of Judgment, he supposed.

"Now what?" Lazander asked, kneeling in the grass, resting on the back of his heels. It was a position he took before battle, if he had time. He would kneel, slow his breathing, and focus on every muscle with razor sharp precision. Usually it calmed him, but this time his body refused to relax. He found himself bracing for an unexpected blow.

"Wait. Watch. *Do not* move," Imani repeated. She crossed her arms and leaned back against a tree. Eyes closed, she looked completely at ease.

Lazander found his fists were clenched tighter than when he'd sparred with her. This was a test, he knew. Why else would she bring him here? The what and why of it however, escaped him.

Which was exactly what worried him.

Minutes passed, and the ravine was silent but for the gurgle of the river below and the gentle chorus of birds overhead. At any other time Lazander would have been happy out here in the wild. Now his heart pounded as his eyes flitted about, searching for a threat.

He heard the beasts before he saw them.

They howled, the blood curdling cry of the hunt—a cry he knew well. He got to his feet, but Imani was somehow at his side, her hand gripping his shoulder. He'd been beaten and bloodied by her countless times, but it dwarfed the strength with which she now forced him down.

She'd been holding back before, he realized.

"Ripperbacks!" he said, pointing at the opposing side of the ravine where the forest was thick and close. "A pack is close, ten strong I'd guess. We need to move, *now*."

"Be still, Champion," Imani said, her voice uncharacteristically soft. "Trust me on this, if nothing else. It is… easier this way."

He frowned. Ripperbacks were deadly reptilian creatures that favored the colder climates of northern Freylen and southern Navaros. Hunting in packs, they tended to swarm smaller, weakened prey—ripping it to shreds before sharing the spoils amongst themselves. They kept to isolated areas, avoiding towns and cities. He'd never seen any so close to the Ivory Keep before. In truth, they were more of a risk to unguarded livestock than they were to people.

With one exception.

During a hunt, ripperbacks whipped into a frenzy bordering on insanity. They would cut down anyone and anything to reach their prey, even ripping out the throats of their own packmates if they couldn't keep up. The howls in the air spoke of such bloodlust. Surely Gallow didn't intend for him to fight a pack of ripperbacks with nothing but bruised knuckles? He'd be slaughtered.

Then he heard her—a small, panicked voice that cut through the echoing howls. Imani's nails dug into his shoulder.

A girl of no more than twelve burst through the undergrowth on the other side, her screams of terror cutting Lazander like a blade. Exhaustion dogged her movements, and she ran blindly but slowly—far too slowly. A chasm lay between her and Lazander, an impossible distance to jump, and there was no rope bridge in sight. He wouldn't reach the girl in time. But in his heart, Lazander was and always would be a Gilded Knight.

He forced himself to his feet, fighting Imani's steel grip on his shoulder.

"Damnit, Imani, let me—"

"Has Gallow commanded you to save her?"

"What? Imani, the girl has *seconds*. Stop this!" He abandoned any sense of chivalry and elbowed her sharply in the ribs. The Champion took the hit, barely moving. A howl sounded again, closer this time. The girl tripped, falling hard. Her choking cries of fear were impossibly loud.

"*Has Gallow commanded you to save her?*" Imani asked again, shaking him like a dog.

Lazander turned to the darkened shape of the boy beside him. "Please," he said, addressing Gallow for the first time. "Please, she's just a *child*."

The boy simply stared at him.

Lazander took a breath—and drove his knee into Imani's stomach with every ounce of his strength. She doubled over, more from surprise, but it was enough. He ran at full sprint for the edge of the cliff, his body moving before his mind could protest the idiocy of what he was about to do.

With a whisper, a prayer, a hope, he didn't know which, he reached the edge— and jumped. Cold air whipped past his face. With his new strength, he'd thought there was a slim, maybe insane chance that he could jump far enough to reach the opposing cliff face. Using the river moss that dogged its crevices, he'd scale the wall and pray he reached the girl before the ripperbacks. That, or he'd fall to his death. In that moment, he would have died in peace, knowing he'd tried to uphold the values Marito and Gabriel had instilled in him.

But Lazander did so much more than jump.

He flew across the ravine, covering a distance as absurd as it was impossible. He landed like a cat on the opposing side, rolling to absorb the momentum. Allowing himself a single heartbeat of shock, he was up again, running toward the girl who lay a few feet from him. He risked a glance at Imani, who made no move to follow. She simply watched him—an old, aching sadness in her eyes.

He shoved thoughts of the Champion away as he reached the sobbing girl. Curled up into a ball, she covered her face with tiny hands as if that would protect her. Lazander knew he had seconds. The ripperbacks hadn't appeared yet, if he could get out of their line of sight and downwind, he could—

Something huge and scaly burst from the trees, jaw unhinged. Lazander grabbed the girl, rolling to one side as claws dug into his back. He gasped, pushing himself to his feet with one hand as he dodged a tail the width of his leg.

The ripperback was the length of a man and twice the width. It ran low to the ground, its four legs built for short bursts of deadly speed. An elongated neck snapped and twisted, moving at impossible angles as it whipped about. A chorus of scrabbling claws sounded as four more of the beasts appeared, their scales a melody of forest greens and browns.

Anyone else, even a seasoned knight, would hesitate. Ripperbacks and their bloodlust were infamous. The only way to survive without a fully armored regiment at your back was to run and pray luck and speed were with you. But Lazander was more than a knight—he was a Gilded. And while that didn't mean much to the king, or Navaros anymore, it did to him.

"Imani!" he yelled, a tail catching him in the ankle as he leaped over the snapping jaws. "I'm going to throw the girl. Get ready!"

"For what?" she called out, her tone that of someone asking what the plans were for a cold, rainy day.

Lazander gritted his teeth, stumbling as claws grazed the girl's back. She cried out, shaking like a leaf in his arms. He couldn't keep this up.

"To catch her!" he roared.

Imani turned to her side as if speaking to an invisible companion—Gallow, he knew. She looked back at Lazander. "Gallow has not commanded me to help you, or the girl," she answered, arms crossed.

Lazander wanted to throttle the Champion, and Gallow too, for good measure. "Why was Gallow doing this?" He wanted to scream. What reason could a god have for letting a child be ripped apart? But with no armor, weapons, and his arms full with a bleeding girl, Lazander had no attention to spare for philosophical arguments. He simply yelled, "Imani, *please*."

The Champion shook her head.

A tail caught Lazander in the knee and he stumbled. Ripperbacks' scales could shatter steel—only a mace or a greatsword wielded by someone as strong as Marito could pierce the creature's skin. Lazander knew this, but anger triumphed instinct. Words sprang from his lips as he drove a fist into the creature's skull, hoping to buy a desperate second to get out of range of its jaws.

"Bend to his might, break before his Judgment," he roared. He felt rather than saw the shape of Gallow at his back. Lazander's fist, instead of bouncing off the ripperback's skull as he expected, kept going.

The crunch of scale and bone beneath his knuckles felt like the splitting of soft, rotten wood. The ripperback's skull didn't just cave from his punch, it *exploded* from the force, the beast's entire body going limp as its brains splattered Lazander and the girl. Claws, jaws, and scales harder than steel descended as the ripperbacks swarmed him.

***

"You're squeezing the girl to death, Champion," Imani said, her tone surprisingly gentle.

Lazander opened his eyes to find he was on his knees, his fingers digging into the girl tight enough to bruise. "I'm sorry! Are you all right?" he asked, relaxing his grip. She didn't move, didn't so much as look at him, and he feared the worst, but then he noticed the rabbit-like pulse of her breathing. The poor thing was terrified.

"You're safe now," he said automatically. It was only as the words left his lips that he realized he had no idea what had happened. He turned to ask Imani, who now stood by his side, and he froze.

Blood and gore surrounded him, the torn limbs of the ripperbacks arranged around him in concentric circles like an art piece. He looked down at himself and the girl to find them both soaked in graying blood. "What did you do?" he asked Imani, his memory scrambling to fill in the blank spaces.

She shook her head. "This was all you, Champion. You used his gifts well, for your first try. Even if it was a touch… explosive."

A whimper in his arms brought Lazander back to the present.

"What's your name, little one?" he asked gently. "I'm Lazander, a Gilded Knight."

Imani huffed at the title but said nothing.

"Little one?" he asked again, but the girl shook her head. Her eyes squeezed up tight.

"… hurt me," was all he caught.

"What was that?" He bent his head lower.

"Please don't hurt me," she whispered.

Lazander's heart broke at the clear terror in her voice. He carried her away from the worst of the gore, making sure to set her down so she faced away from the carnage he had wrought. "Where are you parents?" he asked, kneeling down to face her. "They'll be worried about you. I can take you home—"

The girl ran the moment her feet touched the grass, running as if ripperbacks still chased her. Instinctively he went to run after her, but Imani stopped him with a soft hand on his chest.

"She kept crying for you to stop. You didn't until you'd killed every ripperback. Even the ones that tried to run," Imani said quietly.

Lazander forced himself to take a steadying breath. As a Gilded, he'd rescued children countless times—it had been the times he'd been proudest to be a knight. He'd never, however, had one run from him, terror naked in her eyes.

"She's—she's safe," he said, more for his benefit than Imani's. His eyes strayed to the bloodied, gory remains of the beasts he'd ripped apart with his bare hands. "That's all that matters."

"Tomorrow, we'll practice using Gallow's gifts without losing ourselves to them," Imani said, looking at the orange sky. "For now, we'll call it a night. Clean yourself off at the stream before we return to the Ivory Keep, or you'll scare everyone there too."

Chapter Thirty

"What do you mean, 'if you die, I die'?" I said, the words making even less sense the more I repeated them.

Lukas grimaced. "I knew you didn't know. You wouldn't have left me behind if you did."

"All I know is that I am incredibly confused."

"When you... entered my mind, you didn't just pull me back from the beast within. You *tamed* it. And a beast broken is a beast owned." He sighed. "At least that's how the stories tell it."

"I still don't know what you're talking about."

"You haven't noticed?" he said, smiling in disbelief. "At first I thought it was just an act you wouldn't drop. That's why I got in your face the other night. If I'm going to be someone's dog, I want to know what I'm in for." He stood, gesturing to himself. "Tell me to do something."

"Like what?"

"Anything, Zara."

I sighed, still waiting for the punchline of what was clearly a terrible joke. "Stand on one foot?"

"Not like that. *Tell me.*"

I rolled my eyes. "Stand on one foot!"

He lifted his foot with a jerk. Balancing, he gestured for me to keep going.

"Jump up and down." He did while staying balanced on one foot.

"Stick out your tongue.

"Put your left hand in the air.

"Wave at me with your right hand."

He abruptly followed every instruction. Veins stood out from the side of his neck as if he was fighting against something. I crossed my arms, annoyed—I didn't know what Lukas was trying to prove with Simon Says, but it was getting more and more annoying.

Lukas kept jumping. Resolving not to give in to whatever this stupid game was, I said nothing. He kept jumping.

And jumping.

And jumping.

It was only when his breath ran ragged, and he looked on the brink of collapse that the truth hit me.

"Stop, *stop*!" I said.

He fell down with a wheeze. Legs splayed, he laughed bitterly. "Took you… long enough."

"But how… you're…"

"I'm your whipping boy. Thrall. *Slave*," he said. "You saved my life, and now I'm bound by blood. Your aunt had—has—several such pets at her beck and call. The molger don't have such magic. Only the *vaxion*."

I remembered the vision Zara had shown me of Ashira, her aunt and leader of the vaxion. In it, she forced a woman trapped in the form of a bloodthirsty monster to become human. At the time, I thought Ashira had done it to save the woman's life. It was why I'd done the same to Lukas.

Now, all I felt was horror.

"One of her 'slaves' tried to do a runner once," Lukas said. "Ashira called him home, no idea how, but he tore his fingernails out trying to stop himself crawling back. She gave him a metal cup and a single order—'eat.'" He looked away. "Blood poured from his mouth, his teeth cracked, but he ate the whole thing. Even the handle. The *shi'ara* had to cut his stomach open to remove the shards—his intestines had healed around them."

My stomach lurched.

"And you thought I'd do the same to you?" I asked quietly.

"If you were really Zara the Fury? *Hell yes*. You might not be Ashira's kid, but you're not far off it. I thought you leaving me behind in H'tar was some kind of test. That you wanted proof I'd be a good little pup." He laughed bitterly. "I ran myself ragged trying to catch up to you."

I hesitated, then moved to sit next to him. "That's why you told me to drop the naive do-gooder act."

He nodded. "I was trying to figure out how to approach you when you called down the lightning—all I could think of was the Moonvale Mountains burning after Zara had a temper tantrum. It was only the thought of that metal cup that made me stay."

My mind struggled to wrap around the fact that a person, a real living person, was bound to obey whatever someone said. I shivered, thinking of all the times I'd accidentally ordered him about. "God, Lukas, I didn't know. I swear it."

"I know. And for the record, I don't think you're like Ashira—if you were, I'd... well, I like to think I'd have been brave enough to end it," he said, a shadow passing over his eyes. "But I can't deal with this weird helpless Zara act anymore. Who are you, really? And—and what are you going to do to me?"

The fear in his voice broke my heart. Gone was the cocky, cheerful Lukas who could ramble for hours and ran around doing everything from gathering food to cooking up a storm—things I now saw were acts of self-preservation. He'd probably spent every waking moment afraid I'd drop the mask and order him to kneel.

"You're right—I'm not Zara," I said, struggling to find the words. "In fact, I'm not even from this world..."

***

"... and now I'm here," I finished lamely. The fire had burned to embers, but neither of us were willing to stop and tend the flames. Night had fallen, and stars speckled the sky. Instead of being comforting, however, I was keenly aware of how strange and alien I was in this world. I didn't belong here, and running through the trees with claws or tossing boulders off a waterfall wasn't going to change that.

Lukas narrowed his eyes in disbelief. "So you're some kind of... spirit, who is inhabiting the body of Zara the Fury, who is actually still *alive*, but is locked inside your *brain*, and you speak to her when you're asleep. Am I missing anything?"

"Well, no, but when you put it like that, it sounds—"

"Insane. It sounds *insane*, Zara. Wait—not Zara," he said, jumping up. "You could order me to walk off a cliff, and I don't even know your name!"

"I—I don't know my name either."

"You don't… Of *course* you don't," he said. "How about the person you work for, the one who told you to make the wallow-tail 'shine.'"

"It's called the 'Operator.' I—I don't know its real name either," I said, wincing.

"Great. *Amazing*," he said, sarcasm dripping from every word. "Does it also only speak to you when you're sleeping?"

"Well, yes, actually."

"What? I was *joking*. Bloodied Void," he cursed, throwing his hands in the air.

I opened my mouth to explain further, then shut it again. I'd initially tried to be as honest as possible, but after spending ten minutes trying to describe an arcade game, he'd looked like he was seriously considering going back to the river to drown himself. After that, I'd kept it as simple as I could, but it didn't help. Lukas had grown paler with every word.

Now he paced, forming a neat line in the dirt. Forward. Back. Forward. Back. The urge to apologize was nearly overwhelming, but I quashed it.

"Why are we even out here with a crystal that tried to murder us?" he asked suddenly, pointing at the wallow-tail that sat as dark as the night sky—the brief glow I'd seen earlier long gone. "Why aren't we, I don't know, relaxing on a beach with a pint in each hand? That sounds more fun."

"If I don't do the Operator's…" I fumbled, not wanting to use the word "quests." "If I don't do what the Operator says, it takes something away from me as a 'punishment.' Zara's famous for her fire magic, right?"

Lukas stopped his pacing to nod.

I held a hand out to the embers. "I once called a column of fire down from the sky. I can't even make a spark now."

Lukas' eyes widened. "Your boss took your fire magic? *All of it?*"

I nodded. "I failed a 'job.' He wasn't happy," I said, settling on "he" for the Operator. It felt awkward calling him an "it," no matter how alien his desert plane felt. "It's not all bad though. If I do as he says, and do it well, he rewards me—I can call down lightning because of him. Oh! And he gave me a pack, sort of. An invisible one. Look!"

A glow formed in my hand. Lukas leaned forward, but I gestured for him to back up right as a boulder the size of me hit the dirt. He leaped back, his claws bursting from the tips of his fingers.

"Sorry! Sorry. I should have warned you."

"Are you telling me," Lukas said, poking the boulder with a suspicious finger, "that you've been skipping through the forest with a boulder in your 'pack,' happy as a tree-topper in the rain…" He pointed at his bulging pack, bedrolls peeking from the top. "While I've been carrying this on my back the *entire time*?"

"Oh… that's a good point, actually."

Lukas didn't so much sigh as expel air in a sound of pure exasperation. He went to sit down but was blocked by the stone. "Would you *mind*?"

I placed my hand on the boulder, and it vanished in a dull glow. Lukas sat down in the dirt, his head in his hands. He'd done that a lot this evening.

"I'm sorry," I said, unable to hold it in any longer.

He sighed. "Of course I would end up bound to a crazy spirit lady. Of course!"

"Lukas, you can leave. If you want!" I said, afraid to give anything that could be interpreted as an order. "I won't call you back—I don't even know how."

He raised a suspicious brow. "You'd release me? Just like that?"

"Without hesitation," I said. "Even though I'd really, really miss your cooking."

He smiled at that. "I believe you. Alas, that's not how this works. This is old magic summoned by duty and blood, as the *shi'ara* would say. Vaxion have always been dramatic, but our witches even more so." He gestured between us. "You didn't just save my life—you gave me a *new* one. I owe you. And until that debt is paid… well, it carries a mark."

For the first time since we'd met, he removed the bracer from his right arm. My mouth dropped.

Claw marks dug deep into his flesh, carving out strange symbols I couldn't read. Running from the crook of his elbow to his wrist, it looked painfully fresh and bloody. Normally I'd wince at such a wound, but instead I found myself fascinated by it. There was a beauty to the blood, an elegance I couldn't name. Transfixed, I found myself reaching out, my index finger tracing one of the bloodied lines.

The wound glowed with a dull reddish light, making us both jump. It shrank slightly, curling in on itself by a centimeter.

"Ah—I was wondering how it kept tally," he said, turning his arm. "It seems dumping you in the river shaved a bit off my debt. Once it's paid, then you can release me, but not a moment sooner. Kindly do enough stupid things that I can keep saving your idiot self, but not enough that you croak before the debt is paid."

He leaped up, cracking his back. "Well, now that that's all sorted, I'm *starving*. Dinner?"

"I—sure," I said, struggling with whiplash. He'd gone from looking like the head of a funeral procession to his usual chirpy self. The mask was back up, I knew, feeling sad.

"Eggs? Eggs! Oh—and two things," he said, whipping out the frying pan. "One: as 'crazy spirit lady' is a little long, I'm just going to call you Zara. And two: I need to be debt free by the time the *real* Zara gets her body back. I have no idea how this works if the driver changes, but I don't fancy my chances with a murderous psychopath."

He grinned as the oil started to sizzle. "No pressure though."

Chapter Thirty-One

The girl was dead. Not an hour past he'd risked his life to save her, tearing ripperbacks apart with his bare hands. Now she lay still on a dirt road. Eyes wide. Body broken. *Dead.*

Covered in blood, it had taken Lazander time to scrub himself clean of gore. Once Imani was satisfied he wouldn't "stink the place up," the two Champions had begun the walk back to the Ivory Keep in stony silence. The dirt road that had been deserted that morning was now thick with horses, donkeys, and carts full of stone and wood as people struggled to make it to the Keep before the gates closed for the night. The king was offering generous contracts to anyone who could lift a hammer, and journeymen had been flocking to the Keep in droves to help with repairs.

Lazander and Imani arrived after the accident. He'd seen an overturned cart filled with stone in the distance and heard the panicked cries of the driver screaming, "She came out of nowhere!" to anyone who would listen. Eager to help, he'd run ahead while Imani trailed behind. As Lazander got closer, he saw limp, bloodied limbs poking out from piles of heavy stone like exclamation points. And a face, half buried, but for eyes that would not leave his.

Large.

Wide.

Judging.

Lazander fell to his knees, staring. "Why?" as all he could muster.

"I don't know," Imani replied heavily. "Maybe her death inspires another to join Gallow's cause. Maybe, she'd have sided with the Tyrant. Or maybe this has nothing to do with Gallow, and it was all pure coincidence." The Champion sighed, sounding ancient. "I don't know. Nor is it our place to know. Humans have a choice. We don't. That's the price we pay to protect this world."

Men and women gripped the fallen stones, struggling to lift them as they frantically searched for survivors.

"What's the *point* in having these powers if I can't use them to help people?" Lazander said, resisting the urge to grab Imani and scream in her face. "Why would Gallow do this to us, if not to torment us?"

"In another life, in another world, perhaps a different god saves us—the God of Bunnies and Rainbows, perhaps," Imani said, her tone no longer gentle as she knelt to meet Lazander's eyes. "Alas, the gods turned their backs on us when the Tyrant conquered the world. We were a single soul away from complete and total subjugation, yet not one of them heeded our cries. Only Gallow, the God of *Judgment*, answered when the First Eternity lay on the torturer's rack, her eyes ripped from their sockets. I won't lie to you and say life as a Champion is easy. Or that there won't be nights when you wish you had failed your Judgment and simply died."

Lazander blinked in shock at her confession, and Imani twisted her lips in a bitter smile. "I was human once too, Champion. It took me time to leave that life behind—but you *will*. It's the only way to survive."

"No. I won't stand by and let *children* die."

"If he wills it, then you must," Imani said, gripping his face with iron fingertips. "We're brutal because we *have* to be. Because when the Tyrant returns… when *Calamity* returns," the word carried a whisper of power that made Lazander shiver, "we might not be saved this time. Not unless we're willing to do what the First Eternity did. Not unless we're willing to sacrifice everything we love, everything we *are*. This is what I've been trying to teach you, Lazander. You have to rid yourself of this knightly do-gooder attitude and learn the harsh truth—not everyone deserves to be saved."

"If that's what Gallow demands, how is he any better than Calamity?" Lazander spat.

Imani's backhand sent him flying. He landed with a crunch, his shoulder dislocating as he hit the dirt.

"Never speak of Gallow like that again," Imani said, eyes dark and furious. "Now get up."

Lazander stood, knocking his shoulder back into place with a wet, popping sound. Without a word he walked toward Imani, who nodded in approval. "We're up early for your next session," she said, looking to the Ivory Keep still some distance away. "We need to—"

Lazander brushed past her. He could feel Imani's eyes boring into the back of his skull, but he knew now she wouldn't intervene—not when people were watching.

"Is that *Lazander?*" came a whisper.

"A Gilded? Well, he ain't Gilded no more…"

"You haven't heard? He's dancing to Gallow's jig now. Not surprised he strayed, with Marito gone…"

Snatches of rumor, awe, and even disgust followed Lazander, but he ignored them. Bending to grip one of the rocks, he thought of the strength he'd felt when fighting the ripperbacks. It had overwhelmed him to the point of blacking out, but he refused to fear it. Instead he'd conquer this new power the same way he had everything else in his life—with quiet determination.

"**Bend to his might,**" he whispered, the words easy and natural. "**Break before his Judgment.**" The boulder became light as a feather as strength flooded his body. The crowd gasped when he threw the rock to one side, bending immediately to lift the next.

He'd failed the girl in life. He would not fail her in death.

***

Imani watched Lazander with two fingers on her temple. It had taken months for her to use Gallow's strength without passing out, yet here was a newborn foal of a Champion channeling his power with ease. She should be pleased, she knew. It would take everything they had to defeat Calamity. But all she felt was unease at this boy who questioned a god. A boy who would surpass her in weeks if she wasn't careful. Beneath that unease, however, was a thread of something she hadn't felt since she'd called herself human.

Envy.

She swatted the emotion away. There was no one who could best her in hand-to-hand combat, not even Malik—Eternity's very first Champion. Lazander, a boy who refused to stop playing knight, was never going to best her. *Never.*

Lazander picked up speed now, throwing rocks to the side with a frantic energy. The path cleared, he knelt in the dirt, breathing hard as he cradled the broken, mushy remains of what was once a young girl.

Imani turned away.

As a new Champion, she'd tried to save her mother from the blades of debt-collectors despite Malik's warnings. Much like Lazander, she'd succeeded, feeling joy and triumph in her new abilities. The next day, the family's fishing boat, a steady vessel that had served them for decades, overturned in the water—drowning her entire family.

Imani hadn't questioned Gallow since. She'd held firm, even when her conscience screamed otherwise, and in time, she'd come to understand what Gallow had been trying to tell her. What was her mother's life worth when weighed up against the lives of every single person in the world? The lives of her little brothers, her sister, her father?

Now she'd have drowned them all herself if it meant keeping the Tyrant locked away. It was the toughest lesson for any new Champion—that no cost was too high, no price too bloody in the war they waged. She'd tried to show Lazander that today. Had tried to teach him as she'd been taught. So why hadn't it worked? Why couldn't he see he was only making things harder for himself? Imani sighed. This was going to be... difficult.

***

Lazander collapsed on the freshly-laid cobblestones of the Ivory Keep.

He'd unearthed four bodies—a generous term for the hunks of gristle and bone left pulverized by the fallen stone. He'd turned to the crowd, who'd simply watched the entire time he'd worked. "Who were they?" he'd asked. "The little girl—where are her parents? Does anyone know?"

The crowd had shrugged awkwardly, eyes on the ground.

They began to leave, one by one—pulling on packs, shifting stubborn donkeys, righting carts as they moved, parting around the dead like they were potholes.

Alone, he dug their graves, crafting makeshift markers. He couldn't bring himself to leave the traditional bird's skull or copper coins for Gallow's blessing. Instead he carved words into fallen branches, laying one on each mound of freshly turned earth. He'd paused at the girl's grave, lost for what to say. He knew someone out there was waiting for her. In his mind's eye, the table was set for supper, the door open as they listened for her footsteps. Footsteps that would never come. Eyes filled with tears, he wrote only two words on the girl's grave marker.

"Somebody's darling."

By the time he'd reached the Ivory Keep's gates, they'd long shut for the night. He should call out, identify himself, then wait for the guards to confirm. It was protocol, he knew, but the last thing he wanted to do was speak to anyone, and so Lazander did what he had rarely been moved to do—he broke the rules.

Calling on his newfound strength he scaled the Keep's walls. Using his new power for a third time in mere hours made his vision swim. It was only the dagger of spite in his heart that kept him upright. He wouldn't give Imani the pleasure of finding him battered and unconscious outside the Keep.

Safely within the courtyard, he forced himself to his feet, the world blurring. Instinct led him down a path he'd taken a thousand times. Past the ruins of the Resplendent Farrow, the tower Eternity called home, and around the back of the army's barracks to the one place he'd always felt peace.

The stables.

Closer to a barn than a stable, it had been the queen's gift to him when he'd first joined the Gilded. It was large enough to hold his menagerie of beasts as well as all the animals he'd bonded with: Merrin the hawk, Mabel his horse, even Galora—a dragon as magnificent as she was ferocious.

He pressed his hands against the stable doors, the thought of his animal companions making his stomach drop. He'd tried to call out to them when he'd awoken from the dead. Had been desperate for a familiar voice. But the bond was cold. Silent. The magic that had made him famous as a Gilded and had allowed him to finally speak with the creatures he called family was gone.

He heaved the beam that kept the two gigantic wooden doors closed. Only Mabel would be here. Merrin would be out hunting, and Galora—well, the dragon was her own beast. She kept to the mountains unless Lazander called out to her, and without the bond, he wouldn't be able to—

Something burst through the stable doors, knocking him to the ground. Sprawled on his back, hot air blew in his face as rough scales carefully nuzzled his chest.

"*Galora?*" he cried, astonished at the golden dragon who filled the width of the doors. A neighing followed as Mabel squeezed past Galora, the horse shaking her head in irritation at the dragon who ignored her and nuzzled Lazander harder. Mabel joined in, her thick tongue licking Lazander's face before she changed her mind and chewed on his hair—her favorite snack.

"Hah! Stop it you two, stop," he said, half laughing as he smiled harder than he had in weeks. Begrudgingly Galora pulled back. Mabel trotted behind him, "helping" him up by knocking her head against his back—making him stumble.

"What are you *doing* here, Galora?" Lazander said. He hadn't seen her since the night they'd rescued Eternity. She huffed, making her wings tremble ever so slightly. Then she stared at him with large, expectant eyes.

"Ah…" He automatically reached for the sigil on his wrist, the one that bound him to dragon and horse alike. But Mabel's gentle soul and Galora's immense presence didn't answer his call. The hole in his heart widened.

"I… I'm sorry, girl," he said, reaching out a hand to run his fingers over her snout. "I can't hear you anymore."

Mabel shook her head, shoving him into the stables. Laughing despite his grief, Lazander stumbled inside. "How did you even know I was coming?" he asked, knowing they couldn't say.

He got his answer anyway. A shriek came from above that he would know in his sleep, and something small and feathered flew into him. "Merrin!" he cried, holding out his forearm. She landed carefully, spreading her taloned feet wide so she wouldn't cut him. She could have sliced him to ribbons at that moment, and he wouldn't have cared.

"You were watching for me, weren't you? And you told the others?" He rubbed a finger under her chin. She chirped gently, nuzzling him. Mabel followed, rubbing her head against his cheek while Galora wrapped her neck around his legs.

It was there, surrounded by Galora, Merrin, and Mabel, creatures who without words would always be his friends, his *family*, that Lazander finally broke. Marito and Gabriel lay dead, Valerius had returned to kill him, and the cost of his new life were unseen shackles that bound him to a god who forced him to watch a little girl die.

Mabel whinnied, and Galora huffed in distress, but Merrin simply nuzzled closer, chirping gently.

Chapter Thirty-Two

"Until his 'debt' is paid, if I die, he dies! What kind of magic is this?" I said, pacing the darkness. Zara was in her vaxion form as always, her back to me, but instead of curled into a tight ball she now lay on her side. She was still ignoring me, but I was going to take this as an improvement. A *slight* improvement.

"Why can't I just let him go?" I said, knowing I was just venting at this point, but I had no one else to talk to about this.

"Because he is weak."

I froze mid-step at the low, throaty growl from Zara. "What—what do you mean?" I asked tentatively. This was the first time she'd ever willingly spoken to me.

"The *kath'ckh*—the blood debt," she said, back still to me. "Vaxion refuse death. We face our fates head on, unwilling to be broken. To be ruled. My aunt beat that into me the moment I grew claws. If you are so weak as to give ground to the beast within, as Lukas did, well… he deserves to be owned. Even by a worm such as yourself." With an elegant crack of her spine, she stretched out like a cat, her claws unsheathed. "It's why Magnus has never been able to break me, even after all these years." Her tendrils haloed her in a dull glow as she towered over me. The collar at her neck strained when she bent low, eyeing me with brilliant purple irises ringed by fury. "I refuse death. I refuse to be broken—no matter how long he torments me in here."

"Magnus has nothing to do with this," I said. A memory flashed of his arm burning to a cinder as I rained down fire. "The last time I saw him—"

"*Silence.* Lies upon lies. So thickly laid even you cannot see them," she huffed. "Once I thought you his agent. I see now I was mistaken." I felt a flicker of hope—maybe I was finally getting through to her. "You are far too stupid. You are simply a pawn to him—one who keeps me locked in this dark prison."

I sighed. Never mind.

"I want to give you your body back and get out of here, Zara," I said, trying for rationality. "But first I have to figure out how to make the wallow-tail 'shine.'"

Her tail swished behind her. "So you have said. Yet you have already tried and failed. The boy had to save you from your own idiocy—a pattern, I sense."

My cheeks burned, but I forced myself to meet her eyes. The muscles above Zara's violet eyes twitched in a mimicry of a raised eyebrow.

"I am *trying*—" I began.

"The wallow-tail is a creature who feasts on magic, spitting it back at you tenfold," Zara said, cutting me off. "You already know how to feed its heart, to make it 'shine,' as you crudely put it. You saw me do so in your slave's *tul'gra*."

I cast my mind back to the fight in Lukas' mind where his vaxion, molger, and hybrid form fought for dominance. My eyes widened at the memory. If she was suggesting what I thought she was, I'd have one chance to get it right.

Or I'd die.

"You hate me," I said bluntly. "Why this sudden desire to help?"

"Simple," she said with a yawn. "I am *bored*."

***

"If this is your attempt to make our deaths as flashy as they are painful, then *bravo*," Lukas said, clapping slowly. It was morning, and the wallow-tail was as smooth and still as a lake in the dawn light. Birds chirped, claws scarpered—all in all it was an idyllic scene.

Except for the fact I was probably going to die.

"Well, unless you want to transform into a vaxion and shoot me with lightning—"

"*Absolutely* not," Lukas snapped.

"—then I can't 'test' it. I have no choice but to do it."

I'd woken immediately after my conversation with Zara and had lain awake staring at the sky for hours. She'd flipped from furiously angry to cool and detached in the blink of an eye. It was quick enough I was beginning to suspect she wasn't the angry, tormented soul who lashed out because she was in pain.

She was just a psychopath.

But I had no idea how to deal with the wallow-tail, and despite every bone in my body protesting, I believed Zara. I sighed. Maybe she was right—maybe I was stupid.

The light caught the wallow-tail's crystal, a shadow flickering within. When I blinked it was gone, but my heart was beating like crazy. If I didn't do this now, I was going to chicken out. "Zara, let's try something else," Lukas said, stepping in front of me. The sky darkened as electricity flickered between my fingertips.

"Get back," I said.

He grimaced, his body jerking away like a puppet whose strings had been yanked. I belatedly realized I'd made it an order. I strode toward the wallow-tail before my nerve failed, calling out, "Sorry!" behind me. My heart sped up as electricity shot up my arms, the peach fuzz there rising. The world took on a sheen of white as excitement bubbled up in my chest—Zara's. She wanted me to do this.

"**Strike me in fury,**" I said, pointing at the wallow-tail. "**Strike me in death!**"

Wrath's Storm Activated.

Lightning struck the crystal, enveloping it entirely. It glowed, light shimmering within. I braced myself. "Come on," I whispered, fists tight. The crystal turned a deep, angry blue. "*Come on!*" Fire erupted from the crystal, a dazzling blue that stretched like a phoenix taking flight. In any other circumstance, it would have been beautiful. *I can do this. Probably. Possibly. Maybe?*

It shot toward me.

"Death," I said, "has no dominion over me."

The fire struck me, engulfing me in its entirety.

When I'd seen Zara use *Vengeful Rebuke* from the distant shadow of my mind, she'd simply laughed—throwing her head back in ecstasy. It's why I thought this wouldn't hurt.

I was wrong.

Fire coated me inside and out, greedily eating into my flesh. Zara grew in my mind. I could hear Lukas screaming my name.

"Death," I hissed again, "has no dominion over me."

"*Liar.*" Zara laughed. "*You may as well demand a wolf to bow, girl. Give in. Let the fire take you.*"

I thought of my nephew, Noah. Of Eternity's hand in mine. Lenia pawing the ground in her molger form as she charged. The tears in Lukas' eyes as he looked up at me—human again.

"*You stand on the shoulders of others. Without them you would fall.*" Zara scoffed. The fire bent, spinning into an inferno that wrapped around me like a tornado. I leaned back, closing my eyes as I stopped fighting the flames.

Watch what happens, Zara, I thought, buoyed up by the flames on my skin. *When you realize the whole damn world isn't your enemy.*

"**Death!**" I yelled. "**Has no dominion over me!**"

Vengeful Rebuke Activated.

The flames vanished from around me, spinning toward the wallow-tail. The crystal inhaled it greedily, the light within flaring even brighter before spitting the fire back toward me once more.

And thus, the game began.

The tower of blue-fire grew as we passed it from one to another, flames greedily reaching for the sky. Minutes became hours, but still the flames grew.

> **WARNING.**
> **WARNING.**
> **MANA DEPLETING.**

The pop-up angrily flashed before my eyes. I fell to one knee, breathing hard. My dress, or rather, Lenia's, had long burned from my skin. Naked and covered in ash, I dug my fingers into the soil. The last time I'd used up all my mana, I'd ended up curled into fetal position as the Calamity System drove what felt like an ice pick into my brain. But if I stopped, the fire would engulf me before I could run.

Breathing hard, I got to my feet. The crystal shone with a startling blue light. Before, only its center would glow. Now light filled every inch of the wallow-tail until it burned like a small sun. I took a breath, feeling strangely at peace.

I can do this.

Fire erupted out of the crystal, a tidal wave three-stories tall.

I can do this.

The fire struck me, but instead of burning like it had so many times before, it felt warm and welcoming. It cradled me, wrapping around my limbs like an old friend. Power, dark and fierce, filled me.

"**Death**," I whispered softly. "**Has no dominion over me.**"

Vengeful Rebuke Activated.

The flames exploded out from me, disintegrating trees and rocks in a wall of fire that rushed the crystal. The wallow-tail didn't break—it exploded, leaping into the air in a brilliant shower of crystal and fire. It hovered in the sky for a moment before falling in a gentle arc, pattering against my skin like warm hail. My vision blurred.

The dim shape of a bird, its entire body made from blue-fire, emerged from the center of the broken crystal. It was huge, three times the size of the crystal that once contained it.

The wallow-tail, I dimly thought, smiling at the ferocious creature who hung in mid-air, its wings stretching outward until it threatened to engulf the entire forest in flames. *It's... beautiful.*

A bloom of white fire twisted from the top of its head while the edges of its wings burned a deep navy blue. It had no eyes. Instead sockets of white flame turned to face me.

I fell to my knees.

The bird dipped its head to me—an elegant, regal movement before it shrieked a cry of joy that rattled my bones. The last thing I remember before I passed out was Lukas running toward me as the Menu flashed.

WAR... NING... WARN... ING.
CALAMITY... SYS... TEM... COMP... ROM... ISED.
MA... NA... DEPLE... TED...
PEN... ALTY... PENALTY...

Chapter Thirty-Three

The Calamity System Menu swam into view. My mind was foggy, stinging with the throb of remembered pain. It took several minutes before I could read the pop-up.

QUEST COMPLETED: MAKE THE WALLOW-TAIL SHINE

GRADE: B+

I mentally punched the air—it wasn't an A+ like my last one, but I'd take it.

Blessing of the wallow-tail—Bonus

No NPCs sacrificed—Bonus

I frowned at that last one. Sacrificed? The hell did that mean? The thought was swept away at the next pop-up.

QUEST REWARD

Yes! What would it be this time? Health potions? Ability stones?

The Menu darkened, and I saw the rough outline of something that looked like a mannequin take shape. Confused, I squinted. Rewards in the *Knights of Eternity* arcade game were mainly potions, balms, and sometimes weapons if you got very, very lucky. But I'd never seen this.

The image solidified. Thick, leather straps wound around the torso of the mannequin while heavy pleats fell over the thighs—creating a type of skirt I'd seen gladiators wear in history books. Sections of silver metal were laid over the heart, stomach, and back in overlapping sections.

Armor. It was *armor!*

It automatically moved to my Inventory, and I immediately scrolled to examine it.

Item:	Calamity's Teeth
A shiver runs through you at the sight of this armor—though be it of fear or delight, you can't tell. This armor increases the wearer's natural strength by 20 percent and allows the wearer to dance through fire itself. However, let the wearer beware, for your heart will be open to darkness and shadows.	

I frowned, wondering at that last line. It sounded like the armor would leave me vulnerable to shadow magic, but Gabriel of the Gilded Knights was the only character I'd heard of who could use it. I hadn't met him yet, but I *had* been nearly barbecued several times. Shadow vulnerability seemed like a small price.

The name of the armor though—Calamity's Teeth. A reward from the Calamity System… it didn't take a genius to see a pattern. What "Calamity" was, however, I had no idea. It meant "disaster." Did it refer to a specific event? Or something else? I resolved to ask Lukas about it in the morning. Before the wallow-tail I'd have twisted myself into knots trying to figure out how to ask such a thing. Now I wouldn't even blink—Lukas had heard far stranger things from me.

A pop-up appeared.

NEW QUEST AVAILABLE
WOULD YOU LIKE TO PROCEED?

I tried not to sigh. I knew two quests wouldn't be enough to *Summon Eternity*, or whatever it was the Operator wanted from me, but it had been a nice thought while it lasted.

Proceed.

NEW QUEST
BECOME ONE WITH THE CRESCENT MOON

The urge to set fire to a table and flip it lasted only briefly. Maybe I was getting used to these nonsensical quests. That was a disturbing thought.

As eager as I was to wake up, try on the armor, and set off on my next quest, I had something else I had to do. I brought up the Origins tab.

ORIGIN OF PLAYER CHARACTER: ZARA THE FURY. STATUS: AVAILABLE.
WOULD YOU LIKE TO SPEAK TO ZARA THE FURY?

She was the only reason I had even figured out this quest. It might have been only because she was "bored," and she may have taunted me through it, but I was beginning to suspect that was Zara's love language. Hope in my chest, I thought, *yes*, eager for the Menu to fade to darkness.

***

"You were right, Zara," I said as the glow of her vaxion form swam into being. "*Vengeful Rebuke* did the trick, though it drained me of mana. You should have seen the wallow-tail. It was gigantic, and—"

Fangs snapped inches from my nose. I stumbled back as Zara lunged again, her jaw inches from me. Scrambling, I landed awkwardly, backing up as Zara roared—the coils that haloed her head whipping and cracking as lightning zapped between them.

"Zara, what is it? What's wrong?" I asked, fearing the Operator had hurt her.

The lightning built, spreading out in a deadly fan around her head... only to fizzle out, vanishing in the darkness. "Argh! Blasted *chains*," she spat, violently shaking her head. The collar dug into her neck as she shook, blood lining its edges.

"Stop it!" I cried. "You're hurting yourself!"

"How did you do it?" she growled, eyes wide and murderous.

I *felt* the saliva build in her mouth as she imagined ripping out my trachea and feasting on my writhing flesh.

"How did you survive the wallow-tails flames? Only a *shi'ara* should have been able to release it. You should be charred flesh and *bone*."

All at once her willingness to help me and her anger as she taunted me made sense.

"You were trying to kill me," I said, mouth agape.

"Of *course* I was trying to kill you, you festering boil!" she hissed. "You think us bosom-buddies? Playmates in the dark? You are my *enemy*."

"Zara, we don't know what will happen if I die—it could kill you too!" I said, getting to my feet.

"I *care not*!" she roared, gouging at her neck with her sharp, vicious claws. The silvered collar glowed but didn't move while her claws cut into her flesh. To anyone else, she just looked angry, but I knew her well enough now to see it was more than that.

She was scared. No—terrified.

"I—I will not be broken! I will not be bound! I—I refuse death. I—" Her breathing sped up as she flailed, and I recognized the panic in her eyes. I'd felt it almost every day of my life until I'd come here.

"Zara," I said, holding up my hands. "You need to take deep, slow breaths and—"

"What—what magic is this?" she said, shaking. "I cannot breathe! And my heart, it's exploding."

"It's called a panic attack," I said, risking a step forward. Her claws skittered, fighting for purchase as she backed away from me.

"I—I do not panic. *I do not*," she barked, an order for herself, I knew. She screwed up her eyes, her breathing rough and ragged as she hunched down. Abruptly she wrapped her coils around her face, trying to hide herself from view.

My chest tightened in sympathy. The first time I'd had a panic attack, I was sure I was dying. While Zara had just admitted to trying to kill me, I couldn't leave her like this. Even if it was the smart, well, *sane* thing to do.

"Look at me," I said. I knelt down but kept my distance. I wanted to help her, but I wasn't going to be stupid about it.

Her shoulders heaved as she struggled to breathe. With a jerk, she swayed and fell.

Dizziness, I guessed. "Count with me," I said.

"I—I am not an infant who—"

"One," I said, slowly and aloud. "Two. Three. Four…" I kept going, my voice low but steady. By the time I hit twenty, I heard her start to whisper. At thirty, her voice grew louder, keeping time with me. By the time we hit one hundred, Zara's coils had fallen away. She lay on the ground, head low, eyes closed. I watched her carefully, noting her breathing had steadied.

The darkness began to fade, the threads of dawn piercing the night. I got to my feet, sighing. "Magnus didn't do this to you, to *us*, Zara. The last time I saw him, I burned his arm off. In return, he stabbed me in the back with a blade of ice."

Only the tensing of her paws let me know she was listening.

"I'm still going to let you know what we're doing—that's only fair, I think. But I'm not going to stop by every night like I have been," I continued, even as she began to fade. I wondered what happened to her when I wasn't here. Did time pass for her as it did for me? Was she left staring into the darkness until I showed up? I hoped not. It sounded lonely.

"I'm not your enemy, Zara," I said, unaware if she could even hear me anymore. "I promise."

Chapter Thirty-Four

I opened my eyes to the dim light of dawn. A soft layer of dew tickled my skin, and I rubbed it away, enjoying the light, refreshing feel of it. The forest was quiet but for the soft snores coming from Lukas, who lay spread eagle on his bedroll, half in the dirt. I was back at camp and dressed in one of Lukas' shirts, which while long on me, barely fit my shoulders. Mortified, I realized he must have carried me back here and dressed me.

I carefully stretched out, examining myself for injury. While Lenia's dress was ashes, my hair was miraculously still intact. To my relief, soot covered my skin—Lukas hadn't tried to give me a sponge bath. If he had, my soul would have left my body from embarrassment. I flexed my fingers. Despite facing off against the wallow-tail for hours on end and draining my mana dry, I felt fine. Better than fine, actually. I felt *great*.

Slipping from my bedroll, I headed into the forest.

We'd camped some distance from the wallow-tail on Lukas' insistence. At the time, I thought he was just being overcautious, but seeing the charred tree trunks and scorched earth scattered throughout the forest, I was glad.

When I finally reached the crystal, I gasped.

A huge crater lay in the center of what was once the wallow-tail's prison. It was deep enough that if I jumped in, I wasn't sure I'd be able to get back out again. Heavy chunks of crystal littered the hole and the area around it. I touched one of them, the memory of the blue-fire fresh in my mind, but it was cold to the touch, almost freezing.

I was excited I'd finished another quest, proud even. It was another step closer to getting home. But I was also surprised by how sad I felt. If Zara had had her way, the wallow-tail would still be trapped, and I'd be nothing but charred meat. I'd been so desperate to make her see I wasn't a bad guy that I almost got myself and Lukas killed.

I'd been naive. Stupid even. It was a mistake I'd made in my old life too. Back then, there had been days I wanted so badly to be liked, I'd let people walk all over me. I'd tell myself they didn't mean it or I was the problem. Here...

Here I could be different.

I returned to the waterfall where days ago I'd joyfully thrown boulders. I summoned the Inventory, visualizing Calamity's Teeth—my new armor. The shirt I'd "borrowed" from Lukas flowed, lifting from my skin. In seconds it vanished, the armor appearing in its place. Leather wound around my waist, bound in place by straps tightened to fit me perfectly. The sheets of metal that covered my heart caught the light, turning white. I tapped it with an elongated claw—*plink*. The sound was high and piercing. Was this thing even metal? Straps wound around my ankles, the tops of my feet and my shins covered by the same metallic substance while my toes and feet were exposed. I wiggled my feet. If I summoned my claws, nothing would get ripped.

It was like it was made for me.

I mentally brought up the Inventory, relieved to see Lukas' shirt sitting in one of the slots along with the myriad of rocks and sticks I'd popped in while testing it. *I'll have to buy Lenia a new dress*, I promised. *When this is all over.* I knew there was a slim chance of that happening, but the thought made me feel better.

"Looking snazzy," called Lukas.

I smiled. I'd heard him stumble out of bed ages ago. It was odd—my hearing and sense of smell seemed to sharpen every day. I needed *Tithe of Beasts* less and less.

"You're not going to ask where I got it?"

"Lady, I am quickly learning the less questions I ask, the happier I'll be," he said, yawning as he cracked a shoulder. "Though, I will be so bold as to request *fewer* jobs in which we release a blazing bird of fire that nearly kills you."

I clenched my fist, driving it into the ground. The stone splintered beneath, cracks spreading outward like a spiderweb. I was stronger, *faster* in this armor—I could feel it. And the more quests I did, the stronger I would become.

"Are you having a breakdown, and do I need to start running?" Lukas said, appearing at my shoulder. "Because I haven't had my breakfast yet."

"We're going to free you from this stupid debt, get Zara her body back," I said, punching my fist into my open palm. "And I'm going to find a way home."

Lukas yawned. "Yes, master."

"Don't. *Please*," I added at the last second.

"Oh, *now* she remembers the 'please.' Anyway, where to next?"

I grinned, knowing he was probably going to hate this. "Any idea what a crescent moon is? Other than the obvious, of course."

***

Eternity watched the ink dark lines on the page swirl to form Zara striding around in leather armor layered with pure dragonscale. The vaxion looked ferocious, or would have but for the huge smile on her face. It made Eternity smile in turn for the first time in days.

She was back in the Ivory Keep's tower but without the dinner of rice and beans the Head Disciple had threatened. Harrow's anger at her had vanished without a word when the sages announced the Tyrant had returned. Now the Gallowed Temple was aflutter as the news spread. The message was being passed, slowly but surely, from temple to temple. It would only be a matter of time until it reached the public. Eternity wasn't sure what would happen when it did. Either all hell would break loose, or people wouldn't care.

Even after all these years, she still struggled to understand people.

She banished the image of Zara from the page. The vaxion hadn't sensed Eternity checking up on her, for which she was glad. Eternity had no affinity for divination magic, and her first attempts at summoning Zara's image had been clumsy at best. But Eternity was a prodigy, even before she became Gallow's Chosen. It hadn't taken her long to figure out how to cloak her presence from Zara's eyes, though she wasn't sure why she was so keen to hide herself. Zara wasn't her enemy, nor was anyone in the Ivory Keep even remotely concerned with the vaxion fugitive anymore—Valerius' attacks on the Gilded and the Keep had seen to that.

Yet Eternity found herself drawn to the page, found herself wanting to see Zara's face whenever she couldn't sleep. When she felt sad. *Lonely*. Something had become a daily occurrence. When Eternity first became Chosen, she thought she could have a regular life, *and* serve Gallow, and for a while, she'd succeeded. She'd had a handful of friends, and even a lover or two—though stealing kisses in the meditation hall wasn't nearly as romantic as she had pictured it.

Then someone would come to her, begging to be Judged, and Eternity would do her duty as Gallow's Chosen and lay her hand on their forehead. As her eyes turned black with the Void, the pages of the penitent's life laid out before her for Gallow's Judgment, the inevitable happened. Gallow found the penitent unworthy. And those dear to Eternity would have to watch in horror as a human being turned to ash beneath her fingertips.

They usually avoided her after that.

It didn't take long for Eternity to realize it was easier to strip back her life until all that remained was a singular purpose—find Gallow's Champions. She'd sacrificed friends, family, love, and even part of her humanity to carry out her duty. It was all for the greater good—to save the world she loved. Now that the last of Gallow's Champions had been born, she found herself rudderless. Without purpose.

Lost.

Tears pricked her eyes. She watched as the sun rose, waiting for the two figures who strode out the Keep's gates like clockwork every morning. Right on time the first appeared, brushing down his clothes as he carefully shut the stable doors. Usually the sight of Lazander made Eternity beam. Not anymore.

It had only been a week since Lazander started training with Imani, but already she could see a change in the knight. He was taller, stronger, and moved with a new lightness. She kept waiting for him to look up and wave or to call on her at the tower. But they hadn't spoken since they'd visited Gabriel and Marito's tombs together.

The look on his face when he saw the wilted flowers and pitiful offerings for his brothers-in-arms broke her heart as well as his.

While Eternity might be locked in a tower, she wasn't the type to sit idly by. When Lazander didn't call on her, she had decided to go to him, knocking confidently on the stable doors. But every time she went, an apologetic stable hand would say she had "just missed him," his guilty eyes straying to the open window at the back of the stables. She stopped visiting after her third attempt when Galora huffed at her, the gigantic dragon's breath warming the room with a single breath. It confirmed her worst fears.

Lazander was avoiding her.

Now she saw him the only way she could—from her tower window. Imani appeared at Lazander's side as if by magic, her loose clothes at odds with her stern expression. Imani, too, was barely speaking to Eternity these days, only appearing once at her doorway with a single word. "Come."

Together, they'd entered the winding labyrinth that was the Gallowed Temple. Imani was silent as they made their way down the long corridor to the First Eternity's Heart, and the pocket of darkness that housed the only thing that remained of the world's savior. When Eternity approached the withered fist of flesh, Imani finally spoke.

"Call them. Tell them, 'Twilight descends.' Nothing more."

Eternity mentally opened the door to Void where Gallow lay—the First's Heart beating with Gallow's magic, even a thousand years after her death. Blood dripped from her nose as she reached across countries and continents, searching for the thread that connected those blessed by Gallow.

Malik responded first, his rich baritone filled with joy at Eternity's call, turning serious only once she had relayed Imani's message. "I'll be there soon, little one. Rest now—you've done your duty. We'll take it from here," he said.

Vivek didn't answer her first call. Or her second. It was only on her third, when she'd simply said, "Twilight descends," that he finally replied, "On my way." He cut the connection immediately after.

When she told Imani this, the Champion shook her head. "You'd think Vivek would learn some manners, but then, he was like this last time we were all together. It's been some twenty years since then, hasn't it? Back when Evergarden had locked you up like a prized peacock?" Imani rolled her eyes. "Humans and their wars. They were fortunate Gallow didn't command us to rescue you. There would be little of Evergarden left if he had."

Eternity nodded, barely listening. She heard water falling in the background when Malik answered, and the clash of blades with Vivek, but she had no idea where the Champions were, or what they were doing. It was for the best, she knew—the

Tyrant's eyes and ears could be anywhere. It was something she'd never questioned until she watched Imani and Lazander stride out of the Ivory Keep's grounds. She wanted to know where they were going and what they were doing. Wanted to stop feeling like an outsider, just for a moment.

Eternity settled into her perch by the window, resolving to stay there for the day. She knew if she did otherwise, she would simply summon Zara's image again. She shook her head—she was a grown woman, and a Chosen of Gallow. She shouldn't need to see a vaxion fugitive in order to feel calm.

Despite her best efforts, Eternity found her mind wandering back to when she and Zara had first met. What would have happened, she wondered, if the Gilded Knights had never shown up? Zara would never have let her leave with Magnus, she knew. She'd have found a way to save Eternity. But what then? Would the pair have come back to the Ivory Keep? Or perhaps they would have wandered Navaros together, free as birds as Zara now did?

The thought made her smile even as tears filled her eyes.

If she was with Zara, she wouldn't be sitting here alone—ignored by Lazander, her only other friend. She wouldn't lie awake at night, thinking of all the people who'd died so she could find Gallow's Champions. Wouldn't be wondering if it had all been worth it. Fat, full tears trailed down her cheeks.

At least Zara was happy.

Chapter Thirty-Five

"*Crap. Crap. Crap!*" I panted, kicking my foot out. It caught Lukas squarely in the side, his ribs cracking as he flew backward, missing the jaws that snapped at his neck by inches. I winced. I was still adjusting to the strength boost the armor gave me. I'd kicked him hard.

Too hard.

He skidded in the dirt like a skipping stone, crashing into bushes with an undignified yelp. It would have been funny—if I wasn't surrounded by ripperbacks.

A reptilian head snaked past my guard, teeth grazing my hip as I dodged. My armor moved seamlessly with me, the creature's fangs barely leaving a scratch.

Enough.

"**Untethered, the beast screams,**" I hissed. Fur rippled down my shoulders, my flesh shivering. Howling, the ripperback bit down on my arm, its jaw breaking when my forearm and bicep doubled in size. Claws shot from my fingertips, bursting out the back of its skull, coating me in the soft, squishy warmth of gore.

Partial Transformation Activated.

With a flick of my arm, I threw the dead creature to one side, blood spilling over the grass. The pack circled me, cautious now. I flexed my claws, cracking a shoulder for good measure. Fifteen of them surrounded me, their scales of deep forest green and brown nearly blending with the surrounding trees. A week before I'd have been terrified of their strange, elongated necks, long jaws, and low, scuttling bodies.

Now I felt no fear. Only *excitement*.

I leaped.

They howled.

***

I pinned a scrabbling ripperback with my knee, its claws scraping uselessly down my armor. Claws raised above my head, I readied myself to rip out its throat when a sound cut through the growls and whines of the fight—a loud, high-pitched cry. It was a sharp, almost mechanical sound that made my head hurt.

Grimacing, I slapped my hands over my ears. It only grew louder, and I realized it hadn't come from the forest, or the ripperbacks.

It came from *inside* my head.

As one, the ripperbacks froze—their bodies locked into place. Their eyes shifted, and I could tell they could hear it too. The world stilled and narrowed to the noise, and I retched, my stomach flipping inside me.

Abruptly the ripperbacks howled, claws kicking up dirt as they sprinted madly into the forest. Under my knee, the one I'd pinned flailed—eyes wide, frothing at the mouth. Instinctively I backed up. It didn't even glance at me as it ran after the others, their scales blending into the forest until no hint of them remained. Nothing that was, but the bloodied remnants of the four I'd killed.

No, I thought, counting the bodies, *five*. Not bad.

"Next time you save me, could you kindly *not* kick me so hard you break a rib?" Lukas yelled. It had taken me a couple of seconds to find him crouched high up in a nearby tree.

Hands on hips, I frowned. "One—you're welcome. Two—why are you *hiding in a tree?*"

"After getting hit in the head with a piece of spine, I thought it best to stay out of your way," he said, dropping to the ground in an easy crouch. He looked bright and as fresh as he had this morning. I, on the other hand, was soaked from head to toe in thick, clotting blood. I tried to wipe the blood from my face but only managed to rub it into my eyes.

Squinting, I asked, "You can change into a *vaxion* and shoot *lightning* from your head. You didn't think that would be helpful as I'm getting attacked by *fifteen* ripperbacks?"

Shrugging, he looked away. "You were having such fun being all bloodthirsty and murderous, I didn't want to ruin it." His voice was light, but his entire body tensed. He gestured to the forest. "Nice trick, scaring them off. How did you do it?"

"You didn't hear it?" I asked. "The high-pitched noise?"

He shrugged. "Not over the sound of you cackling, no."

I was about to protest that I hadn't been laughing, but I honestly wasn't sure.

"Oh, well," he said, linking his fingers behind his head. "It's the Ivory Keep's problem now. I'm sure they'll hit the Keep in a few hours, in which case the darling Gilded will take care of them."

He walked off, stopping only when I didn't follow.

"Zara?" he said, frowning. "All okay?"

I shivered, dread creeping up my spine like icy fingernails. That sound, the ripperbacks… something about it felt wrong, but I couldn't figure out what. "Yeah. Just please tell me there's a lake on the way to the crescent moon. I'm *filthy*."

"You don't need a lake, Zara, you need a *waterfall* and enough soap to drown in. But worry not, I know a spot. The crescent moon is about halfway between the Ivory Keep and the Moonvale Mountains. That's *if* my guess about the crescent moon is right." He strode into the forest, calling out behind him, "It definitely is, but it helps to be humble."

Shaking my head, I picked my way through the offal and gristle of the ripperbacks I'd killed—no, slaughtered. It had been easy. Effortless.

And I'd loved every second of it.

I jogged to catch up to Lukas.

***

I was wide awake, my belly full and happy. Lukas lay snoring beside me, his shirt halfway up his chest. For a man who'd spent years tormented by his neighbors, then got trapped in the body of a monster, and was now bound by ancient blood magic, he slept *blissfully* well.

Part of me was glad. A larger part was jealous. Rolling onto my side, I gave up on sleep, summoning the Inventory instead. I scrolled until I found the second ability stone the Operator had gifted me for the *Stop Aerzin* quest.

A dull glow warmed my fingers, my hand dropping slightly as the stone materialized. The amethyst was rough to the touch, and I rolled it between my thumb and index finger. The center pulsed with power, and my heart thudded in response.

With a start, I realized it reminded me of the glow of the wallow-tail within its crystal prism.

Curious, I cupped the stone in my hands.

Lightning was wild, fierce, and unpredictable—much like Zara the Fury, but it could also be precise and measured. The air grew dense around me as I focused on the stone. Electricity zapped in-between my fingers, sending a shock through my spine. Opening my hands, I saw the stone had split in two.

LIGHTNING CLAW UNLOCKED.

Excited, I sat up, crossing my legs. Another Calamity System mystery solved. It didn't, however, tell me anything about how I could use my new ability. I could wait until I fell asleep, pull up the section of the Menu that described my powers, and try to figure it out from there... but where was the fun in that?

Flexing my fingers, I whispered, **"I am death's mistress—bow before me."**

Fury's Claw Activated.

The name *Lightning Claw* suggested it had something to do with my claws. Wiggling them, I jumped when lightning flashed between my fingers. Breathing slowly, I let the lightning spark, watching with amazement as it chased itself around my knuckles, my palms, and then curled itself around my wrists—a snake of pure energy.

Curious, I reached out to a half-rotted log nearby, touching it gently with my index finger.

Words came to me, dark and instinctive. **"Scream at the bite of nature's lash."**

Lightning Claw Activated.

The log exploded, splinters bursting into the sky.

Something huge blasted past me in a rush of hot air. Trees rustled and branches snapped as it crashed into the undergrowth beyond. I turned to find Lukas' bedroll empty.

Hands raised in surrender, I winced. "Sorry, Lukas! I, uh, was trying to figure something out."

A snout poked out of the bushes, followed by small, beady eyes. With an angry huff, a huge molger covered in mahogany fur trundled out on six paws.

"Sorry..." I said again.

Lukas padded toward me, dipping his head. A sharp, wet crunch sounded when his back broke, but he didn't even stumble.

I'd seen plenty of molger transform back in H'tar village. It was a slow, painful-looking process in which muscles slid over bone, and eyes too large for their skulls threatened to burst from lids. It also took several minutes. Yet in three paces Lukas' entire body went from six legs of writhing flesh to his two-legged human form.

He was also completely naked.

"Could you kindly not 'figure it out' in the *middle of the night?* Damn it all, that was my favorite pair of pants." He gestured at himself nonchalantly while I fought very, very hard to keep looking at his face.

His eyes locked on mine, frowning. Eyes wide, he burst out laughing.

"You gleefully ripped a bunch of ripperbacks to shreds only hours ago, but the sight of my manhood has you blushing?" He was practically giggling.

"No, I—it's not. Could you put on pants, *please?*" I said, turning around.

"Never thought I'd meet a prudish vaxion."

"I'm not a vaxion," I corrected him. "Not really."

"Sorry, 'crazy spirit lady' doesn't quite roll off the tongue." He appeared at my shoulders, mercifully wearing trousers.

"How did you transform so fast?" I asked, eager to change the subject.

"Ah, you've seen the molger change? They're as slow as a wet week, but that's normal for them. Vaxion, on the other hand, can naturally shift quicker—something they're *very* proud of. But ever since, well, *you,* it only takes me seconds." He shrugged. "A benefit of the blood debt or because you've made me a beast who can change into molger *and* vaxion? Who knows."

"Do you have a preference?" I asked.

"Why?" he said sharply.

"I was just wondering." I said, hands raised in mock surrender.

He sighed, settling down into his bedroll once more. "Sorry. The topic is a little… unpleasant. I'd never shifted to vaxion before you—didn't even know I could. I've little time for my murderous kin, as you know, but I never thought transforming into one would feel so… freeing. Like I've finally been made whole. When I'm molger though, it feels like coming home." He sighed. "Probably because I look like my dad.

Apparently our molger forms are near identical. When I'm human though, I'm the image of my mother—or so I've been told."

I remembered his parents from his memories. His dad stood on one side, his mother on the other next to Ashira. The leader of the vaxion had asked Lukas, who was barely a boy, "Be you the molger, Lukas? Or the vaxion, Aerzin?" He'd chosen the molger—had chosen his dad. But I hadn't seen him in Lukas' memories since then, or in H'tar village.

"He died soon after we arrived in H'tar," Lukas said. He chuckled at my shock. "Your face is an open book. Good for me, but terrible for your pockets should you ever gamble." He settled back into his bedroll, closing his eyes. "Dad caught some kind of sickness. Some of the elders did too, before we left Moonvale, but Dad was the only one to die."

I recalled Lenia talking about how she and her husband got together. He'd mixed up an antidote for Lenia's mother after she came down with a mysterious illness.

"I thought there was a cure? *Blackroot Cleanse?*"

Lukas shrugged. "There was. The ingredients for which were back in Moonvale where the vaxion were busy killing anyone stupid enough to stay behind."

A pause.

"I'm sorry," I said. It was a useless platitude, but I couldn't think of anything else.

"What about you?" he asked suddenly. "Who's waiting for you back in your world?"

The question made my stomach tighten. I knew I had at least one sister, but I couldn't remember her face or name. I had fragments of memories—dark hair, laughter, and cries of "*Mom, she took my shoes!*" All I had of my mom was the sound of the kettle as she went for the fifth cup of coffee.

"My mom. Sister. My nephew, *Noah.*" I said his name more forcefully than I'd intended.

"No father?"

I shook my head, furious when his name and face came to me instantly while my own family's didn't. "I don't have one. I *had* a cowardly sperm donor who did a runner when I was a kid."

Lukas was silent for a long moment. "I've never understood parents who abandon their kids," he said quietly, and I knew he was thinking of his mother.

"They don't deserve us," I said sharply. I waited for Lukas to crack a joke, or change the subject, but he only nodded sadly.

"No. They don't."

He rolled onto his side without another word while I lay looking at the stars, realizing that had probably been the most honest conversation we'd ever had.

Chapter Thirty-Six

Lazander darted forward with a punishing right hook, throwing his whole body into the punch. Days before, Imani would have dodged it, but she wasn't quick enough. Not anymore.

Blocking with her left hand, Imani's eyes widened as she skidded back from the force. Lazander had taken her words to heart—his "do-gooder" ways wouldn't help him win. Not against her, anyway.

He kicked her in the back of the knee, snaking his hand around her neck. Wrapping her in a headlock, he threw them both to the ground. When it came to a straight up fight, he still couldn't hold a candle to the Champion's strength. On the ground, however, they were far more even.

Imani drove a vicious elbow into his side. His ribs cracked, but he gritted his teeth and held on, jabbing his heels into her thighs as he wrapped his legs around her. Beneath his forearm, the warm flesh of her throat began to cave. She coughed, choking.

The old Lazander would have released her immediately. But he'd spent days getting beaten to within an inch of his life. He was tired. Bitter. *Angry.*

Imani kicked the air, ramming her elbow into his ribs. Her strikes were growing sloppy. Lazander held on. He'd release her when she tapped out, and not a second more before.

"Yield, Imani," came a stern voice. "You've lost—have some dignity."

Imani slapped Lazander's forearm twice. He relaxed his hold instantly, and she rolled onto her side, coughing and spitting.

"Well done, boy." A shadowed figure blocked out the sun above him, blinding him. A hand gripped his, hauling him to his feet so roughly he almost fell. "I've never seen anyone pin little Imi."

"Little Imi?" Lazander sputtered at the nickname. There was nothing "little" about Imani. She was built like a workhorse and was twice as stubborn.

"You always did like to make an entrance, Malik." Imani coughed, getting to one knee. She glared at Lazander as she rubbed her throat. "Not bad, knight. There's hope for you yet."

Malik laughed, the booming sound belonging to a giant of a man, yet he barely came up to Lazander's shoulder. He was short with broad shoulders, his chest twice as wide as Lazander's. Dark hair curled around his ears, rough and needing a cut, while a long beard trailed inches past his chin, tied at the end by a small, silver bead. Ancient gray eyes sat in a face that looked barely thirty, yet his stance, speech, and demeanor spoke of a man twice his age. It was unsettling.

"Well met, Lazander. I'm Malik—first of Lady Eternity's Champions." He held out a shovel of a hand, pumping Lazander's fiercely. There was a twinkle to his smile that made Lazander relax, despite his reservations.

"Where's Vivek?" Imani asked, scanning the forest.

"Likely sulking in a tree, you know how he—"

"I do not *sulk*," came a velvet smooth voice at Lazander's back. He jumped, instinctively bringing his fists up to find a tall, skeleton of a man who looked as though he'd eaten nothing but bread and water for weeks.

"No, you don't, Vivek," Malik agreed. "But you do pop up like a daisy in the snow whenever I say otherwise."

Vivek sighed with an air of suffering. Long hair the color of starlight was raked back from his forehead in a tight braid, giving him the appearance of a bleached skull. His features seemed to shift as he turned to glare at Lazander.

"At least say hello, Vivek." Malik sighed.

"**Bear thine soul before his gaze,**" Vivek replied, power making his words sing as he fixed his gaze on Lazander. Dull as night-black pools, his eyes cut through the knight, making Lazander's breath catch.

"His heart is filled with doubt," Vivek said, looking away.

Released from the Champion's gaze, Lazander let out a shuddering breath, hand coming to his chest.

"He's angry with Lady Eternity for blessing him and wishes he'd died with his fellow knights."

Lazander froze at Vivek's words and the truth he hadn't dared to say aloud. "How…"

"As Gallow has blessed you with *Righteous Strength*, our god saw fit to grant Vivek *Eyes of Truth*. It allows him to see into another's heart," Malik said, brow furrowed. "But it's *not* something he should use on his fellow Champions."

"He's no *Champion*. He neither trusts Gallow's word, nor is he grateful for his new life," Vivek snapped, glaring at Lazander with naked hatred. "I'd sooner face the Tyrant alone than fight with him at my back." Without a word, Vivek strode into the forest, his dark cloak whipping about him.

"Blooded Void," Malik swore.

"He's not wrong," Imani said. "Seven times an Eternity has scoured the world for those worthy of Gallow, yet this is the first time in a thousand years that four Champion have stood back-to-back. And who is this glorious fourth? A prissy 'knight in shining armor' who questions the God of Judgment."

"I watched a little girl die for neither rhyme nor reason," spat Lazander. "If that is what a god asks of me, then I refuse!"

Lazander knew this would cause an argument, the same he'd been having with Imani for days. That every death was for the greater good. That Gallow was their only chance against the Tyrant. That they had to win—no matter the cost.

"Gallow chose him for a reason, Imani," Malik said instead. "Do you doubt his word?"

"Of *course* not."

"Then leave. I wish to speak with the boy."

Imani raised an eyebrow, her lips pursed.

"Imani."

She rolled her eyes but walked off without a word, blending into the forest like a shadow. The older Champion sighed, saying nothing for a long minute as Lazander watched him carefully, preparing for the usual proclamations about Gallow.

"Imani is scared," Malik began, surprising Lazander, "of the Tyrant. Of letting the whole world fall because she wasn't strong enough. Wasn't willing to make the hard choice. She's tough on you because she doesn't want you to make the same mistakes she did."

Lazander said nothing. Imani's words were nails, her fists hammers. She was confident. *Arrogant.* He couldn't imagine her being afraid. Then again, his days in the army had taught him that the loudest and brashest were often the most terrified.

"And Vivek? Is he 'afraid' too?" Lazander asked.

"No, he's just an ass," Malik replied, making Lazander laugh.

"Vivek is the least… flexible, of us. He accepts nothing but total dedication to Gallow. I, on the other hand…" Malik leaned in, his gray eyes twinkling. "… have found there's nothing wrong with asking questions. So long as you're asking the *right* ones. Walk with me?" There was no demand in his voice. If he wanted to, Lazander knew he could refuse.

Which was precisely what made him nod in agreement.

Malik walked in front of him, heading deep into the forest. Between the lazy afternoon sun, and the gentle chorus of the forest, it felt like they were simply taking a stroll. Malik made no attempt at small talk, which Lazander was grateful for—until he realized where the Champion was taking him.

Lazander stopped abruptly. Malik spoke without looking behind him. "We're going to talk, that's all. No one will be hurt, and no blood will be spilled—you have my word."

Fists clenched, Lazander strode past Malik, desperately wishing for Merrin and their old bond. The hawk would be able to see beyond, to tell him if Malik was telling the truth, or if this was another one of Gallow's "tests." He pictured her now—the snap of her wings as she dove through the air, her warm chirp as she nuzzled him. The thought calmed him enough that when he reached the ravine, his heart barely stuttered.

The stream gurgled below, splashing softly. A slight breeze made the river moss along the cliff rustle where the sun was warm and soothing. It was only the bloodstained grass that spoiled the idyllic image. He knelt, pressing his hand into the soil, remembering the girl's screams and the ripperbacks' snarls.

A noise behind him made Lazander turn to find Malik was unbuckling his pitch-black armor. Like Imani's it fitted him like a glove, making his body appear like one elongated shadow. "A gift from Gallow," Malik said at Lazander's look. "Vivek believes he gifts it to us when we prove our worth. I think it's when Gallow gets tired of us almost getting killed."

"That happen often?" Lazander asked.

"It does—though Imani would deny it. She likes to act like she's invincible. Don't get me wrong, she's damn close to it. But we can die like everyone else and easier than you'd guess." Malik sighed in relief when he removed his chest plate, revealing leather padding underneath. "Would you mind…" he asked, gesturing to his back. Lazander unbuckled it quickly, and Malik stripped down to dark, loose clothes.

"I wouldn't trade this armor for the world, but damn if it doesn't make me sweat." He sat cross-legged in the grass, patting the ground next to him—a clear invitation. Stripped of his armor, Malik looked younger, more fragile.

Which was exactly what he'd intended, Lazander thought, making a point to leave a large gap between him and the Champion as he sat. He was aware, as always, of Gallow, who stood off to the side in the form of a young boy. The boy was still and watchful, his dark outline blurred. Lazander focused on the blood in the grass and the memory of that little girl crushed beneath rocks.

"What do you know of Gallow and the Tyrant?" Malik asked, breaking the silence.

"The Tyrant spent a year conquering us. Everyone in the world bowed to him but for the first Eternity, who refused to yield even as he tortured her. Gallow, so impressed with her will and sacrifice, granted her the power to beat the Tyrant back. After finding men and women to fight by her side, 'Champions,' Eternity gave up her life to imprison the Tyrant—who will one day return," Lazander said quickly, the words flat and emotionless.

Malik chuckled. "That's part of it, yes."

A pause.

"There's more to it?" Lazander asked, his curiosity winning out.

"Why don't you ask him?" Malik said with a smile. The dark outline of a tall boy on the cusp of manhood appeared in-between the Champions, his hand a hair's breadth from where Lazander's lay. The knight snapped his hand back, eyes darting between Gallow as a boy and the shadowy figure who sat by him—at least a decade between them.

He knew Gallow appeared in different forms to his Champions, but he had never seen anyone else's. While his Gallow stood off to the side, stiff and statuesque, Malik's practically lounged, his long legs stretched out as he rested back on his elbows.

"The more you let him in, the greater the bond—the greater the ease," Malik said, resting a hand on his Gallow's shoulder. The young man didn't move at the touch, but Malik's face relaxed instantly, his expression serene. Lazander's eyes must have betrayed his distrust because Malik smiled. "Ask him. Ask him about the Tyrant. Ask him why we *fight*."

The Champion lay back in the sun, stretching out alongside his Gallow. "You may be surprised by the answer."

Lazander turned to look at the young boy, curiosity and anger warring inside him. As much as he didn't trust the God of Judgment, he still had the desperate need to ask the most human question of all.

"Why?"

Gallow appeared by his side in a heartbeat, his small icy hand pressed against Lazander's forehead. Lazander's eyes widened as the world expanded, and his body vanished.

Chapter Thirty-Seven

Lazander felt the warmth of the sun and the cold, wet kiss of clouds. He opened his eyes to find he was soaring through the sky, the trees below him smudges of green, the mountains mere pebbles of blue and gray. He laughed in pure joy as he stretched out his hands, clouds splitting around his fingertips. It was a dream—an impossible dream. One he relished as he dipped and weaved, knowing this was the world Merrin saw every day.

He would have been jealous, if he wasn't so deliriously happy.

A loud, high-pitched cry cut his joy in half. Sharp as a dagger, it drove into his skull, shredding it. Instinctively he slapped his hands over his ears, but the sound simply drove deeper into his brain.

HE COMES.

The voice was so loud, Lazander could almost see the words being transcribed before his eyes. It obliterated the high-pitched noise—allowing the knight to think again. He instantly recognized the booming, domineering tone. *Gallow.*

BEHOLD.

A speck of darkness dragged Lazander's eyes to the blue sky above him. He frowned, straining to see what it was when a blast of energy sent him spinning through the air as a thick, inky line split the sky in two. Lazander could only watch in horror as fingers the length of a scarlet sunder and twice as thick pushed through the soft membrane of the darkness. They gripped the edges of the split—and pulled.

HE WAS. HE IS. HE WILL BE.

Hot air blasted Lazander's face, his cheeks blistering. Abruptly he hit a wall, his head cracking painfully as an invisible force gripped him, forcing him to face the darkness as the sky tore, the edges ripping like jagged cotton. A hand the size of the Keep's courtyard punched through, long inky fingers reaching for Lazander.

Fear, icy and cold, washed over him—vanishing all thought. All reason.

HE IS INEVITABLE.

The sound of bone cracking, and suddenly Lazander was falling. He hit the ground face-first—or what was left of it.

Soil crumbled in his shaking fingers as he got to his knees, his mouth a grave of ash, his eyes blurred by the smoke that blocked out the sun. At first he thought he was alone in this new, lifeless wasteland, until he heard the thud of hundreds of feet.

HE CHOSE THIS WORLD BECAUSE IT IS WEAK. PLIABLE. WORTHLESS.

Forcing himself to his feet, he stumbled forward—nearly falling to his death as his toes grazed a cliff edge. In the dim light, he could see row after row of people below him. Thousands, no, hundreds of thousands of people all lined up—neat. Obedient.

An army, he realized.

At the head of the army, a column of darkness touched the earth, its every step an explosion of dark energy that made its soldiers cry in triumph while Lazander's stomach churned. He fell to his knees, vomiting as the sound began again—a high-pitch mechanical cry that made the world spin.

YET ONE STOOD AGAINST HIM.

A hand gripped Lazander's shoulder. He turned to see a short, pale woman with beautiful blonde hair. Bright blue eyes met his, and she smiled. Lovely. Soft. Unafraid.

Eternity—she was the image of Eternity. *His* Eternity.

THE FIRST.

Bright white light burst from Eternity, cutting the darkness in half. Yet her eyes remained locked on Lazander's. The army before him fell in a cacophony of screams and pain as her light cut them down, racing to the tower of darkness.

The light struck the darkness, and hope fluttered in Lazander's heart. But the light merely crackled, dissipating into the shadows. The whine in his ears grew louder.

SHE REFUSED TO BOW. TO BREAK. AS THE WORLD FELL, SHE PROVED HERSELF WORTHY. PROVED THAT THIS WORLD WAS WORTH SAVING.

Four figures appeared at Eternity's back, their faces blurred. Only their armor, dark as pitch and as impenetrable as a shadow, was visible. Champions.

SHE GAVE HER LIFE TO BIND HIM.

The light died in Eternity's eyes, becoming as glassy as a doll's—cracks spidering along her cheeks as she grew pale and brittle. "Eternity!" Lazander cried, knowing what was coming a second before she crumbled.

YET HE WAS. HE IS. HE WILL BE.

A faceless Champion stepped in Eternity's ashes. Kneeling, they drew a sword.

ONLY YOU CAN CHANGE THIS WORLD'S FATE.

Eternity's face flashed in his mind. Her smile as she walked through the courtyard, her hand on his forearm, her laugh as she sat with Marito, Gabriel, and Lazander beneath the stars. The woman who's blessing from Gallow had saved his life. The woman he had spent days ignoring, unable to look her in the eye—angry at her for the fate she had forced upon him.

Shame and determination gripped him as he reached for the sword.

The world fell away until only darkness remained. It wasn't the darkness of a windowless room or a starless night. It was so deep, he could feel his heartbeat, *hear* his blood flow. It wasn't darkness.

It was the *Void*.

A single star appeared, its white-hot center blinding Lazander. From there, it split—one half growing larger, streaking across the sky like a comet.

I KNOW THIS BECAUSE HE IS ME. AND I AM HIM.

The other half shriveled—becoming small and twisted.

RETURN HIM.

RETURN HIM TO ME—AND SAVE YOUR WORLD.

***

Lazander gasped, coughing and spluttering as he returned to his body, his lungs screaming.

Malik slapped his back. "Get it out, boy. You'll feel better."

Lazander wanted to ask what he was supposed to "get out" but got his answer when he retched—a gray cloud of ash bursting from his mouth.

"Ah, wasn't too bad for you. Imani hacked up a bathtub's worth," Malik mused.

Lazander rolled away, remembering with horror the First Eternity's skin crumbling to ash. Malik held out a waterskin, and Lazander gargled, spat, and gargled again, wanting to take a blade and scrape it along his tongue.

"Gallow and—and the Tyrant…" he finally managed.

"Are two gods born of the same Void-star, yes," Malik said, standing now.

"Then why the hell are we following Gallow's orders? And why has he let the Tyrant run rampant this whole time?" Lazander said, throwing the waterskin on the ground.

Malik sighed, hands on his hips. "Joining with the Tyrant and returning him to what he once was, a Void-star, is the only way to kill him. But it won't kill just the Tyrant—it'll kill Gallow too."

"What?" Lazander said stupidly.

"Don't you see, Lazander? This is why he pushes us so hard. This is why he's spent hundreds of years looking for people who know the meaning of his tenets— Honor. Obedience. *Sacrifice*. It's why Eternity had to burn through thousands of people to find *us*." Malik's eyes were alight with the same fervor he'd seen in Imani's. "Gallow is a literal *god*, but he's willing to make the ultimate sacrifice to save this world, to save *us*."

Then Lazander thought of the girl's nameless gravestone: "Somebody's darling."

"If he cares so much, why let her die? A little girl who had nothing to do with this?" Lazander said, fighting to hold on to his fury and disgust because the more Malik spoke, the more his heart whispered in agreement.

"There are a hundred, thousand scenarios in which the Tyrant wins. In which he tramples us, enslaves us, and then moves on to the next world. And the next. Until there isn't a single soul left who doesn't bow to him." Malik gripped Lazander's shoulder, his hand exactly where the First Eternity's had been mere moments ago. "There are a handful, at best, in which we win. I know, brother—I've seen them."

Malik sighed. "Gallow might be a god, but he's not all-powerful. He is carefully, painstakingly, inching this world to victory. Every death we witness, another ten, another hundred are saved. It's why we can only move on his orders. One misstep, and we might *ruin* decades of planning."

Lazander's head was swimming. *Drowning.* Could he do it? Could he stand by and let someone die if it meant saving the world?

He didn't know.

Perhaps sensing this, Malik released him. "I've seen what happens if we fail. If you ask, Gallow will show you too, but I suggest waiting a while. I… I've seen what the Tyrant did to this world's children, back when he first descended. I didn't sleep for a couple of weeks afterward."

"And Eternity?" Lazander asked. "Now that the Champions have been found, where does she fit into this?"

Malik smiled. "Good—now you're asking the right questions."

Lazander didn't tell him the reason he was asking wasn't something Malik would agree with.

"Eternity is our trump card. It's by her hand that Gallow and the Tyrant will be bound. Until then, she needs to stay safe and sound in that tower of hers. But that's not all, I'm afraid. In an ideal world, I'd wait until you settled into your powers, but alas, time isn't on our side." Malik sighed, turning to face the ravine. Only seconds had passed, but it felt like hours to Lazander. "Eternity is Gallow's anchor in this world. Through him, through *her* we get our powers. It's why no Champions found before me are still alive. A Champion's life is tied to their Eternity. Which means if she dies… we die too."

Malik clapped a hand on the stunned Lazander's shoulder. "Our fates, our lives, are intertwined now, brother. Whether you like it or not."

Chapter Thirty-Eight

Buried deep in a field of yellow tenderlip flowers, hidden in an engraved metal box, we found the "crescent moon"—a tulip the size of my thumb. A popular molger bedtime story told of a flower that could heal any wound, cure any ill, and was powerful enough to save an entire village. Or so the story went. Lukas only knew that it grew among tenderlips and appeared to "those in great need."

We weren't in great need, nor did it appear to us—instead, it zapped me hard enough that I saw stars.

We picked through the field of tenderlips for days, finding nothing but, well, tenderlips. Frustrated, Lukas cut his arm at one point despite my protests, on the off-chance it might encourage the crescent moon to reveal itself.

It didn't.

It was only on our third search of a gigantic field that I noticed something. When I stepped on a particular spot, pins and needles shot up my foot—not enough to hurt, but it wasn't pleasant. Curious, I pressed my hand into the soil, feeling the crackle of a brewing storm deep in the earth. Summoning my claws, I started to dig, feeling like a dog hunting for a buried bone.

The more I dug, the more my fingers stung, numbing as the energy built. I pushed on until my claws struck something hard, the tips making a sharp *ting* sound. A bolt of energy shot through me, knocking me off my feet. I went flying through the air, hitting the dirt hard. Flat on my back, I struggled to breathe, unable to move my numb and useless arms.

Hot damn.

Lukas appeared above me, a shadow against the sun. "Can you please stop touching things that try to kill you? Thanks ever so much."

He took over the digging. I watched, afraid he'd get zapped too, but he cleared away the soil with ease, his claws making quick work. In minutes he'd unearthed a large, metallic box. The length of a man and twice the width, it was covered in strange runes that flared whenever I went near but didn't affect Lukas.

Cracking the lid open, we found it almost entirely empty but for an impossibly small, fragile looking tulip. It lay in the center of the box and would have looked silly but for the thrum of power I felt coming from it. With a shrug, Lukas picked it up, looking around furtively. "I'm going to hand this to you now, and if something pops up and tries to eat us, I will yell 'I told you so' with my dying breath," he said, passing me the flower.

Thankfully Lukas was wrong—nothing popped up to eat us. But the moment I took the crescent moon, my body felt lighter, my breath freer. I sniffed the tiny flower, slept with it by my bedroll, even walked with it tucked safely by my heart. But every night my Quest tab still said the same.

BECOME ONE WITH THE CRESCENT MOON

Irritated, I carefully put it in my mouth—surprised at the soft, buttery taste of the petals. After nearly dying to save Lukas, and then again when cracking open the wallow-tail, I was sure the quest couldn't be something as simple as *eating* a flower. Lukas, of course, chose this moment to slap me on the back and ask what I wanted for dinner.

Surprised, I swallowed the crescent moon.

The Calamity System gave me a **GRADE B** that night.

The only bonus I received was for not being injured—which meant there had been another way to do this quest, a "golden path," judging by my grade.

QUEST REWARD

I smiled as the outline of a beautiful, dark cloak appeared, swirling in the darkness of the Inventory as well as another pop up with a new quest. I accepted it, thrilled at how quickly we'd figured out the crescent moon, sure I was finally getting the hang of this world.

The next few weeks passed in a blur.

***

"If the world will not yield, then I will break it."

Monstrous Strength Activated.

The barbed skull of a jackalbite cracked but held as it flailed in the water, struggling against my headlock. Gripping my wrist with my opposing hand, I pulled the fish-like monster tighter against me as it whipped up a frenzy.

"Get out of the water, Lukas! *Please*!" I roared, remembering to make it a request at the last second. He was far from me, half in the water as he slid on mossy rocks, desperately trying to pull himself up. I wanted to snap at him to help me, to transform, to fight back!

But I knew he wouldn't.

"I am *trying*," he snapped, darting out of the way of a jackalbite's jaws as another spun, slamming its barbed tail against the rocks he clung to, barely missing him.

"*Lukas*!" My grip slipped as the jackalbite's tail whipped in the water, raking its spines along my back. The water foamed, stained pink with my blood.

Kicking a jackalbite back, Lukas drove his claws into the stone, cracking it. With a jerk, he hauled himself up and out of the water. The sea churned as the jackalbites swerved as one, charging for me in a vicious wave.

"Strike me in fury," I roared. **"Strike me in death!"**

Wrath's Storm Activated.

There was no build up. No crackle of energy. The magic came easily to me now as the clouds darkened, white lightning bursting from the sky and striking the waist-deep water I stood in.

Breathing hard, the sun broke the clouds—revealing a circle of charred, bobbing corpses. More jackalbites floated behind me. I sagged in the water, exhausted. I was bleeding from at least six different places, and my mana was near empty. I'd killed at least ten with *Lightning Claw* before Lukas could get out of range of *Wrath's Storm*.

"Next time," Lukas called, holding up a ruby the size of his palm. "*You* steal the gemstone worshiped by carnivorous fish, and I'll be the bait. Deal?"

***

"So, children in your world don't have to hunt? Or fish? Surely you laid a trap or two."

I shook my head. "We had big buildings called 'supermarkets' where everything from vegetables to meat was sold. I'd never even made a fire before this."

Lukas grimaced. "Oh, I could tell Zara. I could tell."

I shoved him lightly. "I could also buy chocolate. *Any time I wanted.*"

His mouth dropped. "What kind of chocolate? Did you mix it with sazz bee nectar? Oh, oh! Whip it up with some fresh cream?"

"I was thinking more like Kit Kats."

He made a face.

"You covered cats in chocolate and *ate* them? Remind me never to visit your world."

***

"I can't remember my 'dad' anymore," I said quietly.

Zara lay with her back to me as always, her white vaxion form a beacon in the dark.

"Only time in my life I've missed him. My childhood bedroom. Gone. My favorite food. Gone. My first kiss. Gone." I laughed bitterly. "Though I know it was terrible."

Silence.

"What scares me most is that it doesn't scare me. Not anymore," I said finally.

Zara twitched, and I stopped, wondering if she was going to speak. But she simply stretched, long and languid. I didn't trust her, not after what happened with the wallow-tail, but I kept visiting her every couple of days and made a point to tell her what Lukas and I saw, what we fought. It had started off as a courtesy—I'd go insane if I was locked up in constant darkness and solitude. Now I looked forward to seeing her.

It helped me remember who I was.

***

The beasts were slow and heavy, each step echoing through the forest like a pounding heartbeat. Horns twice the length of me curled out of skulls taller than treetops, a dark silhouette against the moon.

"**Your lies are shadows, my eyes the flames. You cannot hide from me,**" I whispered.

Piercing Sight Activated.

My magic flared, a comforting spark dancing on my tongue as I knelt, trusting my eyes to cut through any illusion in the darkness beyond. We'd spent a week looking for it, but it was here—I could *feel it*. The "Rabid Heart."

"I haven't seen you use that one before," Lukas whispered.

"I had it before, back when I first arrived in this world. I lost it as a penalty, but he returned it after our last job, the one with the bees," I said, the world a sea of black and white as my eyes flitted about, searching.

Lukas shivered. "Don't mention the bees, my tongue will never be the same."

I spotted a flash of pink, almost hidden by thick, corded hair on a trundling thigh. The rough, jagged shape of a heart flashed before my eyes.

"I see it," I whispered.

"It's on one of the xandi, isn't it?" he asked.

"Yep."

"The biggest one?"

"Yep."

He sighed. "You know it took all four of the Gilded Knights to take down a single one?"

"That's why we're to wait until morning. I'll get in close, and—"

"The last time we followed your plan, I ended up swallowing a *bee*. My turn," he said, his teeth white in the darkness. "I'll lead them away, then you go for the Rabid Heart when they stampede. You'll have one shot—make it quick."

Before I could protest, he dropped to his knees, fur sprouting along his body as his spine snapped, his shoulder joints rearranging to hold the four heavy paws that burst from the sockets. Two more burst from his hips. In seconds a molger, huge and barrel-shaped, landed next to me.

"You're going to make them chase you? Are you insane?" I whispered, gesturing at the gigantic xandi. A crown of horns burst out of the back of their skulls like blood spray from a gunshot. Thick, corded fur covered their bodies. They walked slowly, their car-sized hooves flattening the earth with each heavy step. What I found most disturbing about them wasn't their size or the fact that a single step would crush me into a fine paste. No, it was that they walked upright on two hooved feet, their long, skeletal arms brushing their knees. It made them appear strangely human as they lurched about.

Lukas had, of course, plenty of stories about them. Legend had it they were descended from one the Tyrant's lieutenants—a shapechanger who could assume an enemy's face. He'd been quick to reassure me they were now just grumpy omnivores who sometimes accidentally stumbled into a town. Stay out of a xandi's way and they stay out of yours—more or less, anyway.

It wasn't as reassuring as he thought it was.

"One step and they'll trample you to death. Look at the *size* of them. Let's come back in the morning," I said, unable to keep the fear and worry out of my voice. Getting hurt was my job—not his.

Small eyes in a fuzzy face stared at me for a long moment. Lukas' gaze softened as he butted his snout against me.

I'll be fine, his eyes said.

With a roar, he charged forward, quickly picking up speed. A xandi turned, sniffing the air with nostrils the size of my head. Lukas nipped forward, biting it on the ankle just above a dark, mud-encrusted hoof.

That got its attention.

The xandi raised its hoof, stomping the ground where Lukas had been a moment before. He took off at a slow, lumbering run, and I wondered why he hadn't transformed into his more agile, vaxion form—until I saw him pick up speed. Lukas vanished into the forest, the ground shaking as gigantic xandi hooves gave chase.

Molger might not be agile, but they were runaway trains when it came to stamina and endurance.

The largest xandi, the pink outline of the Rabid Heart pulsing on its hind leg, was slower to move. I yanked my hood up. The fabric melted into my skin, elongating me into one long shadow as I moved. Disappearing into the long grass, I silently repeated the cloak's description to myself.

Item:	Calamity's Shadow
Darkness is woven into every thread of this cloak, allowing you to vanish from your enemies' senses. Neither sight, sound, nor spell will find you. However, the longer you wear it, the slower your heart beats, bringing you ever closer to death.	

I could feel the effects even now, the space between each heartbeat growing with every breath. I picked up speed, jogging toward the largest xandi, trusting Calamity's Shadow to hide me. The xandi was huge, its pinky finger alone must have been the size of me. Fighting my fear, I crouched in the dirt—forcing myself to stand still as it charged toward me.

"Untethered, the beast screams."

Partial Transformation Activated.

Muscles thick and corded shot out of my shoulder blades as my arms doubled in size. My legs followed suit, becoming heavily muscled with thick claws perfect for fighting.

Or in this case, climbing.

A hoof slammed into the dirt, soil spraying me. I leaped for it, digging my claws into thick, matted fur as I held on for dear life. The xandi picked up speed, chasing Lukas. Tears streamed from my eyes as the forest blurred around me.

I laughed, partially from the adrenaline, partially from the sheer ridiculousness of my situation. I was hitching a ride on what was essentially a gigantic, two-legged wooly mammoth while it chased my friend, a shapeshifting badger. Smiling, I started climbing, wondering if this world would ever stop surprising me.

Chapter Thirty-Nine

"It was buried in its *leg*?" Lukas asked, frowning as he held the key up by the light of the campfire. Scrubbing it with soap in the river had done nothing to remove the bloodstains. Or the rotting, fetid smell that clung to it. I did my best to breathe through my mouth.

"Not only was it buried in its leg, it was *sewn in*. I could see the scar from where it had been stitched up!" I said.

"Who would hide a key in a xandi?" Lukas asked, twirling it in the light. The top part, the bow, was a solid piece of silver cut in the shape of a diamond. At its center, harsh lines were etched into it in the shape of a star. The key had no "teeth," it was simply a straight line of silver.

"You know, if this was a story of the Gilded, this key would unlock the big bad guy's evil lair," he said.

"Or maybe it'll vanish from my Inventory overnight, like the ruby from the jackalbites."

Lukas shook his head. "We ate chargrilled jackalbites for a solid *week*, and we don't even have anything to show for it." He leaned back but stopped with a wince. He tried to cover it with a stretch.

"What happened? Are you hurt?" I asked.

"I'm fine, *Mother*," he said with an easy smile. "I took a tumble after I left the xandi in the dust. I know it's hard to believe, but yes—even *I* make mistakes."

"Can I see? I asked, ignoring his teasing tone as I grabbed his plate, quickly making space after dinner.

"Zara, it's not a big deal."

"Let me see… please," I said, making sure to keep it a request. It was becoming a habit, but I still had to catch myself.

He sighed, pulling his shirt off in rough, jerky motions. I grimaced at the purple and black bruises that ringed his shoulder, trailing all the way down to his elbow. Closing my eyes, I breathed deeply—letting the world expand around me.

Tithe of Beasts Activated.

"Move your shoulder again, please," I asked. He did, and I heard a loud, meaty click as the bone slid out of place. This wasn't just a tumble. Lukas must have dislocated his shoulder, and then popped it in by himself. I grimaced—that would have hurt like *hell*, but if I mentioned it, he'd deny it. Time to try another tactic.

"I have a… spell that the Operator gave me for finishing the crescent moon quest. Can I try it?"

"I mean, I'll be fine in a day or two, but if it will stop your henpecking, then sure," he said, his back tense. He was sharper than usual.

"Kneel in wonder as I take your pain, your weakness, and thrive," I whispered, placing both hands on his shoulder.

Bloodied Restoration Activated.

The bruises vanished beneath my fingers, sinking into his flesh until all that was left was his smooth, tanned skin. Lukas gasped, flexing his hand in wonder. "Oh, that is *handy*, you kept that one to yourself, didn't you—"

I fell to one knee, gripping my left shoulder as pain exploded. I could *feel* Lukas stumble when a xandi's hoof clipped his shoulder, the sharp crack of bone a death knell. Could feel his terror when he stumbled, a hoof blocking out the moon above him, seconds from coming down on his head.

He would have died, if not for the huge, scarlet sunder directly in his path. He charged for it, slamming his shoulder into the tree at full speed, and knocked the joint back into place. Air whistled past his face as he dodged the xandi's hoof at the last second.

"What is it, what's wrong?" he asked, panicked. I could only shake my head as he pried my fingers away from my shoulder. "Why is *your* arm now covered in bruises?"

"Watch," I hissed, praying I'd understood the ability.

Something warm and wet squirmed in my shoulder. The feeling spread, trailing down my arm and into my fingers. Despite the warmth, I shivered, feeling like I'd stuck half my body into a bowl of cooling jelly. In seconds the pain, as well as the bruises, faded. I wiggled my fingers.

"See?" I said, hiding my ragged breathing as I stood. "Now we're both fine. Which is good, considering you were nearly *trampled by a xandi*."

"How did you—oh, no, no, we are *not* playing the blame game. Why did you collapse, and why did your bruises match mine?"

"It's part of the spell," I said. "Turns out the crescent moon *does* heal, but there's a catch. To heal, I have to *take* your pain."

"I've seen you get mauled by jackalbites and shredded by ripperbacks, and you barely flinched," he said, holding my arm gently, as if expecting it to shatter. "But my little shoulder owie left you gasping."

I sighed. Of course, he noticed.

"When I take your pain, it doubles it. Since your arm was nearly *obliterated* by a xandi, yeah—it hurt a bit." I knew sarcasm wasn't helping, but I couldn't stop myself.

He turned away, his hands in his hair. "You should have told me it would do that."

"And you should have waited for morning. Instead, you made the xandi stampede, and then lied to me. Why would you be so *stupid?*"

"Have you forgotten about this?" he said, grabbing his bracer and ripping it off. The scar there pulsed, red and angry. It was smaller than the last time I'd seen it, curling in on itself by maybe an inch. Since the night he'd first shown it to me, he'd never taken the bracer off, not even when bathing. We hadn't talked about it either.

"I *need* to pay this back somehow. You think I haven't noticed how you do everything you can to keep me out of a fight? How you throw yourself in harm's way while I stand on the sidelines?"

"That's—" I fumbled, annoyed he'd caught me. "That's because you don't want to fight! I know you're scared. Scared you'll lose control and hurt someone."

Lukas blinked in surprise, looking like he was about to deny it. But then he looked away, embarrassed. "That has nothing to do with this. I can't spend the rest of my life being your servant boy."

"Servant boy? But I thought we... have I made you feel like that?"

"Well, no, but that doesn't change the fact that a single word from you and, *boom*." He snapped his fingers in my face. "My freedom is gone. It's like having a noose around your neck while the executioner tells you 'not to worry.'"

My chest hurt, a hollow pit forming. "That's how you see me? As your executioner?" My voice was small and pathetic, but I couldn't help it. I had to know.

"Yes. *No.* I mean—can you blame me, Zara?" he asked, his shoulders dropping. "You have a creature, a monster, in your head, by the sounds of it, whose every word you have to obey, or he punishes you. What happens if his orders stop being about flowers, or keys, or whatever flight of fancy he has, and start being about me? What if you have to choose between hurting me or getting punished?"

I thought of the Operator's alien planet, of the burning agony as sand-touched symbols crawled over my skin and burrowed into my skull. I would have clawed my eyes out to make it stop.

"I'd take the punishment," I said, my fists clenched. "I promise."

He laughed, a sad, miserable sound. "My dad swore he'd always be there for me, and he died days later. Chief promised he'd protect me, but he could do nothing when H'tar made me their whipping boy. So, with all due respect, Zara, I don't believe you." There was no anger to his voice, just a quiet resignation.

Which hurt even more.

"I'm beat," he said suddenly, making a point of stretching. "Let's talk about the next job in the morning." Without a word he lay down, his boots and trousers still on, and rolled onto his side.

I had a sudden vision of Zara, her back to me, her body hunched in on itself.

Looking down at my hands, I thought of all the powers the Operator had given me, of how wonderful and freeing it felt to use them, to *fight*. But what good were my powers or all these quest rewards if people kept ending up bound to me? I was supposed to be a player in this world—not its jailer.

My skin itched with the need to walk, to run, to do anything but sleep. Lukas didn't move as I took off into the forest at speed. He was right—I didn't know anything about the Operator. I didn't know who or what he was, only that he'd brought me here to *Summon Eternity* and then spent all these weeks sending me on nonsensical missions.

I should find out, I knew. I should summon the Calamity System Menu, teleport to that alien plane, and demand answers from the Operator. But even the thought of that desert planet and how much every second there *hurt* made my heartbeat triple. Maybe Lukas was right—maybe if push came to shove, I wouldn't be strong enough to save him.

Maybe I'd just save myself.

I ran until my sides hurt, the night turning red then orange as dawn broke. Exhausted, I stumbled into the clearing where the xandi once camped, nearly tripping on a gigantic hoof print.

Breathing hard, I dug my hands into the compacted soil. *Stop it. Stop feeling sorry for yourself! You need to get your crap together, and get these quests done. The sooner you do, the sooner Zara gets her body, Lukas gets his freedom, and everyone can go their separate ways.*

That last one hurt more than I thought it would. I'd thought Lukas and I were friends, or at least something close to it. Zara would laugh at me for being so naive.

The sun rose, and I closed my eyes, picturing the Calamity System Menu. Slowly the darkness behind my lids took shape. Days before I'd been able to summon the Menu while I was awake—a first, but it had vanished when I'd gotten distracted, so after a grand total of three seconds. Any interruption seemed to make it disappear, and I'd failed miserably every time I'd tried since.

Now exhausted and empty, the Menu came easily—the gold border of the Quest tab appearing in seconds.

QUEST COMPLETED: REVEAL THE RABID HEART
GRADE: A+

My first A+ since I'd rescued Lukas. I should feel excited, I knew—this meant more quest rewards, maybe even more powers, but all I felt was impatient.

Just show me the next quest and let me be done with this.

The Quest Rewards screen blitzed past, showing me a snippet of what looked like a ring before the words that were starting to haunt my waking moments appeared.

NEW QUEST AVAILABLE
WOULD YOU LIKE TO PROCEED?

Yes, I thought, knowing a "no" would result in what the system had only described as "termination."

TEMPER THE VAXION

My blood went cold, every hair on my body raised.

Oh, no.

Chapter Forty

The sky split. Oceans boiled. Lazander watched as the Tyrant grew, and grew, until darkness enveloped the whole world.

Another. Show me another.

In this one, the molger and vaxion are the first to bow to the Tyrant. The Ivory Keep is left burning and bloodstained as bodies litter the courtyard, hanging broken from windows like ornaments. Vaxion prowl the wreckage, their lightning zapping through the air as they build the flames higher and higher. A screaming child, snot running down her nose, is taken between jaws and crushed—her skull popping like a watermelon. Armored molger charge through burning buildings, bringing them down with a single roar.

Another.

The queen's eyes widen in comical surprise, a blade bursting through her chest. She doesn't fall to the floor. Instead, she is kicked, her fragile bones cracking as she hits the marble floor. The king screams, fighting against the many hands that hold him down. Rhys, the king's own second-in-command, a man who has served for over a decade, weeps as he draws his sword.

Lazander doesn't cry out. He's learned that his words, his screams, have no effect on the visions. Instead he simply watches as Rhys presses the blade into the king's neck, whose eyes haven't moved from his wife's dead body. The Tyrant whispers, telling Rhys this is the only way to survive. That if he doesn't kill his own king, the Tyrant will make Rhys watch as vaxion rip apart his newborn son.

Another.

Another.

Another.

In every vision the world bows. In every vision the Tyrant wins. Except one.

In the final vision, Imani, Vivek, Malik, and Lazander stand in a circle, their backs to its center where Eternity kneels. Hands clasped in prayer, the ground glows with the Gallow's power.

Lazander shut his eyes, knowing what came next. Every night Gallow showed him these visions, and every night his heart swelled a little more with acceptance.

"I understand," he said, opening his eyes to find the boy, his eternal companion, his god, before him. The boy's dark outline quivered, then reached out a hand—resting it on Lazander's shoulder.

***

Eternity waited by the tower window as she had done every morning for weeks now, but Lazander hadn't appeared yet. He no longer awoke at the first light of dawn, hurrying after a quick-stepped Imani. Instead Malik would knock on Lazander's stable door, and together they would sit and enjoy the rising sun before heading into the forest to train.

Merrin had taken to perching on Malik's shoulder where he would feed her some of the berries he brought especially for her while Mabel would neigh with jealousy from her stall. Even Galora, who had made it very clear Eternity was no longer welcome in the stable, would snake her long neck out of the double doors to dip her head in greeting to the older Champion. Eternity smiled at how close Malik and Lazander were clearly becoming, even if the sight broke her heart.

She'd given up all hope of Lazander ever visiting her, and so she tried to be content with seeing him the only way she could—from a distance.

When Malik and Vivek had first appeared in the courtyard, their heads bent low in conversation with Imani, Eternity had waved enthusiastically from the tower, calling out, "Welcome!" Perhaps she could give them a tour of the new grounds, she thought. Or they could all get a drink in the rebuilt Resplendent Farrow. Or maybe...

But her plans fell away when Malik didn't so much as glance at her. Vivek openly glared, and Imani, who'd been her shadow since she arrived in the Ivory Keep, acted as if Eternity didn't even exist. Eternity had never exactly been *close* with the Champions—their duties took them to the far reaches of the kingdoms, and she could go years without seeing them. But she'd always thought they had a bond, one that went beyond their ties to Gallow. Surely that merited a wave in greeting?

And then it hit her. She'd risked her life to save the queen's and acted without Gallow's orders—and they were furious with her for it. And while she didn't regret what she'd done, she understood why they were angry. All she had to do was explain herself, apologize, and it would all blow over, she told herself.

It didn't. Days turned into weeks and not once did the people she'd sacrificed so much for come speak to her. Lost to her solitary life, her thoughts turned darker, her mind finding scraps of hopelessness in every corner.

Maybe this isn't about the queen. Now that I've found Lazander, and there's no more Champions, maybe the others don't... want me around. What if they never liked, and were only tolerating, me because I'm Chosen? Am I that awful? That... repulsive?

She dug her fingers into her dress, which was now horribly stained. She'd re-worn her dresses countless times without washing them—the beautiful pieces of cloth she'd once taken great pride in now seemed pointless. She hadn't left the tower in weeks.

Zara had been a saving grace in the long hours between night and day. Eternity had watched her leap through waterfalls, wrestle goober-pigs, and even scale a xandi. Zara's life seemed one fantastical feat after another, like something straight out of a fairytale. All while a tall, blond falsling traveled with her. A stranger Eternity had never seen and yet had taken an instant dislike to. *I wish it was me*, she surprised herself by thinking. *I wish, for one day, I could forget my duties. Forget about Gallow. Forget I'm Chosen.*

A knock at the door. The first in weeks.

Her head shot up. Who could it be? She looked down at herself, she was a *mess*—if the Head Disciple saw her, he'd extend her punishment, Chosen or not. But she hadn't spoken to anyone in so long...

"Come in," she called out, trying to find a hairbrush among the pigsty that was her quarters. "I'm afraid I'm not, ah, prepared for company, but—"

"Eternity?" Came a voice she'd longed to hear.

She turned to find Lazander standing in the doorway. With a hand on the door handle, one foot in the room, he looked uncharacteristically hesitant. "Might I speak with you?"

"Yes—yes! Of course, come in," she said. "I'm sorry, I must look terrible. I've been... well, it's been..."

"A lot," Lazander finished for her.

His eyes moved from her greasy hair to her rumpled skirts, and she smoothed them down, suddenly self-conscious. The air was awkward and tense, and Eternity found herself looking everywhere but at Lazander. She'd desperately wanted to see him, but now that he was standing in front of her, she couldn't think of a single thing to say.

"I'm sorry," he blurted out. "For not coming to see you."

"Oh, it's fine. You're a Champion now, and Gallow asks much of his servants," she replied automatically. She gripped her sleeves, twisting them into knots. "I see you and Malik have been getting along. That's good to see. Imani can be a tough taskmaster, and Vivek is, well, Vivek, so I'm glad—"

Lazander crossed the room in three strides, wrapping his arms around her in a tight hug. Eternity froze at the contact—it had been so long since anyone had touched her, her mind simply went blank.

"I'm sorry. I was angry. Angry that I'd survived when Gabriel and Marito didn't. Angry that I was forced to serve a god I didn't care for. And angry with you—for saving me," he said against her hair.

Eternity's hands hung limp by her side. She screwed her eyes shut.

"I saw you watch for me morning and evening, but I ignored you, even when I saw you grow thin and tired. I was so busy feeling sorry for myself that I let you— someone... incredibly dear to me, suffer. You saved my life, and I reacted like a child throwing a tantrum."

Tears in her eyes, Eternity shook as she brought her arms up, wrapping them tightly around Lazander. It felt so good to be *held*. "I was scared you'd never speak to me again," she mumbled, her voice breaking.

"I know—I'm sorry. But Gallow and Malik... they've taught me a lot." Lazander stroked the back of her head, his other arm clutching her tightly, enveloping her in a comforting warmth. "I've seen what happens if the Tyrant—if *Calamity* wins. And while I can't promise I'll be a good, unquestioning little soldier, I know we're the only chance this world has."

Eternity pulled back. Lazander relaxed his hold, but he kept his arms loose around her.

"So, you're not angry with me anymore?" she asked, aware she sounded like a child but unable to stop herself.

"No. Not one bit. In fact," he made a show of stepping back and offering her his arm, "if you can find it in your heart to forgive my idiot self, I'd be delighted to invite you to luncheon with myself, Galora, Mabel, and Merrin."

"There's nothing to forgive, Lazander." She smiled, wiping her eyes. "Though I'm not sure Galora will be happy to see me. The last time I wandered into the stable she looked like she wanted to eat me."

"She's just protective. Without our… bond, I can't explain things to her so well. But when she sees you with me, she'll be delighted. I promise."

"I'm sorry about the bond," she said, squeezing his hand. "Maybe in time Gallow will return it to you."

Lazander smiled, but it sat awkwardly in his face.

Eternity frowned. She had calmed down enough that she could look over Lazander properly, as he had done to her. He'd grown since his new birth as a Champion, gaining several inches. His shoulders had filled out too, straining against a loose gray tunic that must have been new but already barely fit him.

The physical changes weren't what made her frown though. She knew this was what all Champions went through, had seen it with the others. What worried her was the look on his face. His eyes were duller, his smile strained. If she hadn't known him so well, she doubted she would have noticed, but the Lazander that stood before her felt like a twin to the man she called friend. He looked, spoke, and smiled the same—but something was *off*.

"Shall we go?" he said, offering her the crook of his arm. She took it, shaking off her doubts.

Lazander was the only Champion she'd known before their rebirth. They had died and been reborn, brought back to life by a literal god. She couldn't expect him to be exactly the same… could she?

Chapter Forty-One

It was morning. The forest was silent, the fire long cold. Two bedrolls lay on either side of the ashy remains of a fire.

Lukas didn't wake up—that was too gentle a description for how he jerked upright, swiping at invisible enemies with a deranged snarl. For a second, he wasn't human. He wasn't molger. He wasn't even vaxion. He was a *beast*, a vicious bloodthirsty creature who watched the people of H'tar from the shadows, saliva dripping as he pictured burying his fangs in their stomachs. How good it would feel to feast, to *gorge*. His hands shook, eyes wet as he steadied himself. He had conquered the monster, he told himself. It couldn't hurt him, or anyone else again. But he knew that was a lie. It lay just beneath the surface. Watching. Waiting.

It was a nightmare he hadn't had since he'd joined Zara.

Most people, upon waking up and seeing a blood debt on their arm, would have run into the wilds, praying Zara the Fury would never find them. But Lukas was a man who prided himself on his ability to survive. His plan was simple—get close to Zara, make himself utterly indispensable, then discover and exploit her weakness. He prepared his greatest weapons, his charm and humor, unwilling to believe Lenia's account of a kind, painfully shy woman with more strength than sense.

Turned out Lenia was wrong about Zara. And so was he.

The Zara he met was a quick-witted woman who laughed easily. Who hadn't blinked when he'd revealed the truth, instead promising to free him. Who hadn't pushed him to fight, knowing he was terrified. Her greatest crime was being an idiot (how she wasn't dead was beyond him) and talking with her mouth full.

His eyes welled with tears when he remembered how she'd grasped his paw in hers back in H'tar, whispering fiercely in his ear. "You're the bravest, kindest, strongest person here. Don't you *dare* let these idiots decide who you are." She'd pulled him back from the monster inside and tried so hard to be his friend, and what had he done in return? Yelled and called her his *executioner*. Why? Why did he keep picking fights with her? It was like he was *trying* to make her yank his leash and tell him to bark. Then he could point and say, "Aha! I knew it!"

From the depths of memory, his dad's favorite saying came to him. "Turnips don't dry themselves." Which, admittedly, didn't make as much sense as his second favorite saying. "When people show you who they are, believe them." Zara had shown him who she was, and it was past time he started trusting her.

He sighed. He'd have to apologize, and he *hated* apologizing. Maybe he could just make her a really nice breakfast and act like everything was fine? No, that was too cowardly. Or maybe…

He frowned, his eyes and nose kicking in before his brain did. He took in the cold fire, the empty bedroll, and the words scratched into the ash: Operator sending me to vaxion. Do not follow me. Will ask about blood debt. Ashira should know more.

A shiver ran down Lukas' spine at the thought of Ashira. As beautiful as a storm and twice as deadly, she'd reduced grown men to quivering babes who sobbed at her feet. He reached for his pack, gearing himself up to chase after her but couldn't move. His feet were blocks of stone, as stiff and unyielding as a mountain. The more he pushed, the more his arm burned, like fire bugs were crawling up his skin and burrowing into it.

Horrified, he pulled off his bracer to see the blood debt glowing red and angry. He read the message again, four words jumping out at him— "Do not follow me." The blood debt had to be vocalized for it to be an order. So how…

"Damn it all, Zara!" he hissed, sitting down with a thud. *"Damn it."*

***

I reached up, stretching my body to the absolute limit as I dug my claws into the next rock. I risked a glance down, then quickly regretted it. The ground beneath was a blur of blue-tinged rock spotted by half-dead grass. Freezing cold wind whipped about me, every gust threatening to tear me from the mountain and send me falling to my death. I dug my claws in deeper, *Fury's Claw* the only thing keeping me upright.

Breathe. One step at a time.

I almost laughed. That was something my old life had taught me, if nothing else.

I pulled myself up, reaching with my left hand and thought of Lukas. He was probably awake by now. Would he be angry, relieved, or both?

Both, knowing him.

A pebble struck me, nicking my forehead. I ducked as a shower of rock and debris tumbled down, covering me. Holding still, I gripped the cliff face, waiting for more to fall—but nothing came.

"To hell with this," I said, closing my eyes. "**If the world will not yield, then I will break it.**"

Monstrous Strength Activated.

I didn't pull myself up—I leaped, my claws grabbing a handhold for a split second before I threw myself upward, flying up the side of the cliff. Stones loosened, tumbling behind me, but I picked up more speed, grinning with reckless abandon. Minutes passed, or hours—in the throes of my abilities it was hard to tell. But soon, despite reactivating several times, my strength began to fade and my vision swam.

My hand slapped on level rock, and I hauled myself up onto it, my strength vanishing. I collapsed onto my side, panting hard. Blinking, I pulled up my character sheet.

Current:	
Stamina	10/300
Hit Points	300/300
Mana	250/500

While my mana was still recovering after my fight with the wallow-tail, my stamina had been full this morning. *Monstrous Strength* was an amazing ability, but it drained my stamina. A nap should do the trick. The only problem was…

I looked over the ledge, grimacing at the clouds hiding the ground beneath me. I couldn't even tell how far up I was anymore. Above me, the cliff stretched into the stars like the finger of a god. The air here felt thinner, making it almost impossible to catch my breath. I'd known the vaxion lived in the Moonvale Mountains, but it wasn't until Lukas pointed out the mountain range that I'd realized how insane that was.

"See that? It's the western edge, and yes, that's the *smallest*," he'd said, nodding at a cliff face that pierced the clouds. We'd been in the field of tenderlips, stretching sore backs after hours of looking for the crescent moon. "Most of it's barren rock that nothing but our claws can break—and even that can be a struggle. There's water, rich soil, and even gems we used to trade with humans, but you have to get past the mountains first. There's two ways—or rather, there was: scale the west side and you'll fall to your death or get eaten by gravediggers. Nasty buggers. Or two: go through a narrow bottleneck that they, surprise, surprise, caved in once the molger left." He'd rolled his eyes. "Paranoid as always. They can't even get chocolate now, what kind of life is that?"

I hadn't asked what a "gravedigger" was, nor had I met one yet. Maybe luck was on my side for once.

Shivering, I sat up, rubbing my shoulders and wishing my armor wasn't just fire and lightning resistant. Looking up, I couldn't even see the top of the cliff. It would be insanity to try to climb through the night, but I couldn't camp on a narrow ledge. If I rolled over in my sleep, I'd end up a pancake.

The wind whipped about me, cold and fierce, and then I heard it—a long, low whistle. The sound made my hair stand on end.

Tithe of Beasts Activated.

Focusing, I realized the whistle was coming from behind me—*inside* the rock. I pressed my hands against the blue stone, but it was cold and solid, like the rest of the mountain range. The whistling sounded again, beckoning me closer.

"Your lies are shadows, my eyes the flames. You cannot hide from me," I whispered, eyes locked on the rockface.

Piercing Sight Activated.

The rockface shimmered, then vanished, revealing a cave barely taller than me. It twisted deep into the darkness, and from the depths, the whistling grew louder.

Well, that's not ominous.

The wind picked up, forcing me to crouch or risk getting blasted off the ledge. I could dig my claws in here and try not to fall asleep while I waited for my stamina to replenish. *Or* I could try to find shelter in the creepy cave. I almost took my chances on the ledge. But then hidden among that strange whistle, I caught the faintest whisper of a name.

"Zara."

Zara had been here, I suddenly knew. The *real* Zara.

Droplets of rain fell, so cold they hurt. Arms wrapped around me. I ducked my head, heading into the abyss of the cave and the Moonvale Mountains within.

Chapter Forty-Two

"**Bend to his might, break before his Judgment,**" Lazander said, his body flooding with Gallow's strength. He darted forward, swinging his blade in a wide, deadly arc. The mercenary he fought panicked, bringing his sword up to block, but Lazander's kept going—slicing the man's blade in two before cutting him open from shoulder to chest. The man hit the ground, blood spitting from his lips, gurgling like a newborn babe.

"Finish it, brother," Malik called, burrowing an axe the size of him into the neck of a woman, his blade cutting through her armor like butter. "It's a mercy!"

"N-no," the mercenary gasped, pawing the air uselessly. He was younger than Lazander by a year, maybe two. Freckles dotted his cheeks, half hidden by splatters of blood. "P-pleas—"

Lazander's arm snaked out, cleaving the man's head from his shoulders. As the lifeless corpse hit the dirt, Lazander held the image of the young mercenary in his mind, vowing to remember him.

"Well done," Malik said. The telltale shimmer of dragonscale ringed the edges of the huge axe he hefted on his shoulder. Before he'd become a Champion, Lazander thought only Gilded Knights were "allowed" to own and wield dragonscale.

He couldn't believe how naive he'd been.

Six bodies littered the ground. They were on a dirt road on the path to Evergarden, though Lazander only had a rough idea where they were in relation to the city-state. He'd quickly realized it was easier to just follow Malik's lead.

"Who were they?" Lazander asked as Malik flipped over the body of the woman he'd killed. He undid her straps, pulling her armor off. Lazander gripped the hilt of his sword, watching the Champion carefully. He relaxed only when he realized Malik had removed her armor so he could search the inner pockets of her tunic.

"Why were they here?" he asked when the older Champion said nothing.

Malik ignored him, pulling something small and round from the woman's pocket.

Lazander sighed. "I suppose if I ask what that is, you won't answer either, will you?"

Malik smiled easily as he pocketed it. "If Gallow hasn't revealed it to you, then no—I won't." He rested a meaty hand on Lazander's forearm. "But you can ask a better question."

"Where to next?" Lazander ventured.

"Now you're getting it. Evergarden is just up ahead. Once we're there, all will be revealed, brother." Malik cracked a shoulder, setting off at a quick pace. Their hands hung empty, and their packs carried neither food nor water—only a change of clothes. They traveled by foot, something Lazander questioned until he saw the pace Malik walked at. Despite killing five men, Lazander only felled the last, Malik walked at the same punishing pace, showing no sign of remorse or fatigue.

Lazander looked at the glassy eyes of the dead at their feet, knowing better than to ask if they would bury them. Instead, he called out, "Up ahead? Evergarden is at least five days from here, if not more."

"Not for us." Malik grinned. "Keep up."

"I promised Eternity I'd have dinner with her tomorrow," Lazander said, jogging to catch up.

"Hah! Have you forgotten you don't need to eat?"

"I know—but Eternity does. And she's lonely these days. No one but me visits her, you know," he said pointedly.

Malik was silent for a long stretch, and Lazander wondered if he'd overstepped.

"You know how this is going to end, don't you? Gallow has shown you?" Malik asked gently.

"He has," Lazander replied, feeling defensive. It wasn't something he liked thinking about. "But doesn't that make it more important to spend time with her? Don't tell… is that why you've all been ignoring her?" At Malik's surprised look, Lazander shook his head. "Before you ask, no, she hasn't said a word against any of you. But you, Vivek, and Imani aren't exactly being subtle about it."

"Eternity is… amazing," Malik began, weighing his words. "She found us—*saved* us. And how she wields his power is nothing short of awe-inspiring."

"*But?*" Lazander asked sharply, not liking where this was going. The dirt road vanished beneath their feet, becoming rocky terrain he'd have struggled on before becoming a Champion. Now his breath was even, every step easy. They were picking up speed, he realized, the clouds above zipping past, even though they were only walking.

"Eternity has never let go of her old life, and the... morals that used to guide her. She remembers every failed Judgment and carries those deaths like battle wounds that refuse to heal." He shook his head in disapproval. "I've served Gallow so long, I no longer remember my mother or my siblings. But Eternity does. She keeps letters from her family, even nurses them like a lifeline. And it took her some twenty years to find me. Holding on to these things isn't just unwise—it's dangerous. The Tyrant—"

Shock made Lazander reach out a hand to grasp Malik's, stopping them both in their tracks. They were in thick forest dotted with velvet woodburns native only to Evergarden. Lazander had no memory of entering the forest.

"It took Eternity *twenty years* to find you? How is that possible? She can't be older than nineteen, twenty at most."

Malik's eyes widened in surprise, and then he burst out laughing, a joyous guffaw that brought Lazander no pleasure. "Forgive me, brother, but the look on your face! Like a slapped pig. I always forget it's not common knowledge," he said, wiping tears from his eyes. "Eternity has served Gallow as his Chosen for over a hundred years, give or take. I confess, I stopped keeping track of my own age after I hit a hundred."

Lazander's mouth opened so wide, his jaw almost dislocated. "You're over a hundred years old? That means Eternity is..."

"One hundred and forty, give or take. Ask her yourself. It might be a good reminder for her." He slapped his thigh, pointing at a sign. "Look here, you stopped us just in time. Gallow whispering in your ear, was he? Good. He doesn't always speak to us directly, you know. In time, you'll learn to hear him when he doesn't speak, to obey when there is no order."

With a cheerful whistle, Malik marched ahead on a dirt path so overgrown Lazander hadn't even realized they'd been walking on it. With a start, he stared at the sign. It read: "Evergarden."

They'd traveled halfway across Navaros in the span of minutes.

"Malik, what happened? How did we get here?" Lazander asked, jogging once again to catch up. The man never stopped, not even for a moment, and Lazander was starting to feel like a schoolboy playing catch-up with the "big kids."

"Gallow whispered, and you listened," Malik said. "Tell me, what did he say?"

Lazander was about to say he hadn't heard anything, but Malik crossed his arms with a smile. He wasn't going to let him go without an answer. Sighing, Lazander closed his eyes, emptying his mind of all thought, emotion, and distraction. This was the only way Gallow's words could reach him from across the Void, Malik had said, though Lazander had yet to hear anything.

Until now.

"**Deliver his Judgment with blissful haste**," he said, his body flooding with a rush of power. He opened his eyes to see he was on a cliff edge, his body tipping forward into the open air. The lake below was a mere puddle from this height. His arms windmilled as he fell forward.

"Easy there." Malik laughed, grabbing the back of Lazander's armor and yanking him back. Lazander stumbled to safety, heart hammering, his new reflexes the only thing keeping him upright. He'd been a hair's breadth from falling. From *dying*. He'd no idea what had happened, and he didn't appreciate how funny Malik seemed to find the whole thing.

"You took off like a shot!" Malik chuckled. "Wait until I tell Imani you covered half a day on your first try, she's going to be *furious*."

"What in the hell happened?"

"You tell me, Champion. And no, I'm not being smart. You've got to learn how to keep your head when you use Gallow's gifts, brother. Call this good practice."

Lazander closed his eyes, trying to remember the last minutes. It came to him, slowly at first, but sharpened with every word.

"I was moving, but I wasn't," Lazander started, unable to convey the bliss he'd felt, the speed that thrummed in his legs, begging him to move. "I saw the world pass me by while I stood still."

"*Whisper Walk*, one of Gallow's gifts." Malik smiled. "We go where he needs us and do what needs to be done. You did it earlier without even noticing. What did I tell you, Zander? You're a natural!"

Lazander didn't tell Malik the only person allowed to call him "Zander" was the queen. Instead, he nodded stiffly, following the Champion until they met a freshly laid road, a city in the distance he'd only read about as a child but had never seen.

***

Far away, Eternity's head cocked, a shiver going down her side. "Like someone stepped on my grave," her mother used to say. Mabel nudged her, and she smiled, rubbing the mare's head. "My apologies, Mabel. How *dare* I be distracted from grooming you."

Mabel whinnied in agreement.

"Ma'am. Your, uh, Highlyness?" The stable boy stood in the door, shaking with nerves.

Eternity sighed. Word had finally gotten round that the fourth and final of Gallow's Champions had been found. There would be no more Champions—no more Judgment. But people still stepped out of her way on the short walk between her tower and the stables. On Lazander's advice, she started stopping by to help out and quickly found she loved the work. She'd spend the whole day there if she could, mucking out stables, feeding and grooming the horses, but the stable hands steered clear of her while she was there, only beginning their work once she left. And so, she kept her visits short. Which was why she was so surprised to see the boy. It was rare one of them addressed her—something must be wrong.

"What is it? What happened?" she asked.

"Oh, no, nothing, Your Highlyness, I just… my mum made some extra apple pie. She told me to bring it to you." He held out a plate covered with a patchwork cloth that did little to hide the heavenly smell of apple and cinnamon underneath.

"That's so kind of her. And of you, for bringing it all this way," she said, surprise making her trip over her manners. She took the plate from him, and the boy dropped his head into a deep bow. Eternity sent a spark of her magic through the apple pie, relieved when she found no sign of poison or spells cast with ill-intent. It only took a second, and her smile never dropped, but she hated she had to be so paranoid.

"You don't need to bow, Garret, isn't it?" she said, relieved the stable hand wasn't a child assassin in disguise. The boy flushed a deep crimson. "Also, you can just call me Eternity—if you like."

"Yes'm, Miss Lady Eternity. My mum said to say thanks. For finding all them Champions," he said, taking off at a run.

She lifted the patchwork cloth to find the boy, or perhaps his mother, had lied. These were no leftovers. Instead, a beautiful apple pie filled the entire plate. They had clearly made it especially for her.

Happy tears filled her eyes.

Chapter Forty-Three

"Zara.

"Zara.

"Zara."

With every step the whistle grew louder, the voices hidden within sharper. It was dark, the air fetid with the smell of mold. Outside the wind whipped the mountain up into a storm, and while it was warmer in the cave, I couldn't stop the shiver that ran down my spine. The cave wasn't very large, perhaps only a foot taller than me, but I found myself crouching low, looking over my shoulder every few steps.

It's only a cave, I chided myself, *calm down*. But my heart kept hammering, ignoring the obvious lie. I'd wrestled six-legged molger, been bitten by a rattlespider, and even jumped off a cliff to avoid an enraged goober-pig (long story), but I'd never felt the cold sweat of terror that now dripped down my back. This wasn't "just" a cave.

With my hand against the wall as both a comfort and a guide, it took me a few minutes to realize the rock felt strange. I stopped to squint at the blue stone in the darkness, wishing *Tithe of Beasts* helped my vision too. I trailed my fingers over the crisscross hatching that marked every inch of the stone, even the floor and ceiling. Why did it look so familiar?

"I am death's mistress," I said with dawning horror. **"Bow before me."**

Fury's Claw Activated.

Claws unsheathed, I pressed my hand against the stone wall. It matched up with the deep lines exactly. Flinching, I yanked it back.

"Zara," I said aloud. "I know we're not exactly best friends right now, but what is this place? And why does it scare the hell out of me?"

Silence.

I sighed. I hadn't expected her to answer, but it was worth a—

Screaming. Claws. Flesh. Blood. Blood. Blood.

I fell to the ground, clutching my head at the onslaught of images. The memory of blood filled my mouth. Something sharp and foul coated my tongue, the bile of a burst intestine, I suddenly knew. I wretched, my stomach heaving. I didn't want to know how I knew that.

The visions stopped, vanishing as quickly as they came.

Wiping spittle from my mouth, I shakily got to my feet. The sane thing to do would be go back outside and hide out on the ledge until my stamina replenished. There would be other ledges, other caves, other places to rest—there must be. But I couldn't. A sense of déjà vu washed over me with every step. I knew this place. And it knew me.

Three tunnels lay ahead of me, claw marks lining every inch of the wall where Zara, or another vaxion, had carved out the rock by hand. The whistling stopped. It was so quiet I could hear my heartbeat.

"Which way, Zara?" I asked. "Come on. I know you've been here."

Something pulled at me, and I found myself taking the tunnel on the far right.

The stone grew cold and wet beneath my feet, scree and dirt lining the edges. As I walked, I saw the occasional flash of white and gray abandoned in the corners.

Bone.

I knelt, picking up a large bone that had been snapped in the center—the marrow sucked clean out like a lollipop. It was thick, and long, and while my biology was rusty, I could have sworn it was a femur. I flexed my claws, the hairs raising on my arms.

"What did this, Zara?" I asked, cradling the bone.

Screaming. Claws. Flesh. Blood. Blood. Blood.

The visions returned, splitting my head, but I was ready this time. I winced, trying to breathe through the pain and make some sense of it.

And then I saw it.

Ashira roaring, her face twisting in rage, hands around my neck—around Zara's neck. Behind her a woman, face split in two by a deep wound from temple to chin. A *shi'ara*. A witch. She whispered harsh, guttural words as she drew a blade the length of my arm from beneath her furs, holding it above her head.

"Ravenna, forgive me," Ashira whispered, eyes closed.

I woke up on the ground, soaked in cold sweat, my head splitting. Shaking, I wrapped my arms around myself in a hug. Eyes closed, I brought up my character sheet and checked my stamina—50/300. Not a big increase, which meant I hadn't been passed out for long after… Whatever the hell that was. Not a vision, I knew. A *memory*. Zara hated Ashira, had sworn never to transform into her vaxion form just to spite her. The details I had were fragmented, but I knew Ashira sold Zara to Magnus ten years ago, right around the time the molger were driven out of the Moonvale Mountains.

But why the hell was Ashira strangling Zara? And what was that *shi'ara* doing? Dizzy, I got to my feet. I should go back, I knew, but I couldn't. I had to see.

I had to *know*.

***

Evergarden wasn't idly named. A city-state famed for its gardens, it was a small but proud nation that boasted the continent's finest botanists, alchemists, and architects. As Lazander stood in Twilight Blossom Square, he could see why.

White stone usually reserved for the graves of royalty in Navaros lined every fountain, statue, and storefront here. Even the *cobbles* shone a startling white. Against the ivory backdrop plants of every color and shade burst from flower boxes despite the recent cold spell. They trailed down windows, lined doorways, and even ringed the streets in sturdy barrels Lazander knew would have been tipped over in Navaros. The entire city looked like an artist's rendition of a rainbow.

It was beautiful.

"What is that?" Lazander asked, pointing at a strange arched structure that ran around most of the city.

"Ah, I forget Navaros is still behind the times. Those are aqueducts. They help transport water all around the city," Malik answered. "Give the Ivory Keep a decade or so—they'll catch up."

The Champion gestured for Lazander to follow, and he did, eyes wide as he took in buildings that stood twice the height of any he'd seen outside of the Keep itself. Unfamiliar spices drifted on the wind, and he was surprised to catch snatches of Navrin through the unlatched windows and open doors of taverns. He'd also thought the local dialect was Everos.

As they walked deeper into the city, Lazander was glad it was the middle of the night when the streets were quiet but for the occasional stumble of someone leaving the pub. If it was during the day, he'd have been overwhelmed.

"You said when we got here, all would be revealed," Lazander said, feeling the need to whisper in the dark streets.

"And it will be." Malik smiled. "But first, we're going to the very heart of Evergarden—the Eternal Prism."

Walking through alleys and streets wide enough for two carts to pass without touching, Lazander kept thinking about the Ivory Keep. It was the heart of Navaros, a fortress that made his home country of Freyley look backward and out of touch. He'd always been so impressed by the Keep, but now, standing in Evergarden, he wondered how he'd ever thought that. This city-state made the Ivory Keep seem small and cramped, even destitute.

It was strange to walk in a city that only weeks before Navaros had been about to go to war with. He didn't say that aloud, knowing Malik would only chastise him—as a Champion, he shouldn't concern himself with such things unless Gallow intervened. Instead he said:

"I'd always thought when it came to a fight, Navaros would triumph against Evergarden, but having seen the city, I'm not so sure."

"Oh, Navaros would beat the absolute stuffing out of Evergarden," Malik replied.

"Really? But look at this place."

"That's exactly why Navaros would win, brother. The money, time, and intellect Evergarden has put into its city, Navaros dedicated to its military. Evergarden has fancier war machines, I'll give you that, but King Najar spends most of his year squashing rebellions and putting down bandits as if each fight was Navaros' last stand. His ferocity, and his soldiers, are renowned." Malik shook his head. "Humans are good at two things—creating and destroying. And one is more powerful than the other."

Unable to help himself, Lazander said, "You sound almost sad."

"I am," Malik replied. "I don't remember much of my time before I was a Champion, but I remember the pain. The hunger. I remember thinking the world started and ended with the small patch of dirt I lived on, and kings and queens are no different. Evergarden hoards their knowledge and technology like a spymaster's secrets, and Navaros pours its gold into fighting imaginary threats while their own people starve the moment crops fail. It's all so… pointless."

Malik sighed. "I'm ready to die if it means stopping the Tyrant, but damned if I don't wish I could grab every last human and slap some sense into them. The world is so much bigger than them, and they refuse to see it."

Lazander wanted to argue that there was more to people than that, but to his surprise, he found a large part of his heart agreed with Malik. Uneasy, Lazander found himself looking around at the city he'd stared at in wonder only moments before, the Champion's words and disappointment ringing in his ears.

When they arrived at the city's heart, Lazander didn't need to ask if it was the Eternal Prism—there was nothing else that could have earned the name.

A statue of a woman stood at the center of a courtyard, her hands outstretched, water pouring from holes in her palms and eyes. She had long flowing hair and a cloak that stretched endlessly behind her, curling around her body to form the bottom of a fountain. Lazander had read that during the day the statue caught the light, covering the square in a rainbow that moved with the sun. It had been the inspiration for the city's colorful landscape. He searched the base for a plaque or sign, wondering who the woman was supposed to be. Finding none, he looked back up and realized despite the water that flowed from her eyes, the woman smiled, her expression joyous.

For some reason, this made his heart pound, and he was surprised at the knot of emotion in his chest. He felt the mad urge to kneel before the woman and cry.

"Who is she?" Lazander asked, fighting to keep his tone uninterested.

"One of the old gods, back from before the Tyrant's descent. People tore down their shrines and ransacked their temples once they realized their so-called 'gods' had abandoned them. The only reason this thing survived is because most of the city thinks she's just some pretty woman." Malik snorted. "She called herself the 'Goddess of Truth.' Guess sitting on your ass while your people are enslaved doesn't count as a bloody lie. I don't care how nice the damn fountain is, keeping this thing up is a slap in Gallow's face."

Lazander studied the woman's weeping eyes, which seemed to stare into his very soul. She had sharp features that were softened by her large eyes.

"Mask me from sight, so the truth may follow," Malik whispered, placing a hand on Lazander's shoulder.

The world blurred, and Lazander blinked to find Malik gone—in his place stood a woman with heavy armor and red hair. A woman who looked familiar. She grinned.

"Look in the water," she said, her voice high and melodious.

Lazander leaned over the fountain. A man with plain features and freckles over his cheeks stared back at him. The man he'd killed only two days before.

He leaped back, hand on his sword, his heart hammering.

"Gallow blessed Imani with fists of steel, Vivek with eyes that see truth among lies, and me, well." The woman grinned broadly—a grin that was pure Malik. It was the only thing that betrayed his otherwise perfect disguise. "I can change my appearance as well as that of another. Briefly, mind, and only into humanoid creatures. But you'd be surprised at how it comes in handy."

She cocked her head, listening intently. A serene look crossed the woman's face, and she nodded. "If we pull this off, we're going to save half of Evergarden in the next five minutes," Malik said casually. "Your job is to relax and say nothing, understand?"

Lazander wanted to say that no, he didn't understand—what the hell was going to happen? Then the temperature dropped and Lazander's breath froze into small, icy clouds. The bite of copper filled his mouth—he could literally *taste* magic in the air.

Malik winked. "Here they come, brother."

Chapter Forty-Four

The whistling was back.

When the tunnel carved with vaxion claws narrowed, the whistling grew louder and more insistent. Soon I was on all fours, head bowed as I crawled. A blade of light cut through the darkness ahead, and I pushed toward it, my mind bombarding me with horror stories about people getting trapped in caves. Stories about how they'd starve to death while screaming for help that would never come.

I closed my eyes, rock grazing my shoulders as I forced myself on. My hand reached for the next hold but found only open air, and I fell forward with a jerk, tumbling out of the tunnel. Instinctively I twisted midair, landing on my feet. Awash with relief at not dying in a cramped tunnel, it took me a second to smell the blood.

I was on a ledge overlooking a huge cavern filled with stalactites and stalagmites, like the gaping maw of a long-felled monster. Small holes pierced the ceiling, large enough for one, maybe two people to crawl through. Moonlight flooded through the gaps above, cutting the darkness in half. Except for my pounding heart, the steady drip of water was the only sound in the quiet.

Adrenaline flooded my body. I wanted to run, hide, and scream. No, not me, I realized—Zara. The Fury, the murderous villain of *Knights of Eternity*, wasn't scared. She was *terrified*, and it was taking everything I had not to get swept up in her fear. I leaped from the ledge before my nerve failed.

Landing with a crunch, I looked down to see a skull split beneath my toes. I picked it up, turning it in my hand. It was long and elongated with something that looked like a beak where its jaw should be. Inside the beak were two rows of human teeth. It looked like an unholy cross between a human and a bird.

The whistling stopped.

"*Behind!*" hissed Zara in my mind.

I rolled to the left, instinct taking over as something whipped past me at speed, shrieking. A second followed, diving from above. I caught a glimpse of feathers as I scrambled backward, a sharp beak striking the stone where I'd stood a split second before.

Gravediggers.

"Zraaaa. *Zraaa!*" it shrieked, a high-pitched noise close to a whistle that made me wince. The first appeared behind me, two arms locking around my chest.

Arms?

Shocked, I looked down to see two mottled arms, the skin angry and patchy. What few feathers it still had on its forearms were a deep blue—the exact color of the stone. The gravedigger drove its beak downward, digging into my right shoulder like a shard of glass.

"If the world will not yield," I roared. **"Then I will break it."**

I snapped my arms out in an explosion of strength. The gravedigger shrieked, at least one arm breaking.

Monstrous Strength Activated.

"*Zraaa!*" it screamed, cradling its right arm. I caught a glimpse of two eyes, stuck on either side of its head like a newt before it ducked beneath a wing. The second gravedigger leaped to the first's defense, lunging for me, its beak wide open.

And spat.

Something hot and sticky hit me in the face, and I fell back—blinded. My skin bubbled, eyes burning. I slapped at the gunk with both hands, desperately trying to pull it from my face.

It wouldn't budge.

Get it off, get it off! my mind screamed in panic, any thought of how to remove it gone as I thrashed. Claws raked along my back, and I lashed out—stone shattering beneath my fist. I threw myself backward, the whisper of a claw just missing my neck.

Panicking, I tore at my own face, but my fingers stuck to the gunk, the skin tearing.

"Zraaa. Zraaaraa!" the gravediggers shrieked in unison.

This, of all things, made me stop. I realized they weren't just mindlessly screaming, they were saying a name—Zara's name.

"I'm not Zara!" I yelled, hands outstretched. "I'm not here to, argh, I'm not here to hurt you!"

Pain is just a feeling. Push past it, and think!

The gravediggers fell silent.

Breathe, just breathe. You can't see them, but you don't need to.

Tithe of Beasts Activated.

The world exploded with sounds and smells.

Concentrate. Find them before they find you. I steadied myself, the drip of water from the ceiling suddenly loud and explosive, the crunch of bone and debris beneath my feet rattling like nails in a jar against my ear. And then I heard it, the rhythmic thud of four hearts in two chests.

Got you.

Calmer now I tried again. "I'm *not* Zara, and I'm not here to hurt you. I swear it," I said, head swiveling to where one stood.

The pair whistled, an echoing sound that bounced around the cavern until what sounded like a chorus of gravediggers surrounded me. I winced, the sound head-splitting while I used *Tithe of Beasts*.

"... hatchlings... kill... *feast!*" the first cried.

I could catch only snatches of words in their odd whistling tone, each blending into the other in a cacophonous symphony.

"Smell? ... smell! ... *different*," the second answered.

"No! Zara. Kill. Zara!" the first shrieked in rage, its dual hearts pounding. Rocks tumbled, dislodging as it leaped. The air caught its wings, snapping like a blade as it flew straight at me. I waited until it was almost on top of me.

"I am death's mistress—bow before me," I whispered, driving my fist forward.

"No!" The second's whistle became a scream, echoing endlessly throughout the cavern. Blood splashed on the ground, dripping down my front and onto my feet.

Fury's Claw Activated.

The gravedigger twitched around my arm, the last of its life leaving its body. I forced myself to relax the hand I'd punched through its chest. Feathers rustled against my face. It sighed, its single remaining heart shuddering, then falling still.

The surviving gravedigger screamed, a human sound of grief and pain. Yanking my arm free of the body, and I had to think of it as "the body," I crouched low, all joy at the hunt gone.

"Please, don't!" I cried. "I don't want to kill—" My words were lost as the gravedigger crashed into me, too quick for my claws. We rolled backward, a mess of blood and feathers, each fighting for purchase. My claws kept looking for skin, swiping wildly, but only caught feathers. Suddenly I was flat on my back.

Abruptly *Monstrous Strength* ran out, my stamina gone.

I felt the gravedigger straddle me, its weak arms easily pinning mine, my head swimming.

"Take, take!" the gravedigger screamed. "Babies, mate, everything!"

I felt it lunge, and I knew its beak was about to dig into my throat.

"Scream at the bite of nature's lash," I half screamed in desperation.

Lightning Claw Activated.

***

It took time to get the gunk out of my eyes. The only way to remove it was to stick it to something else. I pawed at the dead gravediggers, yanking fistfuls of feathers from the corpses, then rubbed them over my face. I tried not to think of their last words.

It took a few hours, but eventually the world swam into fuzzy focus as my stamina replenished. Blinking, I looked down at the dead gravedigger next to me. The smell of its burnt flesh made me gag, but I forced myself to look. It had a long beak and eyes on either side of its head. Inside its open mouth I saw a trailing line of jagged teeth and a long tongue.

From the head down, it was a strange mix of human and bird with thin arms at odds with its huge, beautiful wings. The first I killed had a plumage of bright greens and blues on its chest while the second's was darker and more subdued. Their legs were like a chicken's, scaly and with three toes.

Looking around the cavern, it was clear they weren't the first gravediggers to die here. The stone was littered with what I now knew were the skulls of their kin. Their *children*.

"They knew you, Zara," I said aloud. "They said you killed their babies. Did you?"

Silence.

Angry, I got to my feet, stumbling slightly. Zara warned me when the first gravedigger attacked but had stayed silent otherwise. She was watching, I knew, and listening. So why the hell wasn't she saying anything?

Because there was something here, I realized. Something she didn't want me to see.

It took a while to search the cavern and even longer to realize the gravedigger bodies and bones all led toward the eastern wall. Exhausted, I forced myself forward one step at a time.

At the very back, half hidden beneath an overhang, was a circle. Half of it was painted on the floor while the other half crept up the cave wall. Strange, angry sigils, much like the ones I'd seen imprison Eternity at Magnus' castle, were etched onto every available surface. They bound magic, I knew, draining the person at its center of their power. But that wasn't what caught my eye.

A huge collar, rusted with blood and age, was bolted to the wall. I picked it up, my skin crawling. It was too large for a human neck and too small for a molger. I tilted it, noting the claw and bite marks that ran along its jagged edges—edges designed to dig into the skin. Blood stained the ground as well as what looked like old, dried-out feces.

"Zara," I whispered. "What happened to you?"

***

Zara couldn't see much when the invader was in control. Snatches, smells, and sounds pierced the darkness, echoing in a way that made it difficult to understand. Usually she simply lay on her side and ignored the girl child. She would eventually come at night and prattle off her usual report. Zara listened, of course—the invader might reveal a weakness. She was certainly stupid enough, but usually she simply told fantastical tales of a life straight out of a storybook.

Zara found the girl's imagination amusing, if nothing else.

Now Zara stood on all fours, coils haloing her as lightning she could not unleash zipped around her—reacting to their owner's distress. Her world narrowed to the painted circle, the collar, and the blood that stained the walls.

This she saw. This she understood.

And her entire world came crashing down.

Chapter Forty-Five

"You're early," came a man's harsh, suspicious bark. At his words, Lazander realized the man *was* speaking Everos, as had everyone else he'd overheard on his stroll through Evergarden. Yet Lazander could understand it perfectly, despite not speaking a word of it before becoming a Champion.

Another gift from Gallow Malik had forgotten to mention.

"What happened?" the man called. A dark cloak covered his face but couldn't disguise his broad shoulders and towering height. Two figures flanked him, bodyguards Lazander guessed, but they were laughably small in comparison to their boss.

"Bloody Champions," Malik answered in the guise of the red-haired woman. "We barely got out of there alive."

The man turned his head and spat. "You get the package?"

Malik held up the stone he'd taken from the dead mercenary. No, not a stone, Lazander realized—a circular vial the color of night. Malik shook it, the contents within swirling, turning silver.

"Careful!" the man yelled, striding forward.

Malik vanished from Lazander's side, his disguise falling away in a shimmer of light. In the space of a heartbeat, Malik appeared in front of the man, axe in hand.

The bodyguards, to their credit, were clearly not run of the mill thugs. The one on the right, a wisp of a woman, darted in front of her boss, a hefty shield raised, while the one on the left raised her hands—blue light cupped in her fingers.

For reasons that would later keep Lazander up at night, he could only focus on the bodyguard's shield, or rather, the painting on its front. It featured a woman with long, lustrous hair wearing a rainbow cloak. It was rough and poorly done in parts, but he found himself inexplicably drawn it.

And then Malik's axe split the shield in half and kept going—cutting the woman's arm off at the elbow. She screamed, falling back.

Blue light erupted from the mage's hands, her fingers splayed. As the man darted forward, his hood fell back, and Lazander saw strong features marred by a thick scar that ran through his left eye and down his cheek. His eyes were wide and marred by grief.

"Hanna!" he shouted.

Malik shifted his weight, swinging his axe at the man. In a feat of strength that astounded Lazander, Hanna threw herself at Malik's legs, blood spewing from her missing arm.

It saved her boss' life.

Malik stumbled, his swing going wide. The mage flung her magic out, enveloping her and the mysterious man in light. The two of them vanished, leaving the injured bodyguard behind. The man's anguished shout of "Hanna" still echoed around the square.

"Bloodied Void!" Malik swore, kicking the remaining woman. She tumbled backward, head lolling. The Champion sheathed his axe and put his hands on his hips, shaking his head as if inconvenienced by the whole thing. The fight had taken less than twenty seconds, but it felt like hours to Lazander, who'd watched the whole thing in a stupor.

A stupor he quickly snapped out of.

"What did you *do*?" he yelled, running to the bleeding woman. Hanna lay on her side, cradling herself like an injured animal. "Ma'am, let me see—"

Hanna slapped him in the face—hard.

"Don't *touch* me," she hissed, glaring at him as if he were a viper.

Thrown by the hatred in her eyes, Lazander looked away. "That needs to be cauterized and disinfected by a mage," he said to Malik, who stood with his back to Lazander. "Where is the closest House of Healing?"

"Gallow let you grow a conscience, did he?" She spat at Lazander's feet. "Too little too late. We're coming for you, lapdog, and after we cut off Eternity's *head*, this world will finally—"

Lazander didn't hear the rest of the woman's threat. Suddenly her head was flying through the air, sliced from her shoulders with a single swing of Malik's axe. A fountainous spray of blood covered Lazander and the pristine white cobbles of Eternal Prism square.

Her head hid the ground with a meaty thud. Lazander froze, blinking blood from his eyes.

In a flash, he kicked Malik's legs from under him, pinning the shocked man to the ground. Lazander drew his blade, pressing it against Malik's neck, who stared up at him as if he had two heads. The look of surprise on his face only made Lazander angrier.

"You have one chance and one chance only to explain why you *cut off an injured woman's head*," he hissed.

Malik raised empty hands, his face still. Lazander heard a gasp behind him, and the rapid thump of feet on cobbles as someone ran away. They'd been seen, which meant they needed to leave before the local guard came running. Champions or not, standing over a headless corpse wasn't easily explained.

But Lazander couldn't bring himself to care. He pressed his blade into Malik's neck, watching a drop of blood trickle down his throat. Part of Lazander was relieved at the sight. It turned out Champions bled, just like everyone else.

"Easy now," Malik said calmly. "Check her pockets. Mine too, if you like. I won't move from where I am, I swear on Gallow's name."

Lazander hesitated, then backed up. He kept one eye on Malik, his sword drawn, while he searched the woman's cooling corpse. The edge of Lazander's deep gray cloak dipped in blood when he knelt, and lines of crimson crept up the wool like veins.

The woman, *Hanna*, he forced himself to call her, had nothing on her except a note hidden on the inside of her tunic. He only thought to check there because that was where Malik had found the vial on the mercenary.

"What does it say?" Malik asked.

Lazander frowned at what appeared to be a map of Evergarden. Several targets were circled, all of them wells or water sources. "What is this?"

Malik slowly lowered his hands to his pockets while watching Lazander, who nodded. Pulling out the vial with the strange dark liquid, he held it up to the light.

"*Ravenna's Dying Breath*," he said. "So named for the goddess they serve." He pointed at the fountain, and the weeping woman was wrapped in every color of the rainbow. Now, however, the night cloaked her shoulders like a dark promise.

"I thought you said she was the Goddess of Truth," Lazander said, his sword dipping an inch. He'd never heard of Ravenna, nor could he imagine why a goddess enshrined in *rainbows* would have a potion called "dying breath."

"I said that's what *she* calls herself, brother. Big difference." He passed the vial to Lazander, whose hand dropped from the surprising weight of it, the contents turning silver at his touch. "A single drop is enough to poison a whole well."

Lazander looked down in horror at the vial. Most of the circled targets were in Evergarden's center where half a million people alone lived. *If we hadn't intervened, half of Evergarden's people would be...*

"Dead. Or wishing they were," Malik said with his uncanny knack for reading Lazander's mind. "Can I get up now?"

Lazander nodded, only half listening as his eyes darted between the headless corpse, the vial in his hands, and the statue of the goddess, Ravenna. Who were these people? And what could they possibly hope to accomplish by killing so many?

"Now, should I have cut off her head? No. It's a bit hard to question a corpse, after all." Malik slapped a hand on Lazander's shoulder. "But when she mentioned hurting Eternity, well... guess for all my blustering about not being human, I still have a temper—Gallow forgive me."

The square was wide and empty, Hanna's blood already clotting on the cold cobblestones. The fountain gurgled gently, the only sound other than the distant laughter and music from the entertainment district.

"Come, Zander. I'll tell you all I know of Ravenna and her bootlickers—vermin, the lot of them." Malik snapped his fingers and Lazander felt a rush of warmth when the disguise Malik had hidden him behind, vanished—he'd forgotten he was still wearing it.

"For now, we need to leave." Malik smiled sadly. "We may have stopped a genocide, but we failed to root out the source of it. Well, *I* failed. Let's make sure no one suffers for my mistakes." The older Champion made to leave, but Lazander didn't move, his eyes fixed on the shattered remains of Hanna's shield and the image of Ravenna it once depicted.

As if sensing Lazander's distress, Gallow appeared at his side, the top of his head barely reaching Lazander's hip. The god placed his small, freezing cold hand in

Lazander's, tugging him toward Malik. Lazander was about to follow when something made him look back one last time. Later, he'd wonder what it was. A shiver down his spine? A twist in his gut? Whatever it was, he turned, only to see Valerius staring at him with wide eyes.

***

Squealing like a stuck pig, Magnus came tearing in.

"They're here!" he yelled, slamming the door of their small, sparsely furnished tavern room behind him. "Gallow's Champions are here!"

When Valerius and Magnus were still enemies, every word out of Magnus' mouth was wrapped in sarcasm, his lips curled in barely concealed hatred. After only minutes with the mage, Valerius would feel the need to beat the man into a fine paste.

The prince missed those days.

"If any of Ravenna's dogs let the truth slip, we're *finished*," Magnus prattled, shoving clothes into his pack. "They'll know we gave them the vial. They'll know we're close by. Damn it all!" he cursed, struggling to do his cloak up one-handed.

Valerius lay stretched out on the only bed, his hands crossed behind his head. He didn't offer to help.

"I can summon an ice storm out front. That will let us disappear out the back, and—"

"What an excellent way to tell them exactly where we are," Valerius remarked.

A dark look crossed the mage's eyes, the hatred with which he'd once glared at Valerius returning. In an instant it was gone. "Then what do you propose?" Magnus asked with forced politeness.

When Valerius and Magnus were still enemies, Valerius knew where he stood. Now, when Valerius bad-mouthed the Tyrant's latest orders, Magnus started listing all the gifts they'd been given. When Valerius dared take a break during one of their quests, hoping for some reprieve in the hell that his life had become, Magnus whined and pleaded until they continued. Once, Valerius cursed the Tyrant to burn eternally for what he'd done to them, and Magnus' eyes lit up with rage. Valerius thought he'd finally glimpsed the person, the *player*, Magnus truly was. Instead the mage took his hand, as if he were an unruly child, and told the prince about all the good they were doing. About how much better their lives were because of the Tyrant. About how beautiful the world would be when *Calamity* finally returned. Magnus wasn't a person anymore. Not really. He was a blank space the Tyrant had filled in with an NPC's biography.

Valerius hated him for it. What else could he do when confronted with his worst fear?

"We should leave Evergarden immediately," Magnus said, pulling Valerius back to the present.

Valerius stood, kicking aside the blankets and pillows on the stone floor by the bed where he'd forced Magnus to sleep. Gone was his iconic white armor. Now he wore deceptively simple leather that let him blend in, even in the cheap tavern he'd been reduced to. He pulled on a cloak he'd bought for coppers from the bartender downstairs, relived its stink of stale beer was fading.

"Where are you *going?*" Magnus hissed.

Valerius walked out of the room without a backward glance.

It hadn't taken long to find Malik. Since coming face-to-face with Imani's inhuman strength, Valerius had vowed to learn more about the Champions: their abilities, how they fought, what made them *tick*. Imani's strength, and the ease with which she'd knocked him back, had shaken him. He'd spent too long finishing quests and not enough time preparing for the endgame—the day he'd have to face the God of Judgment and his Champions.

In the weeks since, he'd bribed and beaten several of Gallow's followers but had learned painfully little. They'd claimed their god's so-called "holy warriors" could do everything from fly to breathe fire. And so he'd been reduced to crouching like a gargoyle on a roof that overlooked the Eternal Prism. Below Malik lay pinned by a man Valerius didn't recognize, a headless corpse at their feet.

That must be "the last," the Champion that has Gallow's lackeys blushing like brides. He's something special if he can strong-arm Malik, the golden child.

Valerius' vision shimmered, turning black and white.

Dissect Activated.

Scanning…

Scanning…

Valerius frowned when a pop-up flashed.

Subject: ERROR
Ability: ERROR
Magic: ERROR

In all his years in this world, *Dissect* had never failed to break down his enemies and their abilities into quantifiable measures. He tried it on Malik, only to find the same thing. His fists clenched, thinking of his fight with Imani. He'd learned from it, had replayed it over and over in his mind. He knew he could take one Champion down, but what about two? While the man who pinned Malik was as bland as toast, there was no doubting his strength.

Valerius vanished, *Whispering Darkness* cloaking him from eyes and magic alike. It drained his mana, but he didn't care. He had to see this new Champion for himself. As he approached, he saw Malik's form shimmer for an instant. He vanished from where he lay on the ground, darted toward the headless corpse, and then returned at speed. It was so quick, Valerius would have missed it if he hadn't been watching him so closely. The new Champion didn't even notice and simply reached down to take something out of the corpse's pocket.

The sight of such speed shook Valerius. He couldn't move that quickly, not without every spell in his playbook. He'd have to come up with a way to…

The thought fell away, shock wiping Valerius' mind blank. Without meaning to, he'd let *Whispering Darkness* lapse, leaving him out in the open. The new Champion's form vanished, a red-haired knight suddenly in his place. He was taller and broader than he remembered, but there was no mistaking it.

Lazander. Lazander was *alive*.

His former brother-in-arms looked at him, eyes boring into his soul. Valerius opened his mouth to speak, not knowing what he was going to say, when Lazander's fist drove into his throat at lightning speed.

Chapter Forty-Six

"Zara, talk to me," I said quietly. Exhausted, curled up in that gaping maw of a cave, it had taken time to nod off. While I could access the Menu while I was awake, the Origin tab didn't appear until I was fast asleep, and I kept jerking upright, sure more gravediggers lay waiting in the shadows.

Eventually a broken, uneasy sleep settled over me, and Zara now stood before me. She wasn't curled up into a ball or lying with her back to me. Instead she paced back and forth, unleashed electricity zapping about her.

Step. Step. Turn.

Step. Step. Turn.

"Zara."

Step. Step. Turn.

"Zara, why did that cave scare you so much?"

"I do not *fear* stone, invader!" she snapped, whipping around to face me, teeth bared. But I knew her well enough I could see her anger hid the truth—she was terrified. "Nor will I be fooled!"

She leaped forward, snapping the air, expecting me to step back.

I didn't.

Her teeth grazed my nose, spittle flying onto my cheeks. Blood dripped from the wound onto my lips. When she stepped back, I stepped forward. She growled, daring me to step forward again.

I did.

She lunged, teeth clamping down on my forearm. I'd often wondered if I could get hurt in my own mind—turned out I could.

Gasping, claws burst from my fingers, and I felt her tense up, fangs deep in my arm. Taking a deep breath, I forced myself to go still, retracting my claws.

"I want to help you," I said, voice straining only slightly from the pain. Her teeth were *sharp*. "I swear it—on Noah's life."

Growling, she released me, my blood dripping from her jaws. With a sigh, she looked away. "That was a binding for a *tem'rix*," she said. "Those like Lukas, whose blood sings of weakness. 'Hybrid,' you call it. *Mongrel*, I say. A dog not fit to live."

I fought very hard to keep my expression neutral. Zara had been in that cave, I could feel it. "And the gravediggers?" I asked, keeping my tone light, as if I were asking about the weather.

"They spend their days circling Moonvale, carrion to rotting flesh, but they never descend. They know better." Her coils whipped about her head, agitated. "Yet I... *remember* being here. I remember ripping heads from flesh. A *tem'rix* was bound and gagged. It watched me."

"I know the vaxion's, ah, approach to weakness," I said, struggling to find a word to describe the overwhelming disgust Zara felt for anyone who didn't spend every second fighting to live. "They don't seem like the type to tie up a hybrid and leave them be."

"They're *not*," she said. "Those not killed outright were bound to Ashira in servitude—as was her 'right.'" She huffed at this. "I would pity those forced to kneel, were it not the fault of their own weakness."

"So, you were brought here to fight gravediggers," I said, ignoring her clear barb at Lukas and those like him. "While a hybrid was hidden here, away from the other vaxion. But why would Ashira do that?"

"Who knows?" she hissed. "She must have dragged me here as a child, probably for one of her 'lessons.' It would not have been her first." She looked away. "I watched her save *tem'rix*, only to mark them as they screamed, wishing she'd killed them."

I shivered. "Who was chained up here? A vaxion?"

She closed her eyes, and I realized she was *actually* trying to remember. We were standing here, together, trying to figure this out. Despite the horrifying things she was telling me, it felt like a small victory.

"I know not." In vaxion form, she had no eyebrows and only a slit for a nose. It made it harder to read her expressions, but I could tell she was annoyed. "I remember Ashira's treachery. She sold me to Magnus when I was but a girl. But I... remember little beyond that. My childhood is distant, a mere echo of a memory."

Surprised at the poetic turn of phrase, I nodded. "Me too."

Her eyes narrowed, and I realized too late I'd made a mistake.

"Do not align your fantastical delusions with me," she spat.

I sighed, rubbing my temples as she lay down, her back to me. Every time I thought I was making progress with her, she'd lash out. Would we ever get to a point where we could have a civil conversation?

I had a sudden thought.

"You're not going to ask? Why I'm in the Moonvale Mountains?"

She made a show of yawning, her claws peeking from her paws as she stretched out. "Your business is yours, parasite," she said, trying and failing for nonchalance. I debated how much to tell her—about my quest, *Temper the Vaxion*, or that I planned to speak to her aunt about Lukas.

To hell with it.

"I'm going to meet Ashira," I said, bracing for her rage. Instead, she laughed, a deep throated chuckle that sounded like an engine flaring to life.

"Then you are more stupid than I thought. You think wearing my skin will save you? I was a tool to her, girl—a pawn. The moment she lays eyes on you, she'll crack open your chest to better feed on your still-beating heart." She turned to me, eyes glittering. "Or she'll rip off your limbs and deliver you back to Magnus like a tidy, bloodied gift. Either way, I'll enjoy the show."

But her threats rang hollow.

"You say that, but you warned me when the gravedigger was about to attack."

"Tch," she said. "I owe you no answers, invader."

I sighed, a heavy sadness sitting in my chest.

"Zara, you're one of the most complicated people I've ever met. You're angry, sure. But you're also strong, tenacious, stubborn, *brave*. I don't know anyone else who could go through what you have and still be standing. You don't deserve this. *Any* of this. But I wish you'd see that not everyone is your enemy," I said quietly. "If Ashira hadn't betrayed you, would you be this angry? Would you be happy?" I turned away, my voice a whisper. "In another life, do you think we could have been friends?"

Her eyes widened, for once, speechless.

"For what it's worth, I'd have liked that, Zara," I said.

She vanished as she leaped for me, fangs bared, eyes alight with fury.

***

I woke up with a groan, rolling onto my side, my last words to Zara making my cheeks burn. I buried my face in my hands, mortified. What did I think she'd say? "Golly gee, Ms. Parasite, you're right! I'll just forget I've been tortured, am trapped in your mind, and utterly despise you. Let's be besties!"

I sighed. Sometimes I was so dumb, I even impressed myself. Getting to my feet, I yawned. I'd only slept for an hour or so, but in this cold, damp cavern surrounded by death I wouldn't get any more. I needed to get out of here and find my way into Moonvale itself. For both my quest, *Temper the Vaxion*, and for my sanity.

Tithe of Beasts Activated.

I breathed deep, searching for the thread that would let me escape.

Blood, old and rancid. Feces. Rotting flesh. Growing mold in the dead gravedigger's feathers. I pushed past them all until I found it—the sharp whisper of cold air. Eyes open, it took me only a minute to find a crevice on the far side of the cave where fresh air flowed through. I ran my hands along its edges. It was half my size and looked to get narrower.

I thought of the tunnels I'd traveled through to get here and the claw marks that lined every inch of the walls carved by hand.

"**I am death's mistress—bow before me.**" Sharp talons burst from my fingers, and my feet grew in size.

Fury's Claw Activated.

Driving my hands into the rock, I began to dig.

***

Hours later, I'd eaten the last of my rations. Feeling guilty, I'd taken half of the remaining food from Lukas' pack, whispering to him, "Don't wake up until I leave." I knew orders had to be vocalized for him to follow them, but I'd been sure he actually had to *hear* them.

I was wrong. With ears like a bat, he normally shot awake at the slightest noise, impressive considering how loud he snored, but he hadn't so much as twitched while I thumped about the camp, graceful as an elephant. The last thing I'd said to him, after I'd written my message in cold ash, were three words that would ensure, even if he left camp and I never saw him again, he wouldn't put himself in danger.

"Don't follow me."

It was for the best, I knew. I'd learn what I could about the blood debt, find him after this was done, and we could go our separate ways. Famished, I drew back my fist. Now was not the time to be thinking about Lukas, who had probably found the nearest village, kicked his feet up, and was downing a pint, or ten.

"If the world will not yield, then I will break it."

Monstrous Strength Activated.

The wall shattered beneath my fist.

Light burst through, blinding me after the total darkness of the tunnels. Wincing, it took a few seconds for the world to swim back into focus.

I gasped.

The "camp" Lukas had first taken me to with its idyllic waterfall and scarlet sunders had felt like paradise. But what I saw now made that camp look like a dirt road.

Water poured from deep blue stones that hung *mid-air*, floating through the sky with the ease of a bird. Runes, strange but oddly calming, were etched into the sides of the rock. Some were the size of houses, others no larger than me. All of them weaved through the air in a hypnotic pattern.

Leaning out, cold air whipped my hair into a frenzy. The ground below was a distant smudge of blue-green grass and trees that, after wracking my brain for Lukas' lectures, I didn't recognize. At this height, their beautiful mustard leaves and pink flowers looked like a child's crayon drawing. I turned my head to face the sky and saw the smooth blue rock of the Moonvale Mountains stretch endlessly up and beyond.

The sight made my heart stutter. There was no way I'd have been able to climb over the mountains. Finding that ledge and cave had probably saved my life.

A navy rock the size of a horse idled close to me, water pouring from a hole at its base. I could climb down the side of the mountain, using *Fury's Claw* to make handholds, but I'd already been digging for almost half a day, and my stamina was low. I could either wait here for it to painstakingly replenish once more, or...

I leaped, not giving myself time to think, flying through the air as I aimed straight for the passing rock. I hit it hard, scrabbling as I slid down the cold, damp surface. Drawing my hand back, I shoved my fingers deep into the stone, stopping my fall with one leg dangling in midair. Freezing cold wind bit into my skin as I dug in, hauling myself up to the top of the stone. I squinted at the ground below, making out fields roughly divided by stone walls. That meant farming. That meant people. That meant the *vaxion*.

I smiled. I'd actually made it.

A stone lumbered through the air, lower than the one I rode on and twice the size. I leaped, landing on it with a roll. My bare feet tingled like they had in tenderlip valley when searching for the crescent moon, the sparking numbness of magic. Pressing a splayed hand to the rock, I closed my eyes. Despite the water that poured from the stone, the top was warm to the touch. It reminded me of heat from the wallow-tail crystal—a quest that felt like a lifetime ago.

While the stones that swam through the air varied in size, their speed was consistent. It was simple to leap from one to another, the air warming as I dropped.

The moment I jumped from the last one, landing in an overgrown field on the balls of my feet, the world changed. Every muscle in my body relaxed, like I'd just eased into a nice, hot bath. The cobwebs from a poor night's sleep blasted away, leaving my mind sharp. The grass beneath my fingers, a green so dark it was almost blue, felt like the softest velvet.

I didn't just feel good. I felt *amazing*.

I stood up slowly, unsure of what was happening.

Next to me, what must have been a vegetable patch was overgrown and tangled. I frowned at the rock walls that surrounded me. Clearly man-made, they weren't the clear dividers I'd thought. They were broken, smashed entirely in places, like something had burst through them. Those still standing were in poor shape—weeds crept up their sides, weaseling between the gaps. In a year or two, they'd probably be entirely submerged.

Just beyond the field, I spotted a hut half buried in weeds.

Zara's memories of the vaxion, Lukas' stories, and H'tar's warning rang in my ears. These were the people who had driven the molger from Moonvale, murdered Lenia's husband, and dumped his corpse outside her house. I'd be an idiot to just waltz in like I owned the place.

I pulled Calamity's Shadow from my Inventory, wrapping the cloak around me so I vanished from sight. Activating *Tithe of Beasts*, I listened closely for a beating heart, a breath—any sign that someone was inside. Confident no one was waiting to ambush me, I pushed the rotting door open.

And my blood ran cold.

Chapter Forty-Seven

Lazander drove his fist into Valerius' throat with a rage that yearned to burn the world to ash. The prince fell back with a short, ugly gasp, but Lazander didn't give him a second to recover. He lashed out with a right hook Valerius blocked—as he knew he would.

"Bend to his might," Lazander hissed. **"Break before his Judgment."**

He drove his foot into the fork between Valerius' legs with everything he had. Valerius lifted into the air, eyes bulging out of their sockets. Imani was right, Lazander thought as Valerius fell to his knees, vomiting up watery bile as he clutched his manhood. Fighting dirty really was the only way to win.

"Laza—" Valerius gasped, but the Champion gripped his dark hair, driving his head into the alley wall. It cracked, stone and debris littering the cobblestones.

He slammed Valerius into the wall again.

And again.

And again.

Valerius' hand shot out, and suddenly Lazander was flying back. Twisting midair, he landed awkwardly on his knees, skidding back several feet. He brought a hand to his chest to find his collarbones and ribs caved in, his lungs scraping against one another as he gasped for breath. Valerius stood, eyes wide, a huge hammer in his hands.

Lazander forced himself to his feet. He could feel the flesh of his chest already knitting back together. Eyes locked on Valerius, he flexed his shoulder as his bones popped out like a balloon, breathing deeply. "That's twice now you've killed me, Valerius," he said. "There won't be a third."

His former leader turned pale. "What have you done, Lazander?" he asked, his voice betraying his fear.

"Gallow found his final Champion, Prince Valerius," Malik said, appearing at Lazander's side. "Poetic, is it not, that it would be the very knight Calamity ordered you to kill?"

Lazander's entire body went cold.

"I'd planned to tell you once you'd settled in," Malik said quietly. "But I think Gallow meant for the two of you to meet. Meant for you to look into the eyes of your murderer and see him for what he *truly* is—a coward who serves the very god we seek to kill." Malik's eyes were bright as he pointed at Valerius, his tone mocking. "Behold. Only weeks into this new life, and already you can go toe-to-toe with the greatest swordsman Navaros has ever known. With the man who took *everything* from you."

Lazander barely heard him. Suddenly he was back in the Captain's Barracks, watching helplessly as Valerius drove a sword through Gabriel. Watching Marito smile as he flung himself to his death, giving up his life to save Lazander's. Back when he was just a knight. When he was weak. *Helpless.*

Fists clenched, Lazander leaped forward with a roar of pure fury.

Valerius held up his hand. Fire erupted from his palm, exploding out like a deadly flower.

The heat alone made Lazander flinch as he raised useless arms to protect himself. He couldn't dodge it in time.

Time seemed to slow as Malik appeared at his side with a wink, grabbing Lazander and moving them both out of the way. Flames licked his skin as the fire blasted past them, leaving his face red and burned.

"Well, maybe not quite toe-to-toe yet. But damn bloody close," Malik said, his tone light as he dusted off Lazander's shoulder.

Lazander went to shove him out of the way. He had to get Valerius, he had to—

But the prince was gone.

Lazander tore down the alley, kicking down doors to startled cries, shoving a drunken group of revelers who laughed as he charged past. He needed to hold Valerius down, to beat him until his fists were bloody, the cobblestones were spattered with bone and teeth. He'd never felt so angry before, not even during that fateful fight at the Captain's Barracks.

Malik followed him without a word, keeping close, but not crowding him. When Lazander rounded the corner to find the same street he'd just searched, still empty, the new Champion drove his fist into the ground, splitting the cobblestones with a roar. Valerius was gone. He'd let him get away. *Again.*

Malik pressed a comforting hand to his shoulder. "Remember what I said about Gallow—he doesn't always speak with words," he said quietly. "But that doesn't mean he isn't here. Isn't watching us. *Rooting* for us. Meeting Valerius was fate, brother," he said quietly. "Serve him well, and he'll gift that traitor's head on a *platter.*"

"I don't want his head on a platter," Lazander said, his voice a monotone at odds with the grief and fury that fought to overwhelm him. "I want him to cry. Beg. *Scream.* I want him to suffer as Gabriel and Marito did, a hundred times over, and only then will I rip the bastard's head off."

Malik laughed. "Valerius doesn't know what he unleashed when he killed you, does he?" The older Champion offered a hand to Lazander, looking deep into his eyes. "Give yourself up to Gallow, and he'll give you everything you need to strike Valerius down."

Lazander didn't even hesitate. He gripped Malik's hand, allowing him to haul him to his feet. "Whatever Gallow wants. Whatever he needs—he has it."

Malik smiled fiercely. "We're going to make Calamity *wish* he'd never crawled out of the Void."

***

Two skeletons lay inside the hut, their arms wrapped around each other in a lover's embrace. I edged in, shutting the door behind me, leaving footprints on the dusty floor.

No one had been here in years.

The skeletons were humanoid, though whether they were humans, vaxion, or molger I couldn't tell. Molger, I guessed, based on what I knew of Moonvale's history. I looked away, the sight of them turning my stomach for reasons I didn't understand. The hut was tiny with barely enough room for me, two chairs, an iron kettle, a small table… and the hut's owners. My eyes were drawn to two cups that lay on a small table.

I picked one up, the edges rough—as if it had been whittled by hand. On impulse, I sniffed it.

Vile. Danger. Evil. Bad. Bad!

I flinched as every hair raised, *Tithe of Beasts*, sending a primal warning throughout my whole body. Poison—there had been poison in these. I looked at the bone-white skeletons, how peaceful they seemed, and suddenly understood what had happened.

Doorknob in hand, I was shutting the door quietly when my eye fell on something in one of the skeletons' hands—the smaller of the two. Curiosity won out over guilt, and I pried it from boney fingers, expecting the skull to twist to face me at any moment. Darting outside, I slammed the door behind me, breathing hard, the stolen necklace in my hands.

Like the cups, it had been carved from wood. On the front was a small but beautiful painting of a woman. I turned it in the noonday sun. It was faded, but it looked like she wore a colorful cloak. On the back was an inscription in harsh, twisting letters I didn't understand.

I blinked, and they swam, rearranging themselves into something I could read.

In life and death, may Ravenna guide you.

Love,

Dad

They returned to their original, harsh order, but now I suddenly knew the alphabet—or Zara did. Vytrex, an old script used by the vaxion. Gripping the necklace, the ease I'd felt in the Moonvale Mountains vanished. What had happened to the vaxion inside the hut? Why had they killed themselves? And why had they been left all the way out here to rot?

On impulse, I tied the necklace around my neck. It felt disrespectful to simply put it in my Inventory. Gripping it, I searched the skyline for the curl of smoke I'd spotted when leaping from the flying stones—the only sign of life I'd seen here.

I headed for it, dreading what I would find.

***

"Ack!" Magnus yelped when Valerius dumped him unceremoniously on the ground.

WAR... NING... WARN... ING.

The pop-up blocked Valerius' vision, his head splitting.

CALAMITY... SYS... TEM... COMP... ROM... ISED.
MA... NA... DEPLE... TED...
PEN... ALTY... PENALTY...

He gasped—a lightning bolt of pain striking his brain's center. His skull was erupting, held in place only by the hands that frantically clutched his head. "What the hell do you think you're—" Magnus started, tangled in his cloak. He flipped the hood back, catching sight of Valerius. "What is it, Val? What's wrong?"

Valerius wanted to gouge out his eyes for *daring* to call him "Val," but he couldn't think. Couldn't speak.

PENALTY... PENALTY...

They were hours from Evergarden, a distance he'd covered in a mere thirty minutes using a combination of *Swiftness*, *Levity*, and *Whispering Darkness* for cover. He'd pushed himself to his absolute limits to get away from Lazander and Malik.

No, to get away from Gallow's "Champions."

Black spots dotting his vision, took a deep breath. It had been a long time since the Calamity System had penalized him for draining his mana. It was an... experience he had sworn never to repeat.

But needs must.

"Val—"

With a snarl, Valerius slapped Magnus' hand away. He brought up his Character Sheet.

Current:	
Stamina	10/1000
Hit Points	850/1000
Mana	0/500

"Come on, come on," he hissed. A "one" appeared in his mana bar, and he breathed a sigh of relief, the agony in his skull receding until all that remained was a throbbing echo of pain.

"At the very least tell me what made you throw me over your shoulder like some damsel and tear across half the country! I didn't even have time to grab my vests," Magnus snapped.

"What's our next quest?" Valerius asked, ignoring Magnus.

"Quest? What are you talking about?"

Valerius looked at the mage, at his blank, stupid expression. His small, pale hand that nervously fingered his cloak. The empty space where his arm once lay.

This was his future. An insane, oblivious idiot who could no longer tell dream from reality. Who *truly* believed this was the real world and that they served some all-powerful god. Magnus couldn't even see the Menu anymore. He thought the Tyrant communicated with him through *dreams*.

Valerius closed his eyes and forced himself to breathe. Lazander coming back from the dead was a classic twist, something you'd find in the third act of any video game. In fact, it made perfect sense if he thought about it. What better end to a story than for two knights, the only remnants of the Gilded, to do battle? He should take this for what it was—a sign he was inching closer to the endgame.

With a roar, he drove a fist into the ground, splitting it in half.

Iron Strength Activated.
CALAMITY SYSTEM REINITIATED.

Magnus cursed, his facade finally slipping as he spat vicious insults at Valerius. Instead of answering in kind, Valerius brought up the Menu, scrolling to the Quest tab. His main quest, *Summon Eternity*, hung bright and bold like a guillotine. Beneath it, the Tyrant's bizarre orders to craft and deliver that absurd potion appeared.

GRADE B+

He scoffed. It felt like the Tyrant handed out grades based on *whims*. He skipped through to the Quest Rewards, shrugging when he saw it was a *Replenish*. The mana boost it gave him was helpful, but he'd have preferred a *Healing Void*. Unfortunately the Tyrant rarely awarded those unless the Quest was an A+. Still, he thought as the *Replenish* moved to his Inventory.

The Champions can't use magic, not like I can, and if I have to down every potion I have to burn Lazander and that smug bastard Malik alive, I'll do it.

NEW QUEST AVAILABLE
WOULD—

Yes, he thought impatiently. As if he'd answer any other way.

Magnus was mewling at his side, demanding Valerius stop "treating him like a manservant," and claiming "I've served Calamity since you were a *babe*, how dare…" but the words trailed off as the unlikely pair froze.

As one, Valerius and Magnus received their new orders. Magnus' was a whisper in his ear while Valerius saw the words hang before his eyes. This quest wasn't some flight of fancy, or an increasingly strange shopping list. No, this quest was proof for Valerius and Magus both that they still held the Tyrant's favor.

Albeit for very different reasons.

Chapter Forty-Eight

Something was wrong. Very wrong.

The broken, overgrown walls. The abandoned hut. The skeletal remains. I realized now these had only been the beginning.

The silence in the clearing was thick and heavy. My skin crawled, claws peeking through my fingertips as my body screamed at me to run. I backed up, my foot knocking over a bucket so old and weather-worn, it collapsed on itself. The noise made me jump, breaking the spell of fear that had left me still as a statue. Taking a breath, I took off *Calamity's Shadow*, sending the cloak to my Inventory as I stepped forward.

The buildings in front of me were made of stone with two sticks in front, speared into the ground like tarps for tents. There was nothing left of the doors, only rusted hinges or planks so rotten they had collapsed around the entrance. Ten houses circled a huge stone ring clearly meant for a fire—one large enough for the whole outpost. Or village. Or whatever this was.

I took in these facts. The abandoned, rusty tools. The axe buried in a stump with a handle so rotten, it snapped at my touch. I didn't look inside any of the buildings. Or check for more bodies. I knew there would be none.

They were all outside. Bones half sunk in the soil.

They lay in an orderly row, arranged from large to small. Eleven in total. I looked away from the smallest—a child, if even. To the right of the skeletal remains the ground was thick with deep blue grass, marred by fifteen oblong sections of pitch-black soil. Here no grass grew. No weeds.

Heart hammering, I pressed my hand onto one of these strange, dark soil patches, feeling the barest whisper of magic beneath. Magic that felt just like my own *Fury's Claw*.

These were graves. *Vaxion* graves.

One of the skeletons caught my eye. It lay some way from the rest, curled in on itself. I knelt by it, running my fingers over bone-white shoulders that were huge, even in death. Underneath the corpse lay a shovel. Even in death, the person gripped the handle tightly. I looked back at the row of bodies lined up, one-by-one. Each patiently waiting for a burial that would never come.

"What happened here, Zara?" I asked.

A tingle in the back of my head let me know she was watching.

"I... *do not know*," she said, her voice barely a whisper. Then she was gone.

I shivered, wrapping my arms around myself. My neck prickled, and I whipped around. The forest beyond, where I'd felt stronger, faster, more at ease suddenly felt dark and foreboding. I pulled Calamity's Shadow from my Inventory, wrapping it around myself until I vanished from sight. Someone was out there. Someone was *watching* me.

The yellow trees with their burst of pink shook, the wind rising. The air crackled with a magic I didn't recognize.

I didn't see her. Didn't even feel her. One moment I was alone, the next I felt an overwhelming presence. Zara's magic was a wild inferno, one that threatened to spiral out of control every time I used it. But the magic that spilled from the woman behind me dwarfed Zara's.

Frozen with fear, I stopped breathing—a mouse caught in the paws of a lion.

The wind whipped into a frenzy as a hand twice the size of mine clamped down on my shoulder.

"It's been a long time, *chara*."

***

Eternity was knee deep in muck, a shovel in hand, when they returned.

She'd abandoned her dresses. Now she wore trousers and a tunic that used to belong to Garret's big brother, who'd been a stable hand like his little brother before he'd joined the army. She'd found them half buried while clearing out one of the storage sheds. Garret was embarrassed the first time he saw her wearing them.

"It ain't proper for Gallow's Chosen to wear them old things," he'd said.

She'd simply laughed, saying she wasn't really Chosen anymore. Days before, saying that would have sent her into a spiral. Now she felt a new lightness. Wiping her brow, she stood up, stretching a back that ached from hours of mucking out the stalls. It was a pleasant ache.

"This one is done, Garret!" she called.

"Bloody hell, Miss Eternity. You move as quick as the old hands!" he said, almost invisible behind the giant bale of hay he hauled. She ran to help him. He'd dropped the "Lady Eternity," and his bizarre "Your Highlyness," but she hadn't yet managed to convince him just "Eternity" was fine.

"I have a good teacher," she said with a wink, grinning when Garret blushed.

"Mum wanted to know if you were still up for dinner tonight?" he asked as they dumped the last hay bale together.

"Wouldn't miss it for the world," she said, wiping her hands. "I just wish she'd let me help with the clean-up after."

Garret laughed. "Mum would rather die. But that's not cause you're Miss Eternity!" he said hurriedly. "She's like that with all visitors. It was three years before she let my brother's wife do the dishes. This one time—"

Garret's words faded as Eternity felt the door to Gallow crack open ever so slightly. She started, feeling the darkness of the Void sink in to her bones. Eternity stood, shovel in hand, eyes darting about the almost finished courtyard. Gone was the colossal statue of the king and queen standing back-to-back, as well as the garden they'd both tended. Instead, it had been paved over with plans for a new inner wall being drawn up. The courtyard was still thick with people, from journeymen who flashed passes to the armored guards that now manned every door to the tiny market—a shadow of the once bustling hive the king had ordered halved for "security purposes."

Eternity took it all in before her eyes fell on a long shadow at the base of the tower she called home.

From its depths Imani stepped out, as if cut from the very darkness itself. Her pitch-black armor seemed to soak in the light that bounced from the freshly laid stone, and her hair was shorter than usual, shaved to the quick. With a cloak on her back and a small pack, Eternity could tell she was about to leave the Ivory Keep.

She hoped the Champion had come to say goodbye as Vivek appeared at Imani's side, looking almost skeletal in his matching armor. White hair wrenched back in a tight plait, his gray eyes darted around the courtyard. They rested briefly on Eternity before flashing away without even a hint of recognition.

She sighed, though she refused to let herself feel upset anymore. If Imani and Vivek didn't want to speak to her, that was their business, not hers, she'd decided. But as she watched them scan the courtyard, she realized they hadn't been dismissing her—they were *looking* for someone.

Red hair flashed in the sunlight.

He strode through the heavy stone doors of the Ivory Keep spelled by the palace mages to stay open until the new curfew. The guards didn't stop him. Nor did he so much as glance their way as he cut through the crowd. A silence fell as journeymen dropped their tools, abandoning their work to step back.

He didn't seem to notice.

Malik walked a few steps behind Lazander, smiling broadly, but Eternity only had eyes for the Gilded Knight—disbanded or not, he'd always be Gilded to her. He'd grown again and was now as tall as Imani, she guessed. But more than that had changed. Head held high, he didn't even acknowledge the people who threw themselves to the ground in their rush to get out of his way, where before he'd stop to help them to their feet. He didn't call out "good morning" to the guards he'd once sparred with. Didn't even raise a hand in greeting.

But that wasn't what gave Eternity pause.

Gone was Lazander's leather armor. Now he wore pitch-black full-plate that he moved in with ease, as if he'd been born wearing it.

"Woah," Garret said. "Mister Lazander looks just like a Champion now."

Lazander and Malik joined Vivek and Imani. Imani stretched out a hand, shaking Lazander's with a proud smile. Vivek nodded—his version of a round of applause.

"He does, doesn't he," Eternity said. At her back, Galora snaked her head out of the stable doors. The huge gold dragon huffed, moving to the side when Mabel joined her, neighing happily when she saw Lazander. Eternity glanced up to see a dark spot in the sky and knew Merrin watched from above.

She hurriedly dusted down her trousers, pulling her hair out of the bun she kept it up in these days. A hand on Galora's head, she idly scratched the dragon in her favorite spot while she waited for Lazander to see them, jog over to them and tell them all about his latest adventure as a Champion. She couldn't wait to tell him her own news. How she didn't mind that he'd missed dinner with her. How she'd started spending the evenings with Garret's family. How Garret's sister had invited her to a sewing group. How Eternity might actually, for the first time in nearly a hundred years, be making *friends*.

But Lazander didn't look at her, or Galora, or Mabel. Didn't glance up when Merrin cried out happily, circling lower. Instead he strode out of the courtyard alongside his fellow Champions without so much as a backward glance.

***

I turned, heart in my mouth.

Ashira, leader of the infamous vaxion, stood before me, the all-encompassing storm of memory. The woman who had sold her own niece, Zara the Fury, to Magnus. Who had murdered Lenia's husband. Who had run every molger out of the Moonvale Mountains a decade past.

She was, in many ways, the mirror-image of Zara, only the sheer bulk of her muscled arms and shoulders and the curve of her jaw setting them apart. That and the fine lines that weathered the corners of her eyes and the space between her brows. A dark leather band wound around her chest, leaving her stomach and shoulder bare. When I'd seen Ashira in Zara's memories, intricate black tattoos lined her aunt's biceps. Now almost every inch of skin was covered in thick black lines, winding from her shoulders to her collarbones and crawling up her neck. My eyes fell on a snake-like design that twisted round her left shoulder, my stomach plunging when it began to writhe under her skin.

I forced my head back, craning my neck to look up into her eyes.

I'd spent days wondering how I was going to get to Ashira. In my mind's eye, I thought once I'd gotten past the mountains, I'd find an outpost, maybe some guards. Hands raised, I'd announce myself. If I managed not to get murdered on the spot, I assumed I'd be brought before Ashira, likely in chains, based on the stories. I pictured Ashira on a throne, something covered in fur and made of skulls where she'd glare at me, one leg dangling over the armrest. That was usually as far as my imaginings got, for fear she'd order me killed then and there.

What I had never pictured, not in my wildest dreams, was Ashira standing before me in a forest, her golden eyes brimming with *tears*. She reached out, and I flinched, but she simply cupped my face gently in her warm, rough hands.

"Welcome home, little star," she said quietly, pressing her forehead against mine. "I have missed you."

Chapter Forty-Nine

Ashira held me like that for a long time, her hands cupped around my cheeks, forehead pressed to mine. She didn't say a word, simply closed her eyes while she took breaths so deep and slow, they reminded me of a sleeping mountain.

She seemed at peace. Happy, even.

I, on the other hand, was doing everything I could not to wet myself.

She "missed" me? She's acting like I'm back from vacation! Zara said she'd rip my legs off, not give me a hug. What the hell is going on?

I waited desperately for Zara to say something, but she was quiet. I couldn't even tell if she was watching.

Mind racing, I didn't know how much time passed before Ashira leaned back, gently brushing a piece of hair back from my face. Her golden eyes, so like mine, so like *Zara's*, stared at me intensely as they roved over my face, taking in every detail. I felt like I was under a microscope.

A microscope that could rip my head off.

"You've grown, Zara," she said, her voice a pleasant rumble. "Were it another time, another life, I'd say you were ready to take on the trials of Ravenna's Breath. Your mother did so at your age." She looked away, raw grief in her eyes. "Alas, much has changed since you were here. Come, the *shi'ara* will want to look at you."

She turned without a word, striding past the skeletons of her fellow vaxion without so much a glance. I stood there dumbfounded before common sense kicked in and I chased after her.

When I'd imagined coming here, I'd planned to tell Ashira straight away that I wasn't the real Zara. I didn't know what the Operator's quest *Temper the Vaxion* meant, but I knew 1) it must take place in the Moonvale Mountains, and 2) the vaxion hated Zara. I thought by telling them the truth, I'd have a better chance of surviving. But Ashira hadn't acted like someone who hated me. Or like someone who'd sold their own niece to a mad man.

The gigantic vaxion said nothing as she moved through the forest like a shadow, her bare feet making no sound as she leaped over fallen trees and dipped under overhanging branches. The forest itself seemed to move with her, shifting out of the way while my feet kicked every stone and snapped every twig underfoot.

I desperately wanted to ask about the dead vaxion I'd seen. They'd clearly been there for years. What had happened to them? Why hadn't they been buried? I'd just about summoned enough courage to ask when I noticed the scarred mess of flesh that was Ashira's back. Inches deep, lines curled in on themselves in a strange concentric circle. Every edge was rough and shorn—like it had been carved into her flesh using a dull knife. Starting at the bottom of her neck, it ended somewhere in the middle, though it was hard to tell with the leather band she wore. The scars were nothing like her tattoos, which never came more than two inches close to the horrifying marks on her back—as if recoiling from them.

"I hope he screamed," Ashira said, making me jump. She glanced back at me, golden eyes alight with violence. "And that when he begged for death you denied it."

She stared, waiting for an answer. Having no clue what she was talking about, I decided to simply nod. Thankfully it seemed enough for her, and she looked ahead once more, her pace increasing.

Magnus, I belatedly realized. Who else could she be talking about but Magnus? But if Ashira sold Zara to him, why would she want him dead?

Something wasn't adding up.

Ashira stopped, and I bumped into her, my nose crunching. It was like walking into *stone*. Ahead of us, a gigantic deep blue rock lay on the ground, half sunk into the earth. It looked just like one of the stones that circled overhead. I frowned, noticing the runes inscribed into the sides. It *was* one of the stones. How did it end up down here?

"We are not what we were," Ashira said quietly. "Prepare your heart."

She laid her hand against the stone, and it shimmered. Stepping forward, she vanished into the rock. It was just like the illusion I'd found on the side of the mountains, the one that led to the gravediggers.

Heart in my throat, I followed her.

It took my eyes a second to adjust. While it was bright outside, only a few hours past noon, it was dark and dingy inside the stone. Wrought iron lanterns lined what looked like a tunnel while claw marks on the walls betrayed it had been dug by hand.

"The *shi'ara's* suggestion," she said, running her fingers along the walls, her palm fitting the claw marks exactly. I instantly knew she'd been the one to dig this tunnel by hand. "When the waterstones first fell from the sky, their magic failing, the *shi'ara* could only keep so many afloat. She suggested we use one of the fallen as our own. It was safer, she said. I pushed back, of course. I still clung to the idea that nothing would change." She pulled her hand away, sighing. "We moved here after Umin fell."

"Umin?"

"The village I found you in. It's been so long, I suppose you would not remember their names." She looked away, and I felt a sudden burst of guilt. Mine or Zara's, I didn't know. I hesitated. Wanting desperately to ask more, I was afraid I'd blow my cover. In the end, curiosity won out.

"Why haven't you buried them? The people of Umin?"

Ashira frowned, and I feared I'd pushed too hard, but she said, "To remind us of what we lost. Of the cost of weakness." She turned away, missing the disgust I knew was painted on my face. Her own people died, and she called them weak? That sounded more like the vaxion I'd heard of. Ashira moved suddenly, driving her fist into the tunnel wall. Spiderweb cracks appeared. When she drew her hand back, her knuckles were bloody.

"To remind *me* that I failed them. As I failed you," she said quietly, head bent, shoulders hunched.

She stalked forward without another word while I tried to remember how to breathe. *Zara*. I thought frantically. *Now would be a very, very good time to speak up.*

Silence. I wanted to pull my hair out.

As we walked deeper into the stone, the lanterns grew in size, the air growing thick and humid. At last it expanded into a wide, clearly handmade cavern. Trickles of water crept down the side, pooling into stone basins built into the floor where a man knelt, scrubbing something in the water.

All I managed to take in was him and a handful of people chopping food in silence before Ashira stepped forward. "A good tiding," she called, pulling me forward, a hand on my shoulder. "Zara has returned." Her words boomed across the cavern, though she barely raised her voice.

People froze mid-task, raising their heads. I spotted more vaxion off to the side, hidden behind curtains they now drew back, what looked like bedrooms behind them.

Then I was overwhelmed.

Everyone surged forward, hands cupping my face, forehead against mine before the next person pulled me to them. A blur of faces, some my age, others deeply lined, smiled as they held me.

"Welcome home!"

"I knew you would make it."

"You always were the strongest of us."

My chest tightened, vision swimming, but people kept clinging to me. Later, I would realize that no one had asked me how I had gotten here or where I had been. Not even Ashira.

A sharp clap cut through the noise.

The crowd split, parting down the middle to reveal a woman who couldn't have been older than thirty. Sharp-eyed, she was dressed in flowing robes at odds with the vaxion leather of the others. A blood red line, half an inch thick, began at the base of her throat and rose all the way up to her forehead, splitting her face in half. I thought it was paint, but as she walked toward me, I realized it was an open wound. One I somehow knew never closed.

The *shi'ara*, the "witch" of the vaxion. The same woman I'd seen behind Ashira as she'd strangled Zara, a blade the length of a forearm in her hands.

Now, head cocked to one side like a bird, she stared at me with bright blue eyes too big for her face. I looked nervously at Ashira, but she stood aside with the rest, eyes on the *shi'ara*. The woman didn't walk toward me—she glided. In seconds she was in front of me, despite having started off on the other side of the room.

This, of course, was the moment Zara chose to speak.

"*Parasite, do not let her touch us!*" she hissed.

The *shi'ara* reached for me, hands outstretched.

Why? I asked, taking a step back. Ashira looked from the witch to me with a frown. *I don't exactly have a choice right now!*

"I remember her. She is the one who bound me, who held me down with her magic while—"

The *shi'ara's* ice-cold hands, the opposite of the warm furnace of other falslings, clamped down on my cheeks.

And I was gone.

Chapter Fifty

Zara blinked to find she was in her body once more. But she wasn't in the cavern, surrounded by faces of the half remembered, Jaza—the cook who sang beautifully, Himora—the lazy *shek* who was an even lazier hunter. Tek, the stone-eyed fighter.

Remnants of a dream she'd had long ago.

Instead she was in the darkness of the parasite's mind, her eternal prison. But something was different. She looked down at her hands to see they were half the size they should be, her fingers small and useless. Shocked, she started forward, nearly falling—unused to her new, shorter stride.

She was a *child*. Nine or ten years of age, she guessed.

Zara cursed aloud. It was better than being trapped in her wretched vaxion form, but not by much. In this body it felt like a strong wind could take her down. How was she supposed to escape the parasite with claws the size of needles?

"What happened to you, little star?" came a voice.

Zara spun, pathetic claws bursting from her fingers.

The *shi'ara* stood at her back, dressed in her stonebreaker robes. Each piece, from her trousers to her tunic to the scarf at her waist, were all cut from different stonebreakers the *shi'ara* herself had killed. To damage even a piece was an insult, yet when Zara lashed out, her strike clumsy and wild, the *shi'ara* didn't move. Zara's claws cut through the witch's robes, slicing deep into her thigh.

"Yemena," she said, not wincing when she bled. "You may call me, Yemena."

Zara hissed in reply, the sound closer to a kitten's squeak.

"Tell me," Yemena said, leaning down. "Tell me what happened to you, little star."

"Do *not* call me that," Zara hissed.

"Ah," she said, eyes clouded. Drops of blood gathered in the wound that split her face, dripping down the line but never touching either side, like a bloodied waterfall. "I forget. I am not Ashira. Only Ashira may call you that."

Zara frowned, her claws raised. She might not remember much from her childhood in Moonvale Mountains, but she knew that witches were powerful. Why was the *shi'ara* here, in the parasite's mind with her? Was it Ashira's ploy? Or maybe Magnus'? Her claws, so tiny, so useless, flexed. She would not be used. Not again.

"Even now, Magnus sinks his fangs into your neck," Yemena said, her voice devoid of emotion. "He has made it so you see only darkness and sickness, even in light."

"Keep your vile magic out of my mind!" Zara hissed, swiping at Yemena. The *shi'ara* didn't flinch when she tore at her stomach, shins, and thighs—the only parts she could reach. "My life is gone. My body stolen. I have nothing left but my own *thoughts*."

"A question." Yemena cocked her head to one side. Blood dripped from the wounds Zara had made. "Why did you go with Magnus?"

"What—I did not *leave* with that pustulant vermin!" she roared. "Ashira, my own blood, *sold* me to him."

"Why?"

"What do you mean, 'why'?" Zara said, thrown by the question.

"If she sold you to the mage, what was her prize? What gift was so great she'd betray her own blood?" Yemena knelt down.

Zara considered plucking out the witch's eyes, but something about her question made her pause.

Ashira was a cruel, manipulative *shek*—but she never did anything without cause. Did she sell Zara for power? Hardly. The woman could split a mountain in two. Control? There was no one, neither vaxion nor molger, who wouldn't drop to their knees and lick Ashira's boots at her command. Land? No. The molger left Moonvale months before she was sent with Magnus. So, why?

"I... I do not know," Zara said finally.

"Do you not find that strange?" Yemena asked in the same emotionless voice, as if she were reciting something from memory. "Magnus took pleasure in tormenting you. In causing you pain. His greatest joy came from reminding you that you were alone and your own family did this to you. Yet he never said why. Nor did you ask him. Not once."

Despite her mistrust of the witch, Zara found herself wracking her memories. Magnus had locked her in a cell for days without food or water until she had to debase herself and plead for it. He'd beaten her until she couldn't see—he'd claimed time and again she was a pawn for her own family. But the witch was right. He'd never said why. And in all her years as his slave, she'd never asked. Why hadn't she held him by the throat and demanded the truth, even if he punished her for it?

That… was not like her.

"When you wish to see, come and find me," Yemena said, standing up.

"Wait."

The witch had used her magic to trap her and present her to Magnus like a prized gift, this she knew. But the *shi'ara*, for all their power, were bound by a single rule.

They could not lie.

"The parasite, the girl who stole my skin," Zara said, the words spilling out. "Did she burn Magnus' arm to a cinder as she claims? Is she his enemy?"

Yemena looked off into the distance. Nothing was there, save the dark, yet Yemena cocked her head to the side.

"Yes," she said simply.

Zara vanished.

***

I fell to my knees, head splitting. It felt like someone had driven a knife through my eye and was wiggling it around. A burst of light clouded my vision, and I struggled to open my eyes. Knees scraping rock, I looked up to find the *shi'ara* staring down at me, bleeding from her stomach and legs, the flowy cloth she wore ripped to shreds. Terrified I'd hurt her, I looked down at my fingers, but they were clean.

What happened? Who hurt the witch? And why was she looking at me like—

"Zara needs rest," the *shi'ara* said. "We will feast after morrow's Moon Peak."

She turned without a word, gliding away. People smiled at me, not seeming the least bit bothered that their resident witch was bleeding. One or two of them even cupped my face gently again before scuttling away at Ashira's glare. Struggling, I got to my feet. Ashira didn't offer to help me up.

"Follow," she said, taking off at a slow pace. A series of winding tunnels I quickly lost track of led us to a huge white fur that acted as a curtain. She pulled it to one side to reveal what was clearly a bedroom. A stack of blankets and furs were neatly folded in the corner while clothes were placed in cubby holes that had been painstakingly carved out of the stone. A charm, something made with bones, dried flowers, and stone, was hung up above the area that served as a bed.

Clean, minimalist, and practical. Exactly what I'd expected of Ashira.

"Your room," she said, surprising me. I'd thought it was hers. "I made it when we first moved here." Her voice dropped low, thick with emotion.

Before I could think of anything to say, she beckoned someone from behind her. A woman with deep smile lines and bright eyes appeared, carrying a plate with what looked like half a cow on it. "Seasoned with mushi herbs, your favorite," she said, gently setting it down.

"Jaza," Ashira said, a note of warning in her voice. Jaza simply winked at Ashira before dancing out of the room like a pixie. Ashira huffed in an approximation of a laugh.

"You won't be disturbed," Ashira said, dropping the curtain as she left.

I waited until her steps had stopped echoing to look around the room. It was clearly hand-carved and sparkling clean, even though Zara had never set foot in it. I imagined Ashira coming in here every week and dusting it, waiting for the day Zara would return.

"No!" I said aloud, slapping my palms to my cheeks. "She killed Lenia's husband! She made Zara fight gravediggers in a cave! She'd enslave Lukas!" With each accusation, I slapped myself. These were *not* good people. I had to find out what I could about the blood debt, figure out how to finish *Temper the Vaxion*, and get back to Lukas. That was the plan. The plan was not "feel pity for *maniacal falslings*."

I was about to slap myself one more time for good measure when my nose kicked in. The smell of meat hot off a grill filled the room. I looked down at the massive plate Jaza had left for me.

Seeing no utensils, I picked up a slab the size of my hand. Biting into it, I had to stifle a moan as the meat practically melted on my tongue. Pork? Beef? I didn't know and didn't want to know. In seconds, I'd wolfed down the entire plate.

Jaza might actually be a better cook than Lukas. Not that I'd ever tell him that.

I licked my fingers clean, suddenly overcome by exhaustion. Feeling silly, I glanced around furtively before stripping off my armor. I knew falslings, well, the molger at least, didn't have any issues with nudity, but that didn't mean I liked the idea of Ashira charging in while I was in my birthday suit.

I laid out several of the furs as a base for my bed, then pulled more on top of me. They carried a dull, musky scent that was surprisingly comforting, and I burrowed in deep, my mind swimming with everything I'd seen, everything I'd learned today. All the dead vaxion—their skeletal remains left to rot out in the sun. Ashira's claim that it was a reminder to her for failing them. How she'd *cried* when she saw me—Ashira, the big scary vaxion leader. How happy everyone was to see me.

These didn't feel like people who had sold Zara into slavery. Or if they were, they were very, very good actors. I'd have to talk to Zara about it, I knew, but the thought made me squirm. *Why do I even bother? She hates me. I'm like a dog running back to the master who keeps kicking them. God, I'm pathetic. Just focus on the quest, and—*

The Calamity System Menu swam before my eyes. I hadn't even realized I'd fallen asleep. I idly flicked to the Inventory and the ring I'd picked up during my last quest.

<u>Item:</u>	Calamity's Kiss
When donning this ring, mana courses through your veins, granting you explosive power. However, the longer you wear it, the quicker your magic drains until there is nothing left of you but an empty husk.	

Curious, I equipped it, gasping at my stats. It increased my mana by twenty-five percent! That was a huge boost but sounded like something to use with caution. Maybe in a quick fight where I used *Wrath's Storm* or *Lightning's Claw* in rapid succession? But if the fight went on too long, I'd risk turning into an "empty husk," which didn't sound—

A pop-up flashed.

YOU HAVE A MESSAGE FROM ZARA THE FURY. WOULD YOU LIKE TO READ IT?

Surprised, I hesitated.

The temptation to put her off was overwhelming. As was my mortification from the last time we had spoken. "In another life, do you think we could have been friends?" What was I, five years old? Groaning, I knew I had to put on my big girl pants. I clicked on the tab, expecting Zara to come leaping out at me, fangs bared, tendrils coiled with lightning.

Instead my jaw dropped.

Chapter Fifty-One

A girl with huge golden eyes and nutbrown skin stared up at me. Literally. She barely reached my hip. "Zara?" I said, taking a back step. "How—what happened to your vaxion form? I mean, I know you hated it, but if you could change all this time, why didn't you—"

"Your life would be much improved if you spoke less, human," the little girl said.

I almost laughed. No matter the form, she was still Zara. Like her fellow vaxion she was dressed in leather bands. She wouldn't have looked out of place in the cavern, causing havoc as she ran about, leaping into wash basins. The only thing that spoiled the image was the collar around her neck. It glowed faintly, the chains that bound her trailing off into the darkness.

"You wanted to speak to me?" I asked, eager to get this over with.

"I despise you."

I sighed. "I know, Zara. You don't have to—"

"What did I say about speaking less?" She snarled, a fang peeking from under her top lip. In her vaxion form, I'd be scared. But right now, with her tiny fists clenched and teeth the size of toothpicks, it was taking all I had not to kneel down and call her *adorable*.

Keeping my face neutral, I nodded for her to continue.

"You are my warden. My jailer. The one who binds me to this wretched prison," she began, crossing her arms. "But you are also Magnus' enemy. And while I plan to rip out your trachea and *feast* on it for what you have done to me… I am willing to put that aside. *If*," she wagged a threatening digit, her index finger the world's smallest exclamation point.

"If?"

Don't smile. Don't you dare smile.

"You speak to Yemena, the *shi'ara*, at the morrow's Moon Peak. Refuse, and I shall make it my life's work to torment you from this dark prison, you—"

"Sure," I said.

"… What?"

"I mean, I'm a bit surprised, considering your reaction to her, but sure. Anything specific I need to ask her?"

Zara blinked, speechless.

I smiled, despite my best efforts. "You've never asked for a favor before, have you?"

"This is not a favor, *shek*! This is a—a demand," she stammered.

Stammered.

I knelt, making sure to put both my knees on the ground, so we were eye-level. If I just hunkered down on one knee, she'd think I was being condescending.

"Yemena—got it. Should I speak to anyone else?" I asked, keeping my tone light, as if I was prepping a shopping list. She must have something to say to Ashira. If I was her, I'd have an endless list of questions about what I'd seen today. But I was very slowly learning Zara was like a cat—you had to let her come to you.

"No," she said primly, hands on her hips. "The witch will know what you mean. You need only address her."

"All right."

Silence.

Zara looked away first, shuffling her feet. "You may go now, parasite," she said, flicking her hand in a dismissive gesture.

I nodded, trying to look suitably chastised. The darkness began to fade, Zara's form blurring. But right before she vanished, I caught the barest hint of a smile.

***

I woke up buried so deep in my pile of furs, I'd almost fused with them. With a yawn, I gave a luxurious stretch. That was the best sleep I'd ever—I opened my eyes to find Ashira inches from my face, staring at me intently.

"You slept past First Dawn," she said while I lay ramrod straight, a mouse caught in a viper's gaze.

"I... I did?" I said, covertly pulling the furs up to my neck while I wondered what the hell "First Dawn" was—why was there more than one—and *why was Ashira so close to my face?*

She frowned, her go-to reaction. Midnight dark hair plaited to perfection was draped over one of her shoulders while her sheer bulk blotted out the room's only light, a small lantern that hung from the ceiling. Her leathers were polished and tightly bound, her eyes bright. Not a *single* hair was out of place. It was as if she didn't sleep—she simply materialized this way every day.

It somehow made her more terrifying.

"Jaza put breakfast aside for you," she said. "If you are late again, you will go hungry." Then she strode out of the room. It was only when I couldn't hear her footsteps anymore that I let out the longest breath of my life.

Thus began my first day among the vaxion.

I'd expected many things from the infamous falslings, most of them violent. My mind hadn't imagined much beyond trying to talk my way in, but knowing how proud the vaxion were of their cat-like forms, I'd expected to see them lounging about, lightning zapping through the air as they tortured a bunny rabbit or two. I'd pictured trials by combat or some ridiculous "quest" to earn my place among them. I'd never imagined that the first thing asked of Zara after a decade away would be *chores*.

I was immediately assigned "mopping" duty alongside three others. Cold, wet rags were all we had. No soap. I was still wrapping my head around this when my fellow vaxion knelt. Heads down, they gripped their rags tightly as they straightened their legs.

And *sprinted*.

Up and down the main hall they ran, as if ripperbacks clipped at their heels. Panicking, I'd tried to follow suit but immediately tripped, falling flat on my face. In H'tar, laughter would have erupted and some good-natured ribbing.

Here, no one laughed. No one asked if I was all right. I didn't even get a snarl for falling behind. They simply ignored me and carried on working as if their lives depended on it. They treated their powers with the same discipline. In H'tar, people shifted to molger as needed, human and beast working side-by-side to get the job done.

Not the vaxion.

They didn't shapeshift, transform their limbs, or whip out so much as a claw—even if it would have made their jobs easier. I watched, eyes bulging out of my head when three vaxion used *pickaxes* to break down a stone wall. Pickaxes! Their claws could have done it in half the time. I couldn't figure out if they thought using their powers was cheating or if this was a "First Dawn" specific rule. Either way, it was as intimidating as hell.

After mopping, people silently moved to their next job while I stood there awkwardly. A woman bumped me, covertly nodding at a polished stone table where a knife and a basket of what looked like angry hedgehogs waited. Getting the hint, I picked up the blade, relieved to find the brown, spiky things were vegetables and not tiny adorable woodland creatures.

I dug the knife in, where it immediately got stuck. I flipped the vegetable on its side, tried slicing it downward and was considering just smashing it on the table when a man in his thirties came to my station, despite being assigned to another. He pointedly took a prickled vegetable, cut off the top, and hollowed out its core—revealing the edible part was *inside*. I went to thank him, but he left without a glance.

It was then I realized I'd been stepping all over one of the most important rules in vaxion culture.

When I couldn't find a wash rag to mop the floors, a woman "accidentally" dropped one at my feet. Lost on the way to the laundry room? A man who moved like a dancer made a show of taking his dirty clothes down a convoluted tunnel without acknowledging I was following him.

No one could offer to help. Or appear to, at least. The only one who blatantly skirted this rule was Jaza.

When I'd shown up bleary-eyed and full of adrenaline after Ashira's "wake-up call," Jaza had waved at me furtively, ducking behind a twisted column of stone to hand me a bowl. What looked like mushy corn drenched in fermented milk greeted me. The smell alone made my eyes water.

"You slept like a newborn babe!" she said with a wink. "I'll make sure to rouse you before First Dawn tomorrow."

I knocked my breakfast back, trying my best not to breathe it in. It tasted *chalky*. Why did the milk taste chalky? "*Hankyu*," I mumbled, forcing myself to swallow.

"We're on laundry together later. I'll see you then," she said, waving as she danced off. Over the next few hours I mopped, cut vegetables, hauled stone, and now folded laundry in a cave so dry, my lips split and bled in minutes. My day so far had been an anthropologist's dream as I tried to figure out the strange rules that governed the vaxion. I did my best to act like an outside observer, these were Zara's people, not mine, but as I snapped out a sheet, nearly tearing it, I realized I couldn't.

I was too angry.

Zara had been gone for *ten years*, and while the vaxion had made a show of how happy they were to see her, no one had asked me a single question. No, "So where have you been for a decade?" or, "Hey, are we cool about the whole slavery thing?" or even a, "How are you feeling after spending almost half your life getting *tortured?*"

Zara and I weren't exactly friends, but I was furious on her behalf. Were her own people just going to pretend like nothing had happened?

"Second.

"Second!

"Second!"

A call sounded out, echoing from vaxion to vaxion as it traveled from the main hall, the kitchen, and all the way to the laundry room. Jaza beamed, folding her sheets into impossibly small squares while I still struggled with my first. "Come, Zara! I could eat a whole xandi," she called in a sing-song voice, skipping away. I gave up on my sheet, rolled it into a ball, and ran after her. How did she still have so much *energy?*

"Are we on laundry after lunch too?" I said, taking care not to phrase it as an offer to help.

"Of course not, it's Second Dawn."

"Oh... right," I said, completely confused.

She stopped, her smile fading. "I realize it's been some time, but have you forgotten even this?" Jaza looked on the brink of tears, and I moved to reassure her, when her grin snapped back into place. "First Dawn is for work," she explained brightly, "when the mind has yet to blossom. Second is when we sharpen it."

I nodded, not having any idea what she meant.

Thirty minutes later, I decided I was a big fan of Second Dawn. Sixteen people, ranging in age from thirteen or so, all the way up to their sixties lounged on furs around a low table. The vegetables I'd (poorly) chopped were passed along, starting with Ashira. Each time she got a dish, she took nothing from it. Instead she'd hand it to the youngest vaxion I'd seen here, a boy of about thirteen, who kept stealing shy glances at me. Ashira only took her share when the bowls had done a full round at the table.

To my relief, the silent and furious energy of First Dawn was gone. Instead people laughed and chatted about their plans for "Twilight."

"Who wants to spar? Tek, you owe me a rematch!"

And who would bring what to the festivities at "Moon Peak."

"Himora, were there any spike-hogs in the traps this week?"

I recited these silently to myself, First Dawn, Second Dawn, Twilight, Moon Peak, while trying my best to keep up with the rapid-fire conversation. The vaxion spoke as quickly as they worked. Someone started telling a story about a young vaxion who'd tried to kill two stonebreakers.

"And then, and then," she said, hands raised dramatically, "he raises his claws, the stonebreaker before him gushing heart's blood. He takes a step and... trips! Snapping his neck clean in two!"

All the vaxion burst out laughing, and I hurriedly joined, realizing she hadn't been telling a story. She'd been telling a *joke*.

In the race for best sense of humor, the molger were comfortably beating the vaxion.

I covertly looked around the cavern, or "main hall," as I'd taken to calling it, waiting to see if anyone else would arrive. I'd kept an eye out for the blonde hair and blue eyes of Lukas' mom, but I hadn't seen her yet. Surely more vaxion lived here? But as people tucked in, their voices echoing around the too-large room, it became obvious this was it. Lenia had claimed H'tar was "tiny," but they had triple this many people, if not more.

"How many vaxion live in waterstones like this?" I asked Jaza quietly, thinking it might be weird if I asked for "Lukas' mom." I didn't even know her name. Jaza had been mid-laugh, smiling brightly. A smile that now slid from her face.

"Have some *pakina*," she said abruptly, shoving the hedgehog-like vegetable in my face. "What would you like to focus on this Second Dawn? Tek will be practicing calligraphy, her vytrex is the best in the clan. Fatyr is teaching the young one how to dance the *Moon Shadow*—"

"Stop calling me the young one!" came the sharp indignant cry from the boy to Ashira's left. The leader of the vaxion raised a single eyebrow at him, and he dropped his head, quieting down.

"—he might even perform tonight," Jaza said, not missing a beat at the interruption. "I will be meditating in the undergrotto."

I paused, considering. I could tell I'd disturbed Jaza with some of my questions. I might be better off going with someone else and trying to see what I could find out about, well, everything. My eyes fell on Tek, the one who'd be practicing calligraphy. She was the oldest of the vaxion, with thick, ragged scars down the side of her cheeks and threads of white through her eyebrows. A layer of fat born of age covered the muscles I knew lay under her shoulders and stomach. I'd spotted her earlier on mining duty. She'd been breaking rubble with her *bare hands*.

She caught my eyes and fixed me with a look that could crack stone. Not her, then.

Fatyr didn't appeal to me much either. Tall and lithe, he moved around the table like a dancer, effortless and light. The thought of tripping over my feet while I attempted a dance they might ask me to *perform* tonight wasn't in the cards.

"Meditation sounds great," I said, biting into the pakina.

Chapter Fifty-Two

"Woah," I whispered. Beneath a large wooden hatch in the main hall and down a ladder carved into stone lay the undergrotto. The air was hot and humid, a smell akin to peppermint tickling my nose. Water trickled down the walls, pooling in basins that bubbled gently. I trailed my fingers along the surface of one, surprised to find the water hot, almost boiling.

"Jaza, how does the water heat down—"

She unbuckled her leathers quickly, stripping down to nothing.

"Ashira's magic, how else?" she said with a laugh, as if the very question was ridiculous. "I have told her it is a waste, but she insists. She claims it is for the good of the clan. But she just so happened to finish this on my name day." Jaza shook her head with a smile, tying up her hair while I tried very hard to look her in the eye. Her skin darkened in the dim light, steam and shadows tracing along the muscles that lined every inch of her skin. She must have been in her late thirties, maybe even older. It was hard to tell.

"Ashira appears cold, such is her way, but no one loves as fiercely as she does—even if it costs her dearly," she said sadly, the words weighing heavy in the air. I knew we weren't talking about Ashira making Jaza a cute birthday present anymore.

"Come. Cold first," she said.

Behind two heavy wooden doors lay a much smaller room. A waterfall gushed from the ceiling. This at least, I could take a guess at. "A waterstone?" I asked, eyeing the runic shapes trapped in the roof.

"Indeed." Ashira pulled an active one from the sky, then bound it to her. "It took her many weeks to figure out the magic with which to adjust the temperature. She is like you. Her affinity lies with fire and lightning."

She stepped under the waterfall, getting drenched instantly. Standing as still as a statue, she took several breaths before kneeling, head bowed. Now that her eyes were closed, I felt a bit braver. Stripping off my armor, now my second skin, I reached out a hand, wanting to test the water.

I yelped, jumping back. It was *freezing*. Behind a curtain of water, Jaza smiled, patting the space next to her.

Why didn't I do calligraphy with grumpy Tek?

I stepped in, letting out an undignified shriek when ice-cold needles stabbed my skin. How did Jaza go under without a word? I dug my fingers into my palms, determined to stay put. When my skull throbbed with painful numbness, I knelt, the craggy rock cutting my knees.

How is this meditating? This is the most vaxion idea of relaxation I have ever—

But the thought trailed off. I felt myself detach from my body, drifting in a way that felt both relaxing and highly alert. I became the layers of ligaments and tendons wrapped around bone, each working together to move me with ease. The lungs that expanded with aching slowness, letting me breathe in this strange world. The hands lying demurely in my lap that could kill so easily.

The more I took inventory of my body, the more my mind opened up. I heard the voice in my head that told me I was useless. Pathetic. Stupid. I saw how small it had become since I came here, how it now cowered in the corner of my mind—hiding, but not forgotten. I saw my fears about the Operator and about what I would do if I was forced to choose between him and Lukas. My chest tightened, pulling me back briefly to my body, but I forced myself to relax.

Trust yourself. A voice, soft and reassuring, whispered to me. I didn't recognize it, but felt I used to, back in my old life. *My little girl is strong, tough, and smart to boot. You can do this.*

"Hot, next?" Jaza asked, breaking me out of my trance.

"Ah, sure," I answered on instinct. I tried to get up, but fell, my knees numb and useless. Jaza looked around furtively, then reached out a hand. I took it without thinking, belatedly realizing this was the first time a vaxion had openly offered me help.

After Second Dawn came Twilight, a time to "sharpen the body" (I was sensing a theme). I decided it'd be odd if I kept following Jaza like her shadow so I opted to spar with Tek, Fatyr, and Esia— "the young one."

Despite being at least forty years younger than Tek, and far more agile, Fatyr couldn't keep up with her. In one bout, she held him above her head, throwing him bodily across the room. He hit the ground with a yelp while Tek called, "Roll, you fool." She might have the best calligraphy of the vaxion, but I dearly hoped I never met Tek in a dark alley.

I thought she'd have more patience with Esia, who was only thirteen.

She didn't.

I winced when he swung at her with a right hook. His guard was too low, his footwork all wrong. All Tek would have to do was—

I hadn't finished the thought before the older woman blocked the blow, kicking Esia in the ankle. He went down on one knee, and she brought up her foot, kicking him squarely in the chest with everything she had. He went flying while I tried not to gasp.

The vaxion refused death, never offered help, despised weakness, blah, blah, blah. But Esia was just a kid! Fists clenched, I went to help him up, but Fatyr held out a covert hand, stopping me in my tracks. Together we simply watched as Esia coughed, then rolled up onto his side, his hand clutching his ribs, and crawled out of the rough sparring circle drawn into the stone. The sight made claws dig into my palms.

"You're up," Tek said, gesturing to me. She looked smug. *Arrogant.*

I was going to change that.

I entered the circle while Tek dramatically cracked her knuckles. "Give me everything you've got," she said. "It's been too long since I had a real fight."

I whispered the words I needed under my breath, too low for Tek to hear.

Monstrous Strength Activated.

She cocked her head, but said nothing, raising her fists. I let my hands stay by my side, my stance loose and relaxed. Tek watched me with narrowed eyes, waiting for me to move.

I smiled.

Tek darted forward, coming at me with a left hook. I moved in a blur, her fist grazing my cheek as I slipped past her guard, driving a knee into her stomach with growing fury. She grimaced but stayed standing, Fatyr whooping when she backed up.

I followed, not giving her a second to recover and snapped out a flurry of kicks. Out of the corner of my eye, I saw a crowd gathering, people abandoning their sparring, rock-climbing, and sprints. But I focused on Tek. *You want a "real" fight?* I thought fiercely, my foot catching her shoulder, sending her sliding back. *Then I'll make damn sure you get one.*

Tek swung for me, catching me in the chin. She grinned fiercely, and I smiled in return, grabbing her wrist and snapping my head forward. I drove my skull into hers, a pickaxe to the stone she'd broken hours before. She crumpled like wet tissue, blood spurting from her nose in a wide, almost beautiful arc.

The boom when she hit the ground echoed throughout the hall. She blearily raised a floppy fist as if to strike me, but in a heartbeat I was on top of her, one hand in her leathers, the other at her neck.

"I am death's mistress—bow before me."

Fury's Claw Activated.

Claws inched out, pressing into the soft flesh of her throat.

She froze, eyes wide.

"Only cowards kick the crap out of kids half their size," I hissed. "Got it?"

Tek nodded, smiling, blood coating her mouth and chin.

Wait, smiling?

I looked up to see the crowd around me staring in silence. Then someone clapped, and it broke the damn, and the vaxion began whooping and cheering as they applauded. At first I thought it was because I'd won the fight, but then I realized they weren't staring at Tek, or even me. Not really. They were staring at my *hands*.

"You have *claws*!" yelled Esia over the noise, punching the air. "I didn't think anyone but—"

"*Zara*," called a voice that reverberated through my chest. Instantly the vaxion fell silent, the crowd dispersing in seconds. Still straddling Tek, I looked up to see Ashira standing on the far side of the room, fury rolling off her like a storm.

Uh-oh.

She walked out of the room without a word, but I knew she meant for me to follow. I sighed in irritation, blood still pumping from the fight. What was it now? Did I beat Tek up "the wrong way"? Was there a vaxion tradition of dancing in your opponent's intestines that no one had told me about?

Retracting my claws, I got off Tek, walking off without a backward glance.

Ashira stood just out of sight, hidden by the curve of a narrow corridor that led down to the main hall. The air was sharp and musty with the smell of sweat—me, I realized. I wiped my brow as Ashira stood with her back to me, muscles bulging from the force with which she crossed her arms. "Do you take joy in reminding them of what they lost?" she spat, turning on me.

"I took great joy in educating a grown-ass woman on why you shouldn't beat up a kid," I replied, unable to keep the bite out of my words.

Ashira's lip twitched, the hint of a fang peeking out. "So you chose to taunt everyone with what they will never have?"

I blinked, confused. "What are you talking about?"

She roughly grabbed my hand, turning it upward. "Nature's fang. The gifts Ravenna bestowed upon us when the Tyrant first lay claim to this world."

It took me a moment to realize she was talking about my claws. I frowned, my mind scrabbling. Suddenly the knives used to chop vegetables and the pickaxes to break rock made sense. A slow, horrifying sense.

"You mean… the other vaxion don't have claws anymore?" I asked, shocked.

Ashira's eyes widened. "It is as Yemena said." She dropped my palm. "You do not remember."

Taking a breath, she raised her hand. Claws inched from the tips of her fingers like angry splinters, and her feet grew in turn. Her cheek twitched, pulsing as she ground her teeth. It *hurt* her. Her own claws were hurting her.

"I alone can do this," she said. "Or so I thought. Yet you wield Ravenna's gifts without a second thought."

I didn't mention Lukas, or that he could do it too. Not only was it not my secret to tell, but at that moment he was the farthest thing from my mind. The *enormity* of what she had just said was still sinking.

"Wait, if the others can't use their claws, does that mean they can't transform…?"

Ashira's fists clenched, the dark pain in her eyes making me regret asking. "We thought no price too high," she said quietly. "We are vaxion—we refuse death. It was beaten into me, and I in turn beat it into every one of you. I thought there was nothing worse than ending up dead in a hole, wet soil covering my face." She closed her eyes, grief etched into every line of her face. "I was wrong."

She looked so like Zara at that moment, I had to fight not to reach out and take her hand. "Ashira," I said quietly. "What happened here? What happened to the—to us?"

She looked away, a hand covering her eyes. I thought she would walk off, as was her habit, or maybe yell at me some more. Instead, she sighed heavily.

"Yemena is the storyteller, not I. But I will try."

***

"It started as a cough. Such a small, insignificant thing. One moment, the little ones were wrestling in the dirt, their coils barely sparking the air. The next, they were gasping for water they could not swallow. They vomited until their insides turned out and lay beneath the stars, eyes wide and sightless, bodies left bereft of life.

"It claimed the children first. The young die, of course, if they cannot keep up on a hunt or if they challenge the wrong claw to a fight. It is the way of life. It is natural.

"But what happened to us was anything but natural."

Ashira's shoulders dipped with unseen weight. Her voice was hypnotic, her words so vivid I could almost *see* what happened. As if it were a dream. Or a memory.

Zara's memory.

"Our villages fell to sickness," she said. "Taskir. Gowas. Valo. Xani. Umin, where I found you. That was one of the last. More vaxion fell than we had hands to prepare the soil for their return to Ravenna's embrace.

"The sickness claimed everyone. Everyone that is, except the *molger.*" At this, Ashira burned with a rage that dwarfed Zara's. The gold of her eyes, so like my own, bored into my soul as she pulled me into her hatred.

"It began with the molger. Their elders were the first to cough. The first to hole up in their beds, weak with fever. Yet *they* did not die. They did not watch their young shrivel like sun-dried flesh, torn apart from the inside. The molger, who use their gifts to *dig holes* and hunt for *grubs!*" Spittle formed on her lips. She looked feral. "Exile was a *mercy*. Had I the numbers, I would have slaughtered every one of them as they cowered in their "dens."

There, I thought. There she is. The Ashira of legend. The vaxion rage that tore families apart and left the molger homeless. Carried along by her anger, it took me a moment to put the pieces together.

"That's why you kicked all the molger out of Moonvale Mountains," I said, unable to keep the horror from my voice. "You were trying to stop the disease from spreading. They had no idea, did they?" I asked, already knowing the answer. But I wanted to hear her say it.

"Of *course* not," she said, eyes flashing. "They may have burrowed their noses in Moonvale's dirt, but our ways were separate. Our people secluded. It was the only thing that saved us. Had they known how sick we were, they would have torn through us like gravediggers, robbing us of our lives, our *pride*."

And suddenly Zara's anger and her distrust of everyone made sense. It wasn't something she'd been born with. It was something she'd learned—from Ashira.

A memory sparked from my time with Lenia. She'd been telling me about how she got together with her husband. Her mother had fallen ill with a mysterious illness, and he'd mixed together an antidote for her. The sickness had only affected a handful of molger, and no one had died from it—no one except Lukas' dad. Because it was *curable*.

"Did you… have you heard of something called *Blackroot Cleanse?*" I said awkwardly, trying and failing for nonchalance.

"Do you think me stupid?" she asked, suddenly inches from me, her voice so quiet it was almost a whisper.

"N-no. Of course not—"

"Do not think, as the months wore on, and the molger rose from their beds, fresh as First Dawn, that I did not seek out answers? That I did not press a bloodied claw to his throat and demand he tell me of his '*Blackroot Cleanse'?*"

My heart pounded so loud I was sure she would hear it. She was talking about *Rowan*, Lenia's husband. I almost said his name. "Did you kill him? The one who made the antidote?" I asked, proud at how steady my voice was.

"Of course," she said as if it were the most obvious thing in the world. "The exile had begun, yet the molger dallied. He came to me, begging to stay in Moonvale until his woman gave birth. When I demanded he tell me how he cured the molger, he claimed he was only too happy to help." Her lip curled in disgust. "*Blackroot Cleanse* was known to Yemena. She had mixed it countless times, yet it did nothing. He had our salvation in his paws, and yet he let our young die screaming. He was a liar who did not deserve to live."

"He was telling the *truth*," I said before I could stop myself. "The molger weren't 'hiding' some magic potion that could fix the vaxion. They didn't even know you were sick! And you did a hell of a lot more than kill him. You dumped his body outside Lenia's home with a note stuck to his chest! What is *wrong* with you?" I said, remembering the tears in Lenia's eyes, how she'd blamed herself for her husband's death all this time when it had been Ashira all along.

Ashira's eyes narrowed. She snapped out a hand, quick as lightning, gripping my chin in her hands. "*I* did no such thing, Zara. *You* did."

Chapter Fifty-Three

"Me?" I said stupidly, my mind going blank.

"I ripped out his throat, but it was you who dragged the corpse to his woman's door, splaying his innards wide. You who penned his woman a note, saying 'Any woman worth her claw can raise a babe alone.' You were only eleven years old, yet it was your words that pushed the last of the molger to flee like dogs."

Ashira's fingers slipped to my throat like a vice. God, she was strong.

"You have no memory of the sickness that has left us near extinct or of the mage's deal, yet you claim the molger innocent. You know the name of the molger's woman. How? How do you know this?"

I jerked back, but Ashira held me tightly. I'd need *Monstrous Strength* just to get away. If it came to a fight... I was dead.

I might already be.

"You spoke to them, didn't you? Debased yourself with the very fiends who crippled us!" she spat. "The sickness began with them, yet it was not they who suffered. *You* paid the price for our salvation, yet you *defend* them?"

I struggled to take in what she said. It was important, I knew, another hint, another clue as to the mystery that was Zara and why the vaxion lost their shapeshifting powers, but the words slipped from my understanding like water through splayed fingers. My vision blurred as her claws dug into my throat.

"*Now is not the time for sleep*, shek!" snapped Zara, her voice bursting through the fog like a firework. "*Faint, and Ashira will slaughter us.*"

I slapped Ashira's wrist, but her grip tightened. She lifted me clear off the ground, my legs kicking uselessly.

"I knew such fortune would turn false," Ashira said, her voice low with grief. "For how long have I prayed to Ravenna for your return? For you to kill the mage, so you might return to me? Only now you stand before me—eyes dull, memory fragmented. You are not the Zara I know. The one I was willing to burn for, had Magnus only wanted me and not you."

Ashira pressed her forehead to mine, but it no longer felt comforting. It felt like a farewell. "I should have killed you long ago. But I was weak. *Selfish*. No more. You deserve better, little star."

"*Do exactly as I tell you, human,*" Zara said, her voice calm, despite the death that shone in Ashira's eyes. My mind flashed to the wallow-tail, and the last time Zara had given me "advice."

"*Hah! Don't flatter yourself, parasite. I see now that death would be a mercy. And I'll grant you no such blessing. Listen…*"

My eyes flared open as Zara lent me the fury that was her namesake.

"**If the world will not yield,**" I roared, one hand gripping Ashira's forearm, the other raised to strike her. "Then I will break it."

Monstrous Strength Activated.

Ashira's eyes lit up. She grabbed my raised hand, nearly crushing my wrist as she stopped me in my tracks, but Zara had a different plan.

One hand on Ashira's forearm, my other gripped in her hands, I *swung* my lower body forward, kicking out. Surprised, Ashira twisted at the last second, moving around me in a flash of lightning. I hovered in mid-air, time seeming to slow as she appeared to my left, my head turning in time to see her answer with a kick of her own.

She caught me in the ribs, sending me shooting across the corridor. I hit the stone wall with a meaty slap, blood bursting from my nose.

"*As expected,*" Zara said calmly when I hit the floor, stars in my eyes. "*Use our claws, then repeat what I say. Do not deviate.*"

As expected?! Zara, this is suicide. We can't—

"*WORD FOR WORD, PARASITE.*"

"**I am death's mistress.**" Blood clogged my mouth, making it hard to speak. Ashira approached, her pace slow and measured.

"**Bow before me,**" I finished, my final words a furious whisper.

Fury's Claw Activated.

At this, Ashira's eyes widened. Though whether it was with pride, envy, or loathing, I couldn't tell.

"Refuse death," I said, getting to one knee. "You taught me it is this and this alone that makes us vaxion. Not our powers. Not the beasts who thrum within our souls, begging for release. *Refuse. Death.*"

Ashira stopped, eyes narrowed.

On my feet, I reached for the wall to steady myself but stopped at Zara's hiss. I raised my arms dramatically, ribs crying out in pain. "Yet what do I find, upon my return? You—cowering in a rock like a swaddled babe."

Ashira's eyes flared with rage, her own claws inching out, even as her lips pulled back in pain. Every instinct screamed at me to run, but in that moment, I did the bravest thing I'd ever done.

I took a step forward.

"You stick to the old ways with your little 'First Dawns' and 'Twilights,' playing pretend in this graying shell you call *life*. Where are the vaxion who roamed Moonvale, fighting and feasting as they pleased? Where are the vaxion who hunted *xandi* for the sheer thrill of it?"

I stepped forward again. Ashira stayed where she was, a vein throbbing in her neck.

"And where is the Ashira who would slit my throat for questioning her as I do now?" I raised my chin, daring her to do it, even as my mind screamed I was going to die. The air crackled with tension, and I fought to keep looking into those golden eyes.

Then Ashira *smiled*.

"Perhaps you are still in there, little star," she said, turning on her heel and walking away. "You will sit next to me at Moon Peak. We have much to discuss."

It was only when she'd disappeared down the corridor that I collapsed, clutching my throbbing nose. "*That was not entirely terrible, parasite,*" Zara said, unable to hide the note of approval in her voice.

***

Zara didn't want to talk about the vaxion. The fact that they'd lost their powers, that only a handful remained, or that a mysterious sickness almost wiped them out. No, she only wanted to talk about one thing.

Ashira.

"She *sold me* to Magnus to save her own pathetic skin!" she hissed, yanking at her hair. "She sentenced me to a decade of torment with a *worm*, so she could live inside a *rock*?"

"I think there's more to it than that," I said, trying to keep my voice level. "Remember what she said? That the mage had wanted you, and not her? It sounds like she would have gone in your place."

"Tch. What use is guilt, other than to cower behind one's mistakes? Why paw at the door of forgiveness, other than to avoid punishment?" young Zara snapped. "She is as much a coward as the blood-spiked mongrels she used to enslave!"

I raised my hands, trying to calm her. "It sounds like the vaxion made a deal with Magnus, but there's so much about this I don't understand. Why was Magnus even here? He specializes in ice magic, not healing, so how did he cure a plague? And why did the vaxion get so sick? Do the molger have some kind of resistance to it? That might explain why *Blackroot Cleanse* didn't work. It has no effect on critical ailments."

Zara looked at me with what I had taken to calling glare number four: "I don't understand, but I don't want to tell you I don't understand."

"It isn't meant for serious illnesses," I clarified.

"The how and why matter not!" she hissed. "Ashira should have *died* alongside every other pathetic excuse for a vaxion." If it were anyone else, I'd think they didn't mean it, but I knew Zara better than that.

"Look, Magnus is still out there. Which means everything we can find out about him, and what happened here, is an advantage against him we didn't have before," I said, changing tactics. "Yemena might know more. That's why you wanted me to talk to her, right?" I asked, hazarding a guess.

She hit me with glare number two: "You're right, and I don't like it."

"We have no more need of the witch," she said after a long pause. "She promised to reveal why I'd been sold to the mage—I have my answer."

I hesitated, knowing I had to tread carefully. "Maybe. But something about this whole thing feels… off. We're missing something, I know it."

"Do whatever you want, parasite," she said, throwing up her walls once more. I sighed. At least we'd managed a civil conversation.

"There is one thing I wanted to ask you," I said, regretting it when her eyes narrowed with glare number five: "I'm picturing what your insides look like on the outside." "The other vaxion have been acting strangely," I said quickly. "You've been gone for a decade, but they haven't asked me a single question. Nothing about Magnus or if I'm even all right. I spent the morning mopping floors and chopping vegetables, like you'd never left. Is that… normal?"

Zara's lip twisted in disgust but not aimed at me. "It is meant as a 'gift,'" she said finally, her voice making it obvious she thought it was anything but. "When a vaxion is forced from Moonvale, be it to kill one who has wronged them or because of a flight of Ashira's fancy, they are not exiled. If they *prove* they are vaxion true, they may return, and the clan will wipe the wrongdoing from their minds."

"And act like you never left," I said, understanding dawning. She nodded.

"I used to think it a kindness," she said, looking away.

My heart swelled. "Zara, I'm—"

"Go. Before you are whipped for napping," she said. At her words, the darkness began to brighten, but she didn't look away.

"Thank you," I said as she faded. "For saving me from Ashira."

Zara didn't answer, her eyes locked on mine with an intensity identical to her aunt's.

***

I awoke in my bundle of furs back in "my" room. When I'd walked away from Ashira with a bloodied nose, the rest of the vaxion in the training room had pointedly focused on whatever they'd been doing. Only Tek nodded to me, her face still streaked with blood.

I'd ignored her, stumbling back to my room where I'd fallen asleep in seconds, for once eager to speak to Zara.

I scrambled out of bed, worried I'd slept through the rest of Second Dawn and into Moon Peak, Zara's quip about being "whipped" ringing in my ears. A small basin of water had appeared in one of the cubby holes, next to what looked like a pair of loose black trousers and a long black scarf. Washing the blood from my nose, which thankfully no longer felt like crushed glass, I picked up the clothes. Made of a soft, luxurious silk, they slid through my hands like water.

"Were you thinking a xandi knot or maybe a twisted witterfly? I think either would suit you," Jaza called from behind.

I smiled at her—she'd made a point of stomping down my corridor loudly.

"For Moon Peak?" I asked, holding the clothes up. "And the 'feast' that isn't to celebrate my return but just so happens to be on tonight?"

Jaza laughed, a beautiful tinkling sound. "I see our ways are returning to you, though I wouldn't speak so boldly to the others. They won't find it as endearing as I do. Now let us get dressed."

She removed her leathers, pulling out black robes just like mine. She slipped on the trousers, then began to tie the black scarf around her chest and arms in a complicated series of knots I could barely follow, despite how slow she was doing it for my benefit. When I managed to tie my elbow to my wrist, she gave up all pretense.

"There," she said, stepping back to admire her work. "Not even Ashira could find fault in your knotwork."

"Yes, 'my' knotwork," I said, looking down at the intricate ropes she wrapped around my neck and chest, but left my stomach and shoulders bare. I rolled a shoulder experimentally. Despite how tied up I was, my movement wasn't limited in any way. Stylish yet battle-ready—how very vaxion.

"Come." She smiled. "Tek is bringing her famous honey mead, and Himora managed to scrounge up some spike-hogs. We are in for a *feast*."

Chapter Fifty-Four

Dinner was divine, spike-hog grilled to perfection served on a thin bread that burst with spices. Esia's usual seat next to Ashira was pointedly empty when I entered the hall, and he now sat where I had at lunch. No one commented when I took his seat, nor did Ashira speak to me. As with lunch, she passed the food to the person on her left, me in this instance, without taking anything from it until the second round.

I looked for Yemena, who had left Zara badly shaken, though she'd tried to hide it. I hadn't seen her at all that day, not since her grand entrance when I'd first arrived. But the strange witch was nowhere to be seen, nor did anyone seem worried by her absence. I'd been honest with Zara when I said the more we learned about Magnus, the greater our advantage. But that wasn't the only reason I was hoping to speak to Yemena. If anyone knew more about the blood debt that bound Lukas to me, it was her.

Tek appeared at my shoulder, a clay bottle half her size hefted on her shoulder. She gestured to my empty cup, and I hurried to hold it up to her. With a satisfying pop, she uncorked the bottle, leaning forward. The scent of honey filled the air as golden liquid poured from it, filling my cup to the brim. She made no mention of our earlier fight, but I noticed she was extra polite to Esia now, taking care to gently pass his food to him.

Halfway through the first course, Yemena appeared. While the rest of the vaxion were dressed in black twisting scarves like me, she looked exactly as she had when I'd arrived, the wound that split her face in two seeming to pulse in the dim light.

Yemena took the cup Tek presented to her but didn't sit.

"Ravenna, mother of fang, breaker of tyrants," she said, her voice surprisingly high. "When the world fell to darkness, she gifted us with claws. When the Tyrant's foot split the earth, she blessed the soil—gifting us Moonvale. And when the Tyrant tried to break us?"

"We called down the lightning!" Esia said, leaping out of his seat with excitement.

Fatyr yanked him back down with a smile.

Yemena grinned, revealing teeth stained with blood. I wondered if it was permanent.

"Our flesh became clay, to be molded to our will. Our hearts thrummed with Ravenna's light from which we commanded the sky blade—we commanded lightning!" Yemena's voice rose to a crescendo, and the vaxion howled in answer. Fists thumped the table, almost lifting it from the ground. I cheered along with them, their energy infectious.

"But what Ravenna grants, she can take away," Yemena said, the table immediately sobering. "Long we have toiled within the waterstone, waiting for a sign of her will, of our fate. And now we have it."

As one, the vaxion raised their cups—to *me*. I froze, eyes brimming with hope locked onto mine as everyone but Ashira stared at me. The room was silent, cups raised, arms locked, but the vaxion leader remained still as a statue. The silence dragged on, the air thick with tension as I prayed for the ground to swallow me up.

Zara, I thought at her, *what the hell do I do?*

I could feel Zara watching from the back of my mind, but she said nothing. Then Ashira let out a long sigh. She took her cup and raised it.

"To Zara!" Esia cried, unable to contain himself.

"*To Zara*!" came the resounding cry. Clay cups chinked against mine, and people reached over to pat me on the back while I took an awkward sip of my drink.

"Tek, this is *amazing*," I blurted out. "Honey, oranges, and is that… cinnamon?"

Tek said nothing, but I caught her smiling into her cup.

Once dinner plates were cleared, the dishes to be done during First Dawn tomorrow, the real party started. I quickly learned that the vaxion partied as hard as they worked. Tek's gigantic container of mead was empty by the time the piggyback races started.

Esia served as the judge, and I watched vaxion clamber up on each other's shoulders and sprint up and down the main hall. Fatyr was dancing the *Moon Shadow* by himself for the eighth time, having been abandoned by a mortified Esia. The dance involved scarves and the clacking of two bones together, as well as a partner.

But that didn't stop Fatyr. He snapped out his arms for his non-existent partner to leap into. Jaza eventually took pity on him and joined in, spinning him easily.

While she'd kept her distance from me during the feast, Jaza made a point to pass behind me on the way to the dance floor, her hand touching my shoulder, then Ashira's. I didn't miss how she lingered on Ashira's, squeezing it gently. The leader of the vaxion said nothing, but she did reach for her cup, taking a long drink from it.

I hadn't liked everything I'd seen and heard of the vaxion, and it would be a long time before I forgot the rage in Ashira's eyes when she talked about the molger. But it was hard to stay angry at people who laughed and joked like big, drunken children. Every day I spent in this world taught me that people weren't black and white, and I don't think there was anyone grayer than the vaxion.

Tek unearthed another pot from somewhere, and the vaxion cheered. Despite my protests, cup after cup was pressed into my hands. At one point, one of the piggybackers fell, crashing through the table, which shattered into pieces.

No one seemed remotely concerned.

Three cups later, my head was buzzing pleasantly. As I accepted another cup, I idly worried why I hadn't drunk very much back in my old life. I used to have wine with dinner, I seemed to remember. No, that wasn't right… I'd have a glass on special occasions, like a birthday, or Christmas, and it was always under an adult's watchful eye. Why was that?

I hadn't been old enough to drink, I realized. And I wouldn't be, not until my birthday, which was still weeks away…

I froze, nearly dropping my cup.

My birthday.

When I came to this world, I'd been a month away from my eighteenth birthday. An age I'd been desperate to see, diligently crossing out the days on my bedroom calendar every night. How long had I been here now? Five weeks? Six?

I looked down at my cup. Eighteen. I'd turned eighteen, and I hadn't even realized it.

"Zara," called a voice, cutting through the chatter. Yemena stood at my back, hand hovering over my shoulder but not touching it.

"I told Yemena to show you everything," Ashira said at my side, the first she'd spoken to me all evening. "When she is done, you and I will speak." Her hands gripped her cup, still half full from the single drink she'd taken at Jaza's encouragement.

I nodded mutely, her words feeling like more of a threat than usual.

Head fuzzy, I stumbled after Yemena. Did walking always take this much effort? Behind me, I heard a slap, and then a roar of delight. Things had turned to wrestling about two cups ago, with the slim, lithe Fatyr dominating the ring while Tek pointedly cheered from the sidelines.

Ahead of me, Yemena pressed a hand against the rock, then *pulled* it back. It took me a minute to understand she'd just drawn back a curtain the same color of the waterstone. She held it aside for me, dropping it when we were both inside. Between my swimming head and the darkness, I felt nauseous. I heard Yemena walk on but couldn't figure out which way she'd gone.

Tithe of Beasts Activated.

My hearing and sense of smell expanded. It didn't affect my eyes unfortunately, but I could use it to follow steps and—

"You are as at home in the dark as you are in the light," Yemena said, suddenly behind me. "You need only *feel* it." Her hand touched my shoulder, cold as the undergrotto waterfall. The darkness shimmered, twisting before my eyes as brushstrokes of gray outlined the tunnels that split ahead of me.

UPGRADE UNLOCKED—EYES OF THE HUNTER.

"How—how did you do that?" I whirled, but Yemena was gone, leaving behind only a graying afterimage.

"He binds you. Of that I have no control. But I can loosen your chains."

A rush of power filled the corridor, trailing along my skin like sharpened needles. Ashira's magic was like Zara's—wild and tempestuous. Yemena's was the opposite. Cold. Absolute. Immovable. Yemena beckoned me forward, taking care not to touch me as she guided us forward. I stumbled, trying to think through the mead and magic that clouded my mind. Yemena wasn't as strong as Ashira, nor was she weaker. Instead, she felt like the rod to Ashira's lightning. The anchor to her sail.

"Ashira's magic is tied to her beast. It is why, despite what we have lost, her flame still burns so brightly. Mine is also tied to my beast—the binding of it," Yemena said, her words answering my unspoken question. "I gave up my beast to better serve the vaxion. It is the blessing and the curse of a *shi'ara*. When the others lost their claws, my life was left little changed."

Light exploded, burning my eyes. I winced, deactivating my newly improved *Tithe of Beasts*. Blinking, I looked up to see we were in a small cavern, the walls outlined with the telltale mark of claws. Ashira's claws, I now realized. With the rest of the vaxion unable to use their claws, she must have carved the entire waterstone out herself.

The thought made my fingers ache.

Lanterns lined the walls, nailed into place rather than swinging from the ceiling like in my room and the main hall. The lights here were dim, lending the room an ominous glow. I stepped forward, confused as to where we were, when pinpricks of pain ran up my right foot, leaving it numb.

I looked down, stomach lurching at the red marks on the ground. A blood-red circle was painted onto the stone. I recognized the sigils from the gravedigger's tunnel in the mountains.

A binding. One for a hybrid, a "mongrel." A *tem'rix*.

Wrong. Bad. Run. Run! my instincts screamed, heart pounding. This was a bad place. Worse than the blood-circle I'd seen. Worse than the chains that had been nailed to the stone wall. "The body remembers, even if the mind does not," Yemena said, her voice echoing around the halls, each word vibrating with promise. "This is where you decided our fate, Zara."

Chapter Fifty-Five

"I said you were a sign from Ravenna," Yemena announced, stepping on the bloodied circle as if it didn't send shivers down her spine. "That much is true. But the nature of the sign is your decision. You may kill us. Or you may save us. The choice is yours."

"I—I don't know what you're—"

"Not you, human," Yemena said. "Zara."

I froze. She *knew*.

Yemena glided toward me, head cocked to the side. She dragged her index and middle finger along her wound, digging it into the flesh. Before I could move, she darted forward, pressing bloodied fingers against my eyes.

There was darkness. A darkness I'd seen many times when sitting across from a silent Zara, her back to me in her vaxion form. And more recently when she'd spoken to me as a child. I was in my *own* mind.

"Zara?" I called, looking around. My voice fell flat, almost engulfed by the darkness. How did I get here? Where was she?

Then I heard her voice. A muffled echoing, the words slipped from my understanding. Someone answered in-kind—Yemena. I concentrated, trying to make sense of the words. They crackled one second, then flared to life like a battered radio the next.

Suddenly I could see the bloodied circle and Yemena, but I couldn't move, though my eyes did. Couldn't speak, though my lips formed words—because Zara was in control.

***

"... could banish the parasite, why did you not do it sooner?" Zara snarled. She'd been a fool to think she could trust the witch. They may not be able to lie, but they twisted the truth until it became unrecognizable.

"As I said, I can only loosen your chains. Not remove them," Yemena replied calmly.

"Then what is the point of you?" Zara snapped. "Why dangle the promise of my body, only for the parasite to snap it away?"

"*Zara?*" cried the girl-child. "*Zara, what's going on? Hello? Can you hear me? What's—*" Zara tuned out the mosquito-like cries of the invader. Soon, she couldn't hear them at all.

Yemena sighed. It was the most human she'd ever appeared. "You were meant to come to me in your own time, for the truth is both a gift and a burden. It is *not* something to be forced upon the unwilling. But Ashira insisted."

"Does she know about…?" Zara tapped the side of her head, unwilling to say the words aloud. Shame burned her cheeks. Ashira would never have let a *human* take over her body.

"No," Yemena said. When Zara breathed a sigh of relief, Yemena added. "Though she suspects something is wrong. It is only a matter of time before she discovers the truth."

"When she does, she'll kill me." Zara laughed, a harsh sound. "I'll die wishing she'd done it sooner. Wishing she'd had the courage when I was a child. Anything would have been better than shipping me off to Magnus like a prized *cow*."

"She didn't send you to Magnus," Yemena said.

Zara almost laughed. "Ashira said it herself, witch. Don't twist the truth."

"Did she?" Yemena cocked her head to the side.

Frowning, Zara skimmed through the parasite's conversation with Ashira. Annoyed, she found the witch was right.

"When Magnus arrived at Moonvale, clean and unmarked despite the gravediggers he fought and the mountains he climbed, we thought him a sign." Yemena looked away. "*I* thought him a sign. The people I'd bound my beast to protect were dying, no matter how much magic I poured into them. And then Magnus, a *human*, placed a hand on Tek. She lay blind and deaf from sickness, death a mere breath away. Yet one touch brought her back."

Yemena closed her eyes, her mystic veneer vanishing beneath raw grief. "He offered to save us, asking for one thing in return—you. Ashira refused." Yemena opened her eyes, her voice deadpan once more. "You did not."

Rage flared in Zara's chest. How stupid she felt for thinking she would finally get a straight answer. "*Lies*. No vaxion would accept such a deal! Death comes to those who accept it. If the vaxion fell to sickness, we deserved it! Because we were *weak*. I would *never* sacrifice my life, my freedom for another. *Never.*"

The last word was a violent hiss that echoed around the cavern. In the dim light, the bloodied circle beneath her feet seemed to shimmer.

"You are correct," Yemena said, dipping her head slightly. "That is... was our way. And were it any other time, any other place, you would not have done it. Nor would Ashira have let you."

The witch paused, and Zara felt a rare moment of hesitation from her. "But you did not do it to save us," Yemena continued. "Nor to save Ashira, who had already begun to vomit so hard, she fell unconscious at my feet.

"You did it to become a true vaxion once more—to earn back your place here. You were only eleven years old, but you spoke with the wisdom of those three times your age. I had no right to refuse you. Nor did Ashira."

Yemena held out her hand, which looked pale and small in the light. "Let me show you."

Zara's heart pounded with the weight of a thousand xandi hooves, her world tilting. Part of her, a small, terrified part, could guess what Yemena spoke of. But to speak it aloud would tear apart what little sense of self she clung to with white-knuckled fury. Could she do it? Could she see?

"I—"

The walls shook with a thunderous *boom*. Yemena's eyes went wide, her head jerking left and right with unnatural speed, her body twitching.

Zara wasn't disturbed by the noise, or the witch's strange, supernatural movements. Instead it yanked her out of the spell Yemena's words had woven and the doubt the witch had seeped into her heart.

She knew who she was. And would die before she let Yemena, Ashira, or the *parasite* try to trick her into thinking otherwise.

"They're here! How? It is too much. Too soon. Tek? No!" Yemena's words were a harsh cry, but her lips barely moved. Her body unnaturally still.

"Enough of your riddles!" Zara snapped. "Speak plainly, or I'll snap your neck, Ravenna's fury be *damned*."

"*He* is here!" Yemena flailed, ignoring Zara's words. It was only then that Zara noticed the cloud of magic that roiled behind Yemena's eyes. "The forked path crumbles. The choice is polluted. Fate tainted!"

Yemena's entire body shook while Zara looked on, disgusted at what she deemed mere theatrics. With a jerk, the *shi'ara* fled through the tunnel, back the way they'd come. Zara watched her go with a sigh.

Blasted witches.

"… ra? Zara! Thank goodness. I don't know what happened. I couldn't hear or see for a minute."

Zara sighed. Like all mosquitos, this one had returned with an irritating vengeance.

"Get used to the darkness, parasite," Zara snarled. "I have no intention of letting you chain me again."

She was so focused on the girl, she missed the hairs that rose on the back of her neck and the speed with which her heart pounded. In a way, the witch had been right. The body remembered, even if the mind did not.

"My Fury? Is it really you?" the voice of nightmares echoed through the chambers. Adrenaline flooded her body, the world narrowing to a knife's edge. That voice. The voice that made her want to rip her skin off and stuff it into her ears. The voice she'd do anything to never hear again.

A laugh of relief. Not hers.

"It *is* you. I knew he would lead me back to you. I *knew* it."

She turned.

He stood smiling with too-white teeth, the blond hair he demanded she brush for hours was tied back from his face. Gone were his resplendent robes and silk slippers. Instead, he'd donned worn traveling clothes he'd have once spurned with disgust. He was thinner now and looked closer to the corpse she dearly wished he was. But his eyes were the same—gray, bright, and eager, they locked onto hers, a smokescreen of affection masking the cruelty she knew lay just beneath. Only one thing was different—his arm.

His right arm was gone.

Magnus stepped into the dim light, gasping with joy. He held something in his remaining hand, but Zara's mind couldn't process it. Her claws inched from her fingers.

"It's all right, my love," he said, raising his only hand. In it, he grasped the bloodied head of Yemena, fingers digging into her hair. The witch's jaw hung slack, her eyes wide and afraid as her eternal wound wept even in death.

"I know you weren't in your right mind before. An alien plagues you, but I can get rid of it." He smiled, eyes alight with devotion. "You need only say the word."

Chapter Fifty-Six

Valerius shifted his weight to the side, his hair ruffling as a fist brushed his cheek, slamming into the wall behind him. He smiled when the waterstone shook, the force of the woman's blow splitting the stone.

Good. He needed a challenge.

Gray threaded her eyebrows, yet the older woman was the first to move when he strode into the waterstone's hall, the stink of vaxion, sweat, and mead assaulting his nostrils.

Now she spun to face him, her blunt teeth bared, her still-human hands small. *Pitiful.* He spun his blade, feinting to the right, then leaped forward, driving it through her chest at the last second. She gasped, a small, insignificant sound. With a jerk, he yanked his sword free, his quest shining in his mind.

TEMPER THE VAXION.

One down, he thought, the woman falling to her knees, babbling like a newborn babe. Someone at the table half screamed, half cried, "Tek!"

He'd heard about the vaxion when he'd first arrived in this world. How they transformed into sleek, murderous beasts with the power to command lightning. How they fought with suicidal rage, bringing down countless enemies before death claimed them. He laughed now at the thought.

The heyday of the vaxion was gone. In the place of the legendary falslings he found a handful of sprawling drunks, bereft of their beast forms. Magnus hadn't been exaggerating—he really had crippled them. To think the vaxion had been hiding here all this time, praying their reputation would be enough to protect them… it would've been funny, if it wasn't so pathetic.

"Tek, no! Stop it, get away from her! *Get away!*" The young boy cried again.

"Gu… gu…" Tek babbled, blood dripping from her lips.

With a graceful swing, his sword lashed out, cutting her head off. As her body hit the floor, her head half a second behind, a woman stood. She was the largest of the vaxion, and the others crowded around her with wide, terrified eyes. Valerius' gaze sketched over her, smiling in recognition. Golden eyes, sun-kissed skin, a death-filled glare—she could have been Zara's twin. He snapped his sword to the side, blood leaping from his blade and decorating the floor.

"I'll kill you!" the boy squeaked, his childish rage echoing in the silence. A man held him back, tears rolling down his cheeks. A crying vaxion? Now that was a sight. "I'll kill you, I'll kill you, I'll—"

"He is *mine*," Ashira said, her deep voice carrying easily across the room. Valerius felt a thrill at the power that roiled from her. Either Magnus was sloppy, and he hadn't dealt with this one or…

Valerius cracked his neck loudly. Ashira's lip drew back to reveal fangs already inches long.

… or her own magic trumped the mage's, trumped even the Tyrant's. That, if nothing else, impressed him.

"Ashira, I take it?" he said, dropping into a fighting stance.

"Do not speak my name, worm," she answered, stepping onto what looked like the remnants of a table, broken and splintered. Valerius only laughed at her insult. He loved when NPCs had good banter—it made them more realistic.

"Kitty has claws," he jabbed, enjoying how her eyes flared. "Or the kitties did until Magnus came along. Tell me, how—"

His words were lost as the wall behind him *exploded*.

A shape came flying through the air, almost lost among the spray of stone. The waterstone shook, dust and debris falling from the ceiling. Valerius ducked behind his shield, one eye on Ashira.

The vaxion smiled. It was not a smile he liked.

The air crackled as the temperature dropped, his hair lifting as static clung to it. Above him, thick black clouds gathered. He blinked in confusion. Clouds? But they were *inside* the waterstone.

A piece of the rubble coughed, and Valerius dragged his eyes back to the floor. He sighed when he realized one of the dark shapes was Magnus, regretting the brief moment of credit he'd given the mage. Could the man do nothing right?

A foot crunched on gravel behind him. Valerius turned, his breath vanishing at the gold eyes that bored into him, her rage and hatred intoxicating. Zara stood before him. Not the cowering creature he'd met in Magnus' dungeon. No, in her place stood the storm who made his heart thunder—the *Fury*. She smiled, lightning coiling around her like vipers.

"Hello again, little princeling."

***

Zara didn't know what was going on, nor did she care. Magnus was *here*. And she was going to do what she should have done years ago.

She stepped over Tek's body, her mind only registering it briefly. Tek had failed. She wouldn't.

Magnus curled up like a cowering babe, gray with dust. Zara eyed Valerius, the Gilded Knight who'd once left Eternity out for her on a silver platter. Who'd ensured that when Zara stole Gallow's Chosen, it was without fight or fuss. As expected, the prince did what he did best.

He stood aside.

Zara looked to Ashira with a warning look—*this kill is mine*. She expected her aunt to protest, or nod in approval. There was a first time for everything, after all.

But Ashira's smile slid away when she watched Magnus struggle to his knees, half strangled by his own cloak. Emotions flitted across her aunt's face: grief, anger, pain, before settling on something Zara had never seen in Ashira's eyes.

Fear.

"You said he was *dead*," Ashira snarled.

"He's about to be." Zara shrugged, only paces from the mage now.

"*Now*," Ashira hissed, eyes wide with panic. "Kill him *now*, before—"

"I was ready to welcome you back with open arms. To purge the invader who puppets your body," Magnus said, head bowed.

Ashira narrowed her eyes at his words.

"But I see now that freedom has undone all the good work we did. You're still the ungrateful brat I had to order to eat. To drink. You're still *useless* without me."

Ashira appeared behind him in a blur, her claws fully extended, aiming for the mage's neck. Instead they met Valerius' shield in a flurry of sparks. Ashira leaped back with a growl, and Valerius followed, sword meeting claw.

Zara ignored them.

She leaped for Magnus, years of hate and torment lending her a roar that could shatter stone. Magnus looked up at her, and she saw the mask slip. Saw the dead-eyed look of the man who once made her eat glass. He said only one word.

"Kneel."

She almost laughed. Did he think he still had a hold on her? That she—

Pain lit up her body, her back arching as her knees folded, sending her crashing to the ground. A sharpened piece of stone dug into her leg, deep enough to chip bone, but she couldn't move. Could scarcely breathe.

"Did you think I let you go?" he asked, cupping her face.

She snarled, trying to bite him.

"Don't move," he said.

She froze, her body as unyielding as stone. "*Invader, what is this?*" she thought, refusing to panic. Panic would mean he'd won. "*Whatever magic you force upon me, undo it. He'll kill us both!*"

"*It's not me!*" she answered. "*I have no idea how he's doing this.*"

"You're speaking to it now, aren't you?" Magnus smiled. "Your visitor from another world? He'll be angry with me if I bind it, but I'm willing to do it, Zara. There's no one else I'd risk his wrath for but you."

Zara growled, sweat beading on her forehead as she fought to raise her claws and drive them into his stomach.

"You just have to beg," he said, whispering in her ear like a lover. "I want to hear how much you *missed* me. How useless you are without me."

Zara closed her eyes, revulsion crawling up her skin like ants. "No," she hissed through lips that wouldn't move. "You will not... *break me.*"

He laughed, grabbing her right arm by the wrist and raising it gently. Her world went white at the angry, red scars that trailed along her forearm, lighting up at Magnus' touch. It was a scar she'd seen on the pathetic mongrels who bowed to

Ashira's will. A scar she'd seen on the blood-spiked Lukas who trailed after the invader like a puppy.

"Oh, little Zara. I broke you *years* ago."

Chapter Fifty-Seven

I watched in horror as the scar on Zara's arm lit up. Magnus leaned closer to her, to *us*, and whispered one word.

"Remember."

And just like that, Zara's memories came rushing back.

A young Zara, ten-years-old, the fire-wielding prodigy of the vaxion. She thrived among her kin in the Moonvale Mountains while their molger neighbors were kept at a watchful distance. She was set to become the strongest vaxion of the century, surpassing even Ashira.

And then, Zara's scent changed.

She denied it at first, as did Ashira. But soon her vaxion form, her white-furred pride, became volatile, her body refusing to fully shift as bone and gristle burst from her. The vaxion were no strangers to anger, nor did they shun it. But Zara's outshone even Ashira's, becoming a raging inferno that set fire to half the Moonvale Mountains, earning her her title— "The Fury."

Then the first vaxion, a man, fell to sickness. His death was a blip on Ashira's radar. He was weak. *Deserving*. But then another fell. And another. And soon the vaxion were forced to retreat farther into Moonvale, terrified the molger, the *world*, would discover the infamous vaxion were dying on their feet. Nothing conquered this illness—not Yemena's magic, not the *Blackroot Cleanse* that was the molger's saving grace. Nothing.

When Ashira hid Zara away, she was still conscious, oscillating between human and the feral beast her future promised, fighting it with everything she had. By night Ashira carved the tunnels that would become Zara's home and hunting grounds, by day the vaxion leader carried the sick, dug graves for the dying, and prayed for Yemena to find a cure that would never come.

Zara's world narrowed to the nights when her aunt unshackled her. With the tunnels finally completed, and the gravedigger's home an unexpected and welcome find, she felt the only joy she would for years to come, feasting on the shrieking, bird-like creatures until she fell into a bloodied, exhausted heap. She spent her eleventh birthday chewing on gravedigger hatchlings as if they were candy.

Seeing what she'd gone through, and the revulsion she felt at what she was becoming, I understood why she hated hybrids, why she hated *Lukas* so much. We despise in others the thing we hate most about ourselves.

When Magnus appeared, as if sent by Ravenna herself, he offered to heal the vaxion and ensure those who survived were immune. All he asked for in return was Zara. But he didn't want a girl trapped in the mind of a "half-slobbering beast," as he described her. He wanted the fire-wielding prodigy he'd dreamed of. He'd *obsessed* over.

Ashira refused. She'd rather kill her niece than subject her to such a fate. Yet every day she found an excuse to stay her hand, to wait and pray Zara would find a way to defeat the beast within. Ashira hadn't blinked when other vaxion died, happily killing more than her fair share. But it was easy to proclaim, "refuse death" and to shun "weakness" as if it were a disease when you didn't have to hold your niece in your arms, her fangs digging into your shoulder as she screamed.

She stayed her hand until it was too late. Ashira fell ill with the very sickness that was killing her people. Still, she refused Magnus' deal.

Zara didn't.

I saw her now in my mind's eye. Saw Ashira stubbornly standing, even as she swayed with fever. Saw Zara beckon her aunt to her. "I am vaxion," she whispered in Ashira's ear. "I *refuse death*. Do as he says. Tame my beast. Use Yemena's magic to gift him your new dominion over me. I will wait. I will watch."

Magnus stood to the side. He was different then. Nervous. Afraid. Jumping at every odd noise. Both he and his magic had smelled strange—like rusted blades.

"When I return—a true vaxion once more," Zara whispered, "you will know the mage is dead, and I am free."

And so the devil's deal was struck, for Magnus did as he promised. He saved the few vaxion who still breathed. Made it so the illness that once annihilated them would never again be a threat, but in doing so he *bound* their powers.

I saw it all unfold before me. Saw Zara arrive in a *trunk* to Magnus' castle like a shiny new toy. Saw the endless hours Magnus spent poking and prodding at her, at her thoughts, her memories. Saw him weave his new thread that her family had sold her to him. That she was hated and despised by her own people.

Until one day, his lies and her truth blurred into one.

She'd spent so long under his control, she no longer questioned it. He beat her, *tortured* her, then let her slaughter his horses, butcher his mercenaries, even kill an innocent minstrel in retaliation—all to make her think she had free will. To carefully maintain the illusion she had a *choice*.

Now he was back. And the illusion was gone. A single word was all it took to leave her helpless against him. I hadn't understood Lukas' fear of the blood-debt until now. It was *terrifying*.

I had to help her. But how? I was trapped in here, but even if I wasn't, what could I do against Magnus? I'd used *Inferno*, Zara's ultimate from *Knights of Eternity*, and I hadn't been able to stop him. I paced in circles, wracking my mind. Something was niggling at me, something about the scar on Zara's arm and the control Magnus wielded over her.

And then it came to me.

***

Zara's world collapsed.

Ashira went flying, crashing into the rock with a resounding thud. She was up in an instant, bleeding heavily. One of her claws had snapped, taking part of her finger with it. Blood pumped from it in rhythmic spurts.

Valerius smiled, twirling his blade in one hand in a movement that was as pointless as it was arrogant.

Zara took in these details haphazardly, snatching at them like fireflies in the night, anything to keep her sanity intact. She looked down at the scar on her forearm, proof she was pathetic. *Weak*. That her entire life was a lie.

"Let's start easy, shall we?" Magnus said, smiling. He'd won. And he knew it. "*Bow*."

Her body moved of its own volition, tilting her forward. She didn't fight it.

"Lower. *Lower*."

Her forehead touched the floor, tears pricking her eyes. *I deserve this*, she thought. *I am pathetic. I am weak.* She repeated these words to herself over and over, but they didn't help. They didn't stop the crushing wave of shame and self-loathing that threatened to bury her. Why hadn't she died? Why hadn't Ashira *killed* her? Her rage sparked—a welcome flame. Why hadn't Ashira done her duty and murdered her the moment she showed signs of turning?

I deserve this. I am pathetic. I am weak.

"I won't command you to say it. That defeats the purpose," he said, pressing a hand into her hair. Blood pooled around her from the wound in her leg, and she could no longer feel her knees. "But if you beg me to take you back. If you tell me how much you missed me, I'll free you from his puppet. I'll give you back your body."

She shook her head, unable to stop the act of defiance. *Kill me. Kill me, please.* She couldn't bring herself to say the words out loud, but she thought them with every fiber of her being, praying the mage would grant her that mercy.

Instead Magnus' booted heel came down on the back of her head, slamming her face into the stone, breaking her nose.

"Stupid. *Ungrateful.* Brat!" he yelled with the vindictive rage she knew so well. "I'm offering to defy a *god* for you! I could have rinsed out your mind and left you an empty-headed slave. Instead I gave you some measure of control. I made you feel like you had a *choice.* Your aunt didn't do that for her little blood-spiked slaves, did she? Do you remember what happened to them?"

She did. When they stopped trying to run away, they would simply stare into space, waiting for their next order. Bereft of autonomy, they became mere shells. And she hated them for it. Had never understood why they didn't fight back.

She did now.

"I could've done the same to you," he said. "And you would have deserved it. Wouldn't you?"

I am pathetic. I am weak.

"Yes," she said, feeling her soul sink into a dull grayness.

"Do you want that? Do you want me to do that to you?"

I am pathetic. I am weak.

"No," she whispered.

"Then beg, Zara, and I'll make this all go away. We'll go back to my castle, clear out whatever idiot lord the king has put in my place, and get rid of the creature in your head. *Or you can refuse me now, and I'll scoop out your soul until there is nothing left but a husk.* I won't let you die, Zara. Not for a long, long time. So, *choose*. I won't ask again."

"I…"

"Zara! Zara, I have an idea!" The invader's voice rang in her ears. *"Listen, it's about the mark, the blood debt on your arm. I think—"*

It is over, invader, Zara thought, her words deadpan. *Unless you can kill me, you're useless to me.*

This seemed to throw the parasite, who was silent for once. She could feel her taking in the scene around them, what little she could see with Zara's face nearly crushed into the stone.

Ashira growled at Valerius, who held his sword to Esia's neck, smiling.

Esia was crying, his hands clinging to Valerius' sword, blood pouring from his small fingers as the blade dug in.

The rest of the vaxion, once the most feared falslings in the land, now stood about like dumb cattle. Too scared, too useless to take on Valerius themselves.

The vaxion are no more. We deserve this. We deserve whatever—

Her cheek stung, but not from a blow from Magnus. Instead she felt the invader quiver with rage as she slapped Zara again. *"You are Zara the goddamned Fury. You don't cower, and you don't beg. You get up, and you fight!"*

For what? Zara argued, annoyed at the platitudes. *I'm a slave, a blood-spiked mongrel who doesn't deserve the air she breathes.*

"No. I won't let him do this. I won't let him hurt you, or the vaxion."

Zara laughed aloud.

Magnus, thinking her laughter was directed at him, kicked her in the face.

Blood poured from her already broken nose, stunning her. She could feel the invader's fear but was surprised to see it wasn't for her own skin. No, she was afraid for Zara.

You'll free me, will you? Like you promised to free Lukas?

"Damn right I will. And I'll prove it."

Zara felt herself vanish into her own mind and the darkness that once caged her. Now, however, the invader stood in her place. Zara almost laughed at the sight of her. She was half Zara's size and looked painfully young. *Naive.* It was hard to believe this was the creature who'd stolen her body.

Zara flexed her fingers, looking down at herself. She wasn't in her vaxion form, nor that of a child. She was an adult once more, the blood-debt that bound her to Magnus gleaming on her right arm.

"What do you want, parasite?" Zara sighed, an aching weariness setting in.

The invader said nothing. Instead, she raised her right forearm and *bit* it.

Zara watched in confusion as the girl tore at her arm with blunt teeth, pulling at the flesh until it bled. Taking a finger, she dug into the wound, tearing it wider. It hurt, Zara knew, she could see it in the girl's eyes. But the girl kept pulling and tearing until the cut was inches long and jagged.

"This is my blood debt to you," she said, holding out her bleeding arm. "We're going to stop Magnus. *Together.*"

Zara looked at the girl, whose eyes welled up with pain, but she refused to brush the tears away. Something was happening in the real world to her body, she could tell. The air was growing colder, her breath forming icicles in the air. The girl stared at her, teeth stained bloody, determination shining in her eyes.

It meant little. The girl was her warden. And yet… she'd treated Zara as an equal. Had refused to take advantage of Lukas when it would have been child's play to do so. Zara had mocked them both for it, once. How different she felt now that she was the one being dominated.

Zara's fists clenched. She should bow to Magnus. It was the sane, rational thing to do. If she didn't, she'd end up worse than dead. But if there was one thing she'd never been accused of, it was being sane.

She had one question though.

"Why help me? Do you pity me? Or is this some misguided sense of 'justice'?" Zara asked.

The girl didn't even hesitate. "No. I'm helping you because Magnus is a *bastard.*"

Zara laughed aloud, then reached out, clasping the girl's bleeding forearm. The invader winced but said nothing. The Fury took two fingers, dipping them in the girl's blood and painted a long line between their two arms—joining them.

"The debt is made. Now pay up, parasite."

Chapter Fifty-Eight

Magnus wanted to scream. He'd offered Zara everything, and she *still* pouted like a stubborn child. All he wanted to do was to help her, why couldn't she see that? He stopped himself from kicking her again, knowing even his Fury had limits, and if she died now, she'd win. Instead he placed a hand on her large, strong back. He splayed his fingers, ice bursting forth.

"I'm going to kill Ashira and the others now. You will wait here, unmoving, until I am done. That's an order."

The ice inched over Zara, melodically cracking until she was covered entirely, becoming a beautiful, crystalline statue.

Feeling affectionate, he patted her back once more, then turned to Valerius. The waterstone hall was littered with the bodies of the dead, blood no longer pouring from their cooling bodies. Ashira was somehow still standing, despite the wound that split one of her eyes in two. Valerius held a blade to a young boy's neck and kept taunting Ashira to strike. To prove she was still a vaxion.

The mage sighed. If Ashira still had her full powers, Valerius would be dead. The prince had the tactical acuity of a toddler and knew only one way to win a fight—"brute force."

At this rate, if he left Valerius to his own devices, they'd be here all night. Instead Magnus would deal the final blow, and was that not fitting? To finish what he'd started all those years ago when Calamity commanded him to unleash a plague on the vaxion? To sow chaos, by making it begin with the molger? Back then, he'd questioned his master's wisdom. Why push the vaxion to near-extinction, then leave them to rot? He'd been so new to this world he hadn't trusted in Calamity. Hadn't realized the gift Calamity had given him by bringing him here—to the *real* world.

When he first arrived, he thought his memories of earth, with its skyscrapers and form-fitting suits, were his actual life. The lie had been so convincing, his mind had even conjured up the "real" Magnus of Ashfall, a strange man who lived in darkness.

The man screamed and sobbed, pulling at the chains around his neck, begging to be released.

It was a long time before he stopped dreaming of that man, but he knew that this fake Magnus must have been a test of Calamity's. One he'd clearly passed with flying colors.

Not that it was always easy to please his master. There'd been times he desperately wished someone else had been chosen to bind Calamity to this plane, allowing the Void-star to step forth, unhindered. But every time doubt crept in, Calamity showed him the way. The plague. Zara. Even Valerius, the miserable git. It'd been a part of his master's plan, a night sky of stars that, once in place, would form the most beautiful constellation of all.

The temperature dropped, ice forming on his eyelashes.

"Raise your shield, Valerius," he said, a storm bursting from his fingers.

Ashira turned, eyes alight with fury. She charged for him, fangs bared.

"Too little." He smiled. "Too—"

Squelch.

It was a small sound, but it broke his train of thought. The storm that swept around him vanished, his magic failing. *Why? What...*

Magnus looked down in confusion to see a bloodied fist where his stomach should be.

"*No!*" Valerius yelled, throwing the boy to the side and rushing forward. But Ashira met his blade with her claws, holding him back.

Magnus gasped, his intestines churning as the fist in his guts twisted. With painful slowness he looked over his shoulder at the woman who, even as she killed him, made his heart swell.

"Za... ra?" He gasped, wanting to ask why? *How?*

"I'm not Zara," his beloved said, and he saw it was true. She wore Zara's face, but the tears of rage in her eyes weren't his Fury's. Parts of the ice he'd used to cage her still clung to her, slipping from her skin like drops of glass. "But she's watching. And she has a message for you."

The woman leant in, lips close to his ear.

"You will die as you lived, mage. With piss-soaked trousers and the knowledge that the power of a god couldn't change what you are—a shriveled foreskin of a man." She ripped her arm free of him with a savage jerk.

He tried to call out, to activate the blood debt and force her to save him. But her arm, slick with his insides, was free of the scar that once bound her to him.

Magnus fell to his knees, blood and bile pouring from his stomach.

"We can't *kill* him, Zara. What about the blood-debt?" The woman who wore Zara's skin tilted her head as if listening. "Just because you were bound to Ashira first doesn't mean... okay, okay." She sighed, then held up a hand.

"I am death's mistress—bow before me." Claws inched from her fingers like sharpened silk. The steel in her eyes told him that while her hand may shake, she would do it. She would cut his head off.

Magnus' insides burned, spilling from his body, but he could handle the pain—he'd suffered worse at Calamity's hand. He could even accept the fact that he was about to die. What he would not, could not, accept was that Zara had chosen someone else over him.

"Calamity step forth..." He gasped. The woman hesitated—and that was the only reason he managed to finish the spell. **"... and ruin this world."**

The ground shook as if Calamity himself had descended, his very presence threatening to rend the continent in two. The spell was a gift from his master, something to be used once, and once only. He smiled as the stone cracked beneath him, chasing past Zara, a snarling Ashira, and a shocked Valerius as it raced up the wall, digging into the ceiling above.

The first rock fell.

How fitting, he thought, a memory of that other life, that other world, flitting through his mind as the waterstone collapsed, screams filling the air. That this begins and ends with an earthquake.

He allowed himself one last look at his Fury, who could only stare in horror as the ceiling collapsed. He was grateful. Grateful she'd been his, if only for a short time. That she'd given his life meaning.

Grateful they would die together.

***

Everything hurt.

My gasp turned to a cough that wracked my lungs. I opened my eyes, but it made no difference to the total darkness. I snapped my eyes shut, then opened them again, terrified I'd gone blind.

"Run… little star," growled a voice.

"Ashira," I called out. "What happened? Where—"

She gasped, and I ducked instinctively at the sharp crack of shifting rock. A flame appeared somewhere behind me, lighting up the darkness, and it took me several seconds to process what I was seeing.

I was half buried by rubble. Magnus lay on the ground, eyes closed, the skin around the gaping hole in his stomach burned nearly black, staunching the bleeding. I was sure he was dead, but then his chest shuddered, rising and falling.

A droplet of blood hit my cheek.

I turned my head to see Ashira directly above me, half crouched. Two of her fingers were missing, blood dripping from the stumps. Her fangs pierced her bottom lip, arms bent nearly double from the weight of what looked like the entire waterstone on her back.

She'd saved me. Hours before, she'd tried to kill me, and now here she was, nearly broken in half, fighting to keep me alive.

A snap of fingers made me look back at Magnus and who stood next to him.

Fire danced on Valerius' palm. He stood upright and proud, despite the stone that surrounded him and Magnus. Something flashed white just above his head, forming a sphere—*Kinetic Barrier*, I realized. It was a special move from *Knights of Eternity*. The greater the force used against it, the more powerful the barrier became. The downside? It drained your mana in seconds. Or it was supposed to.

Yet there Valerius stood without so much as a bead of sweat on his forehead.

What the hell is going on? Why is Valerius here? And why is he protecting Magnus? They hate each other!

"Ah," Zara said. "*The princeling arrived with Magnus. He is either a traitor to Navaros or perhaps he serves the same god Magnus does. I suppose it makes little difference.*"

Valerius is a traitor? Why didn't you tell me?

"What the hell are you *doing?*" Valerius snapped. But he wasn't talking to Magnus. He was talking to *me*.

"What?" I said stupidly.

"Did you not read the quest? *Temper the Vaxion?* I know killing Magnus is tempting, I've thought about it myself, but we need him to *Summon Eternity*." He'd begun annoyed but was furious toward the end.

Mouth agape, I stared, dumbstruck.

And then everything clicked into place.

"You're... a player?"

He rolled his eyes. "Yes, and so is Magnus. Now hurry up and kill Ashira. The sooner we get rid of these NPCs, the sooner we can get to the endgame."

The rock above cracked, caving in a few inches. Ashira's knee hit the ground from the force, her one remaining eye shut. The other was gone—a gaping hole in its place. Teeth gritted, she showed no sign of having heard what Valerius had said, and I knew every fiber of her being was focused on holding up that impossible weight. On saving Zara.

With a grunt, I kicked at the slab of rock that buried my legs. Shoving it aside, I wiggled out from under Ashira.

"Leave me," was all she managed to say.

I crouched, pressed my back against the rock, and *heaved*, trying to relieve her. I gasped at the weight, how the hell was she doing this by herself?

"For the love of—Zara, enough!" Valerius hissed. "What part of this don't you understand? Kill the NPC, and *get over here*."

"She's not... she's not an *NPC*," I said, my legs shaking. "These people are real!"

"As real as *Knights of Eternity*, is it? Did you cry when pixels exploded in that ridiculous death animation?" he asked mockingly. "Or when you killed a boss, like Zara the Fury? If you played as much as I did, I know you must have killed her dozens, if not hundreds, of times."

I looked away, and he smiled. "Exactly. This place is just a game, one the Operator rules. And if we want to get back to our world, we *have* to do what he says."

"But—but *Temper the Vaxion* could mean anything!" I said, scrambling. "There're multiple ways to do his quests, right? I had one with a bee where—"

"He does that at the beginning," Valerius interrupted. "Starts you off with easy quests meant to prepare the way for his arrival. Or help you find your way in this world—it's why I got placed with the Gilded. Why Magnus got Zara. The idiot would have died otherwise. Once you power-up, however…" He shrugged. "You learn pretty quickly that a blade is the golden path. Or claws, in your case."

My mind caught on so many things he'd said, racing through my quests. But one thing stood out to me.

"'Prepare for *his* arrival'? What are you talking about? Who is the Operator?"

There was a sharp crack as spiderwebs formed in Valerius' barrier. He frowned. "I'm not wasting a *Replenish* potion to answer questions you're too stupid to figure out." He sighed. "Look, he's someone who can and *will* make your life a living hell. Trust me."

I narrowed my eyes. "The last time I saw you, you threw me off a *dragon*."

"Which I'd *never* have done if I'd known the truth. The Calamity System sent out a notification about a new player once I was back in the Ivory Keep, and by the time I put two and two together, it was too late."

My back burned from the weight of the stone, but it was a welcome distraction from what Valerius was telling me. On the one hand, I was relieved I wasn't alone, on the other, I wondered how many other "players" the Operator had dragged into his game? And what had happened to the ones who came before us?

"Let's start over, okay?" Valerius said, smiling gently. "I'm sorry for hurting you and for dumping all of this on you. I've been here so long I've forgotten how terrifying this must be. To wake up in a body that isn't your own, trapped in an *arcade game* of all things. Even after three years here, it still sounds insane when I say it out loud."

He held out his hand. "But you're not alone. I know the System inside and out. Together, we can finish the game and get out of here. You don't even have to kill Ashira, just—just come inside the barrier."

I hesitated, head swimming. If I did what he said, then what? Sure, I could tell myself that if the rock collapsed on Ashira, killing her, it wasn't my fault, but that was only the beginning. Valerius planned to kill *all* the vaxion. Even if he let me stand by and do nothing, their blood would be on *my* hands.

Valerius' mouth thinned, his eyes darkening like a storm. "*Or*," he gestured at Magnus, whose breathing grew more shallow, "you can stay here, and on the off-chance you survive, end up like *him*."

"Ten years. Ten years he's been trapped in this world. I don't remember my name anymore. Or my parents, or my brothers. But I know I had a family. I know I was only a kid when I ended up in *Knights of Eternity*. This man, on the other hand…" Valerius looked at Magnus, not bothering to hide his disgust. "He *really* thinks he's Magnus, and that the Operator is a god who visits him in dreams. You've heard Magnus talk—he sounds like a cliched video game villain, not a person. And the same thing will happen to *us*. I can… I can feel it sometimes." He looked away, shame burning hot on his face. "When I first wake up in the morning, there's a second where I forget I'm a player. Where I think I really am 'Valerius, Prince of Navaros.' Is that what you want? To spend the rest of your life thinking you're a character in an *arcade game*?"

Chapter Fifty-Nine

Valerius' words rang out, naming my worst fear. That one day, I'd forget my old life entirely. That I'd think I really was… really was…

"*A monster,*" Zara said, making me jump. I'd almost forgotten she was watching.

You scare the hell out of me, Zara. But I don't think you're a monster.

"Then you are not as smart as I thought you were," she said. "A pity, considering you were correct about the blood debt—it is bound to soul, not body. Magnus is near death, and perhaps I will follow. Perhaps not. Either way, our contract is done. What you do now is no business of mine."

Stop it, Zara.

"I have no idea what you're—"

Stop with the act. You may not like me, but we know each other better than that.

Zara fell silent. Valerius watched me, his eyes narrowing.

"I don't trust Valerius, but his words ring true. This is your chance to break the ties that bind us," she said, her voice low. She sounded almost sad.

Don't tell me you'd be fine with it? Killing Ashira? I looked at the giant of a woman and the blood that dripped from her ruined eye. *What about the rest of the vaxion?*

I felt Zara pacing in my mind.

"The vaxion are near death," she said cagily. "Magnus saw to that."

That doesn't answer my question, Zara.

"I owe them nothing."

Zara!

"What do you want from me, parasite?" she hissed. "My entire life is a falsehood. I've spent nigh on a decade believing my own blood sold me on a whim, instead I find I risked everything to save them. I thought… I thought being a vaxion meant spurning weakness and refusing death at every turn. Yet the very woman who beat this into me was willing to become a slave in my place. Would have happily died of sickness to save me, had I chosen to stay."

I tilted my head toward Ashira, knowing Zara wanted to see her. Sweat dripped down the side of her brow, her remaining eye screwed up in pain. She wouldn't last much longer.

"*Who even now risks everything to protect me,*" Zara whispered.

"I won't ask again, Zara," Valerius said, his hand drifting to his sword.

Closing my eyes, I thought of Lenia hugging me goodbye. Lukas laughing as we raced through the forest. Eternity gripping my hand on Magnus' rooftop. The love in Ashira's eyes when she cupped my face.

This world isn't a bunch of pixels and nameless NPCs, Zara, not to me, I said, giving voice to the feeling that had sat in my chest from the moment I arrived here. *Ashira and the other vaxion have a lot to answer for, but I can't kill them. I won't. But if I refuse… then on the off-chance I survive, you're going to be stuck with me.*

She barked a laugh. "*Your freedom dangles before you, yet you worry for mine. Of course I would end up bound to someone so stupid.*"

A smile tugged my lips.

I'll take that as a compliment. Besides, didn't you do the same? Magnus promised to get rid of me, but you didn't even consider it.

She bared her fangs in return, and my claws pushed against the soft flesh of my fingertips in answer. "*Then I suppose we will both die idiots, parasite.*"

The rock shuddered, threatening to collapse. I took a deep breath, yelling, "**If the world will not yield, then I will break it!**"

Monstrous Strength Activated.

I shifted my grip and *pushed*. The rock inched off Ashira, who collapsed, her huge form hitting the ground with a dull thud as she fell unconscious.

"What are you doing?" Valerius hissed, a vein throbbing on the side of his head. "I can't maintain the barrier *and* help Magnus. Get over here right now!"

I gasped, forcing *Monstrous Strength* to the absolute limit as I pushed against the rock. It shifted, pieces cracking and falling, knocking against Valerius' barrier, but I pushed until I stood up straight with what felt like the entire waterstone balanced above my head. When last we met, Valerius towered over me. Now I couldn't help but think how small he was.

"So, you weren't offering to help me out of the goodness of your heart," I said, grinning even as my arms burned. "You did it because you *need me.*"

Valerius grimaced but didn't argue. His eyes flitted upward when more cracks appeared in his barrier. "The Operator will make you. I'm surprised he hasn't already."

"I've been punished for failing a quest before."

Valerius shook his head. "That was just a taste. If you'd been punished, *truly* punished, you'd have gutted Ashira in a heartbeat. He'll come for you, Zara. And it won't be pretty."

The rock shifted, and I hissed in pain, reactivating *Monstrous Strength*. I couldn't keep this up.

Valerius laughed. "You still need to speak to use your powers?" He shook his head. "How I let you get the best of me at Magnus' castle is beyond me."

Sching.

His sword glinted as he drew it one handed. Ashira stirred at my feet. What felt like a thousand fire ants crawled up my thighs and back, burning me from the inside out, but I forced myself to stay upright. The rock was too heavy to throw, and there was too much for me to punch through *and* protect Ashira. So I did the only thing I could think of.

I stalled for time.

"Do the Gilded know?" I asked, the words closer to a grimace.

He stopped, eyes wide.

"Do they know their leader is nothing but a puppet?" I pushed.

Something broke in his eyes at the mention of the Gilded.

"They don't, do they? What would Marito say? Or *Lazander?* He saw what you did to me. How you abandoned Eternity. What did he think of the hero of Navaros?

"Shut up."

"I bet he was ashamed of you. Almost as ashamed as I am."

"*Shut up!*" he said, taking a step toward me. His barrier wavered, but to reach me he'd have to either extend it or cross it.

"You were right, I did play *Knights of Eternity*. Almost constantly. And do you know who my favorite was?" I chuckled, shaking my head. "The Prince of Navaros, leader of the Gilded. The knight who always stepped up and did the right thing. You're the reason I introduced my nephew, Noah, to the game. He's only a kid, but he worships you. Has pages and pages of drawings of you, and when he's had a bad day, or he's struggling, do you know what he asks?" I fell to one knee with a grunt, head bowed. "He... he asks, 'What would Valerius do?'

"I'm asking you now, one player to another." I was pushing it, I knew. All it would take was one step, one strike, and he could kill me. But I had to try. "What would Valerius do? Would he kill the vaxion? Or would he help me *save* them? You've played *Knights* as much as I have. If the game and this world are one and the same, there *must* be a way to beat the Operator *and* finish the game. Hell, that might even be the way to get home!"

"I..." He shook his head, frowning.

"Please, Valerius," I said, thinking I'd gotten through to him. But the moment I said that name, his grip tightened on his sword, and the flicker of hope I had vanished.

"Valerius is gone," he said, raising his sword. "I'm all that's left. And I choose to *live*." He stepped forward, extending the barrier even as I saw it waver. I closed my eyes, knowing if I moved, Ashira would take the blow.

I tried, Zara. I'm sorry.

There was a rumble and the dull echo of a roar.

Valerius frowned, sword still aloft.

The roar echoed, closer this time. A roar I *knew*.

"*The difference between a hunter and a predator is simple*," whispered Zara. I felt her sink into my body, nudging my feet into the perfect position to spring. "*A hunter lays her traps, hides in bushes, and stills her heart while she waits for a chance to strike. But a predator? She does not hide. She strikes fast and true, and all fall before her.*"

The rock on my back grew lighter, but I didn't move or show any sign. Claws scrambled against stone, and I heard something huge heaving rock out of the way.

"*Hold*," Zara said.

Abruptly, Valerius let the flame extinguish.

Tithe of Beasts Activated.

With my newly upgraded vision, I could see Valerius as clearly as if it were noon. I tensed, not daring to activate *Fury's Claw* for fear he'd hear me. At Zara's instruction, I stretched out one foot and kicked a rock. With *Monstrous Strength* still active, it sailed through the air, hit Magnus in the head with a soft *plink*. He groaned, and Valerius whirled, looking away from me.

"*Now!*"

As the rock above me was lifted away, light breaking up the darkness like sharpened blades, I *leaped*.

Chapter Sixty

"Zara, I swear if you're not dead under there I'll kill you myself," Lukas yelled in faux-anger. "Do you have *any* idea how hard it is to *follow you* without *following*—hey!" Lukas jumped back, still half-molger as Valerius and I flew past him. I took in a handful of details—Esia and Fatyr, covered in dust, but otherwise unharmed. Jaza bleeding from a gaping wound in her shoulder, running toward Ashira. And then Valerius and I were on the ground, rolling as we fought for purchase, rubble stabbing us in the sides, arms, and back.

"Is that *Valerius?* Wait, why are we fighting the *Gilded?*" Lukas called.

"Ignore the mongrel. You have claws and fangs, the princeling has blades. He can be disarmed, you cannot. Use that," Zara ordered.

"I am death's mistress—bow before me," I growled.

Fury's Claw Activated.

A patch of sun illuminated the waterstone, or the remnants of it. It hadn't fully collapsed as I'd feared, just a section of it, leaving a gaping hole in the ceiling that hinted at the coming dawn. The walls that circled the main hall were still standing, albeit barely. Magnus hadn't been trying to kill the vaxion and fulfill his quest, I realized. He'd been trying to kill *Zara*.

"Focus, parasite. That castrated meatsack is no longer our concern."

Valerius got to his feet, driving his fist into my stomach. I gasped, doubling over. He hit like a *truck*. His sword was gone, lost in the tumble, but he drew a blade from his boot, swiping for me. I threw myself back, twisting at an impossible angle to dodge it.

"Give him no ground! Left shoulder. Strike true."

Valerius swung at me in a wide arc. This time, I darted forward, letting the blade nick me as my hand shot out, fingers narrowed to a point. Valerius' forearm flew up at the last second, trying to block me. My claws pierced his leather armor… and kept going, cutting through his flesh and bone like a spoon through cream.

"*Good*," Zara said when Valerius howled, falling back as he dropped his blade. Blood poured from his arm, and he grasped it with his free hand, breathing rapidly. "*Next, his stomach, where the flesh is weak.*"

I leaped forward, swiping at his belly. Valerius threw himself back, less a dodge and more a fall as he hit the ground, clutching his bleeding arm. He scrambled back, pain making him panic.

"*He is done. Finish him, girl.*"

Valerius stared at me, eyes wide with panic. Stained with dirt and blood, I no longer saw a knight who butchered innocent people to save his own skin. I saw a kid trapped in a world he was losing his mind to. A kid barely older than Noah when he'd first ended up here, scared and alone.

I might be a player, but that didn't mean I had to be like *him*. "It's over, Valerius," I said softly, lowering my claws. "I'm not your enemy. We don't have to—"

He held up his hand, palm outward. I felt a soft tingle of warmth, almost pleasant, and then I was flying through the air, my body a comet as flames engulfed me. I cut a path through the rubble, hitting the ground, and kept going—but I barely felt it.

"Zara!" Lukas' cry was almost lost as I screamed, fire rushing down my throat. I flailed and thrashed, but it only encouraged the flames. They greedily inhaled my skin, hair, and insides, crackling with dark glee as I burned. The flames built higher and higher, a perversion of the *Inferno* I'd once summoned to kill Magnus.

"*Argh! You are... we are fury incarnate. The... the flames are ours to wield.*" Zara's voice was threaded with pain, briefly pulling me from my own. "*Your master... does not...*"

Her voice fell to the flames.

I tried to remember what it felt like to wield fire, to see it as a friend and not an enemy. But my concentration kept slipping, and the flames refused to move at my command, my affinity for fire stripped from me by the Operator. Rational thought fled as my kicks became weaker, my thrashing duller.

I was going to die.

Suddenly arms wrapped around me. Lukas picked me, screaming for water. I tried to tell him it was too late, there was no river close by, but I couldn't speak. He ran but only managed a few steps before he tripped, crying out when he lit up like the sun, the flames eager for another victim.

Let me go, let me go, you idiot! I mentally screamed at him, praying he'd understand, but he only gripped me tighter, holding me close. Together we burned, the flames building higher and higher.

No.

The thought cut through the pain.

I refuse.

Zara's rage rose in my mind, but not the fury that lashed out at everyone and everything. Instead it was cold and determined. We closed our eyes as one.

We refuse.

WARNING.

ATTEMPTED BREACH OF CALAMITY SYSTEM RESTRICTIONS.

The flames grew taller, whipping around us. I heard Valerius laugh, heard the sound of his sword being sheathed. We lay helpless and burning, and he wouldn't do us the courtesy of putting us out of our misery. No, he was going to stand by, and *watch*.

We refuse.

WARNING. WARNING. BREACH OF CALAMITY SYSTEM RESTRICTIONS WILL RESULT IN SIGNIFICANT PENALTIES.

We refuse death.

The flames blasted from us as if repelled by our skin.

I opened my eyes to find Lukas' arms still wrapped around me. He was staring up at the sky where flames whirled into a vortex above us. I looked at Lukas in shock—he didn't have a scratch on him, and neither did I. Flexing my fingers, I found my skin cool to the touch and free from burns.

"Oh, so *now* you have fire powers!" Lukas said.

INFERNO UNLOCKED.

"*Refuse death, is it? Ashira would be proud,*" Zara said softly.

I shakily got to my feet, holding out my hand to help Lukas up.

He took it, pulling me into a fierce hug. "I'm sorry for yelling at you. I was being a prick. A scared prick, but a prick nonetheless. You're not my executioner. You're… you're my friend." He pulled back, looking at me. "A friend who needs to stop getting set on fire. I only have so many pairs of pants, you know."

"I'll do my best," I murmured, wiping my eyes, my heart full. I couldn't believe he was here, that he'd come to help me even after everything that had happened.

"Bad guy first, then tears of adoration." He winked.

"For once, the boy speaks sense," Zara said with a touch of indignation. *"Let us teach the princeling that a storm cannot be tempered."*

I held up my hand, palm outward to Valerius. He stared at me, horror flashing in his eyes. His hands glowed as he moved to summon something from the Inventory, but I was quicker.

"Burn."

Inferno Activated.

The flames shot toward him, swirling into a vortex of fire and pain. The air crackled with heat and power, slamming into him…

… and vanished, the flames I'd summoned extinguished in a single breath. I growled, raising my claws. I'd used *Inferno* once before, back when I'd first arrived in this world, and it had been powerful enough to trap Magnus in its flames, burning his arm off. Valerius might have magic, but there was no way it was as strong as Magnus'. So how the hell had he stopped it?

Valerius turned to me in shock, looking as confused as I was. Wait, if it wasn't Valerius, then who—

eNOuGH

Pain, sharp as a blade and twice as brutal, drove into my skull. I fell to my knees, gripping my head. I was dimly aware Valerius did the same.

"Zara? Zara, what's wrong? Talk to me!" Lukas gripped my shoulders, but his touch burned, hot needles on my skin. I slapped his hands away, but the pain only intensified. Blood dripped from my nose. My jaw unhinged, and I screamed, but the blade only wriggled deeper into my brain like crawling fingernails scratching every part of my mind, my soul, as it burrowed in.

tO ME

And then I was gone.

***

I knew without opening my eyes I was back.

Red sand boiled against my cheek. Symbols, pitch black and angry, trailed along my skin, digging into me like maggots. Gone were the dark robes Jaza had carefully wrapped me in. Instead I was naked. *Vulnerable.* I screamed, scrambling in the sand, slapping at symbols as if they were ants.

"Shut up… makes him. Angrier," came a gasp. I looked to my right to see Valerius, as naked as I was, the symbols crawling over his cheeks and neck like deadly ink.

BoW

The disembodied voice echoed throughout the desert, the dual suns in the sky glowing in answer. Valerius threw himself forward, his head sinking into the painful sand, bowing as deeply as he could.

Bow TO YouR MaSTER!

An invisible force pushed me down, forcing my head into the sand where it scraped against my skin like sandpaper.

WhAT Is YOUr queST?

"*Temper the Vaxion!*" Valerius cried, his words a rush of pain and obeisance.

Out of the corner of my eye, I noticed someone else. Someone lying on his back, arms splayed, oblivious to both his nakedness and the symbols that chased themselves all over his skin.

Magnus.

WhY HAVE yOU NoT Done SO

"It's—it's her!" Valerius said, trying to point at me, but the movement fell flat as he curled in on himself, whimpering. "Let me go, please. You know I'm loyal. I've proven myself over and over, so please let me—"

SILenCE

Valerius managed one last whimper before doing so.

Something fixed its attention on me, an overwhelming force that pushed my mind to its absolute limits. I knew if it focused on me for too long, my own brain would tear itself to pieces trying to comprehend it.

yOu forCE mE TO dRAG yOu Here AT greAt CoST

exPLaIn

"I-I won't do it!" I managed, gritting my teeth, forcing each word out as if they were bile. "I won't... kill them."

"See!" Valerius cried, pointing at me like a child.

You ARe bleSSed

yET YOu reFUse

yoU ARE ChoSEn

YeT yOu TaMPer WitH tHe SySTEM

UnACCeptAbLE!

The Operator's voice was a hammer on the inside of my skull, every word threatening to shatter it. I screamed, nails tearing at my scalp, scratching it bloody. I had to get the Operator out of my head before it killed me.

YOu WiLL ReMAIN hERE UnTIL YOu OBEY

"And—and me?" Valerius whimpered, face deep in the sand I knew burned him. "Master, please."

yoU DID nOt COnviNCE hEr

YOu mUsT Be pUNished!

Valerius howled, clawing for me, but he could scarcely move. He wept, tears mixing with sand. "Do it! Say you'll obey!" he screamed.

I wanted to. I desperately wanted to give in, to say I'd do it. That I'd do anything if the pain would only stop.

"I..."

Valerius nodded at me, head bobbing, eyes half mad with pain and eagerness.

I thought of him—the once brave knight, the pinnacle of hope and justice in Navaros, reduced to a man who now sobbed on his knees, willing to kill innocent people to save his own skin.

I shook my head.

"You'll... have to *kill me*," I spat.

AS YoU WISH

The pressure in my head increased, my world turning white. Spittle mixed with blood as I screamed. Valerius turned away, but the pain stopped as suddenly as it began, a voice cutting through it.

"You will not touch her, you miserable *shek*."

Paws as white as fresh snow hit the sand on either side of my head. I turned, black spots dotting my vision to see Zara above me, the air crackling with rage as her vaxion coils wound about her head with promised fury.

Chapter Sixty-One

Clouds formed above, hiding the blistering suns. The world darkened—shadows elongating as Zara growled.

"Ho-how? *Why?*" I managed. My head was no longer splitting, but my skin still burned, the Operator's dark symbols burrowing into my very bones.

"If anyone is going to kill you, parasite, it will be *me*," Zara said, her words echoing in my mind as her lips curled in a fang-marked smile. She lifted her head, and *roared*, the sound echoing endlessly in the desert. Sand blasted away from the sheer force of it, exploding into the air and raining down on Magnus, who didn't so much as twitch.

Instantly the burning in my skin lessened. I shook my head, the fog of pain lessening. I'd almost given in to the Operator, almost let him kill me while I just *lay* here. My fists clenched. This might be the Operator's realm, but that didn't mean I had to go quietly.

"Your lies are shadows, my eyes the flames. You cannot hide from me."

Piercing Sight Activated.

The world turned black and white, and I smiled. If my powers worked here, then the Operator wasn't as all-powerful as it liked to appear. I stared at the sand and symbols, understanding dawning. Unsteadily I got to my knees.

"The sand!" I called to Valerius. "It's not the symbols that hurt, it's the sand! Wipe it off!" With clumsy hands, I tried to shake it out of my hair, but Valerius didn't move. He curled in on himself.

"Valerius?"

"He'll be angry," he whispered.

beGOnE BeaSt

yoU ARE NoT WELcoME

A rumble began, the sand undulating like a slumbering monster. Something in the distance caught my eye, and I squinted, trying to make sense of the dark shapes that roiled on the horizon. As they grew closer, increasing in speed, my heart stopped.

It was a *wave*. A colossal wave that greedily inhaled the red sand it raced over, growing larger and larger, reaching up into the sky.

"Zara…" was all I managed. We'd be buried alive.

Zara said nothing. Instead she raised her head… and *laughed*. The air crackled, my hair lifting from my shoulders as the clouds descended. Static tickled my arms, the air thick and fat, but Zara laughed on, the lightning building until I could scarcely breath.

The wave towered overhead. Valerius whimpered, the sand he cowered in pulled from him, sucked up by the wave. As it arched, preparing to smack down on us with all the fury of a god, Zara *struck*.

Lightning burst from her, turning the world blinding white with *Wrath's Storm*. An explosive boom followed, rocking so loud I had to cover my ears, momentarily blind and deaf. When the world swam back into focus, spots of light in my vision, I looked up to see the wave above us. It was still arching, nearly bent in half as it began its deadly descent.

But it wasn't sand anymore.

Instead a wave of glass, frozen and eternal, lay permanently curved, as beautiful as it had been deadly. The skies above, normally clear after I used *Wrath's Storm*, grew darker. I felt lightning build once more.

"Come, little god. You can do better than that," Zara snarled, her claws digging into the metal below. *The metal?* I reached down, realizing the sand had hidden a hard metal floor marked by strange sigils. I only recognized some of them, but they reminded me of the ones I'd seen bind Eternity's magic so long ago in Magnus' castle.

"This is a prison. You're a prisoner here, aren't you? And I…" With dawning horror, I clasped my hand over my mouth. "All these quests, preparing for your 'arrival.' I've been helping you escape, haven't I?"

The voice hesitated. I had a feeling it wasn't used to being questioned.

BoUND fOR mY NAtuRE

BOUnD AnD CAllED TyRANt wHiLE THE OthER RUles

"Oh god. You're… you're…"

yOur GOd aNd mASter

i aM

CALAMITY

Lightning exploded from Zara, blasting through the air as she struck a nearby sand dune, turning it into a twisted sculpture of glass. The clouds above erupted, lightning dancing across the sand like deadly ballerinas, striking the ground again and again. One bolt came perilously close to Valerius. A wave of sand covered him, but he made no move to shake it off.

I moved to help him, but Zara growled. "He chose his fate. As we will ours."

I ignored her, my hands clumsily wiping sand from Valerius. With how tightly he was curled up, it was difficult, but I persevered until my fingers burned.

He cracked an eye, staring at me in shock and horror.

I didn't know whether to smile at him reassuringly or punch his lights out. Probably both.

A boom made me duck.

"What are you *doing?*" I cried when Zara zapped another sand dune, red sand blasting outward.

"If I can neither move, nor see my enemy," she said, panting, "then I will force him to reveal himself to *me*." On and on she went while Calamity, the Tyrant of legend, stayed silent. Her paws shook, but Zara stayed above me, huddling over me protectively.

And then, a noise. So small. So insignificant, I almost missed it.

Zara didn't.

"*There*," she hissed. Her huge jaws reached for me, wrapping around my middle. Snapping her head back, she flung me up and onto her back. I hit it so hard, I nearly fell, hands digging into her fur, but she didn't wait for me to get comfortable—she charged into the desert like a raging bull, sand sticking to her paws, alien symbols greedily swarming up her. Soon she was covered in so many her white fur turned gray, but she merely hissed and ran deeper into the desert.

"Zara! What are we—" I started, but then I saw it. It was tiny, maybe the size of a cat. Small, ink black, and bloated, it crawled along the sand, inches from where a bolt of lightning had just missed it.

"I've never eaten a *god* before." Zara laughed, speeding up. "I wonder how they taste?" The symbols reached her shoulders now, her paws kicking up so much sand

I was covered again, my arms and legs burning. But I didn't scream, despite how much it hurt. If Zara could stand it without a whimper, then so could I.

My mouth twisted in disgust when I saw the "god" that had dragged me from my home, my *family*. The creature who'd bound me to Zara and Zara to me, who'd used Lukas as a tool to help me do its bidding. Who'd wrapped Zara in a bow and presented her to Magnus. The enemy of Gallow, the tyrant who attacked this world—*Calamity*, now frantically crawled from us in the sand, a long, elongated slug that writhed in fear.

The creature curled in on itself, wiggling. Against the red backdrop of the sand, it looked like the symbols that burned my arms. I gripped the fur around Zara's neck as she leaped, roaring with deranged, bloodthirsty joy. It had nowhere to go. Nowhere to hide. It was finished, I thought.

I should have known better.

With a sharp boney crack, the alien plane vanished.

***

Lukas had seen some strange things in his life. While nothing would ever match finding Grandma Fi butt-naked and snoring in the middle of H'tar, a stolen cask of booze in her hands, watching a pure white vaxion fall from the sky was a close second.

One minute Zara was getting ready to cook Valerius like a well-done steak, the next they were gone. He'd barely started to say her name when a boom made him look up, and a vaxion appeared high in the sky.

But vaxion, for as much as they loved crowing about their abilities, couldn't fly, and so the white vaxion began to tumble through the sky. She didn't move. Didn't so much as twitch as she began the long fall to her death.

"*Zara!*" Ashira roared, struggling to her feet.

Jaza hovered over her, softer now than Lukas remembered, her hands trying to hold the bleeding Ashira back. She fell to her knees, cursing.

"Boy!" Ashira barked, golden eyes locking with his. He started, no longer Lukas the man but Aerzin the boy. The one forced to choose between his mother and father while Ashira mocked him. Who bent his head whenever the vaxion leader passed, the back of her hand quick to force his eyes to the ground. The woman who, by exiling the molger, had effectively killed his dad.

"… Lukas," she said, shocking him. She'd used his name. His *molger* name. "Save her, I *beg* you."

***

The girl was screaming. They lay in the darkness of her mind, chains wrapped around Zara's neck once more. She started forward, trying to reach her but was yanked back sharply.

"What is it, what's wrong?" Zara barked, anger masking her fear.

The girl kicked and flailed in answer, her hands gripping the sides of her head as if clinging to a cliff edge.

"Calamity… *Calamity*!" was all she managed before her jaw unhinged, letting loose an unholy shriek, that of an animal in the throes of death.

Zara's eyes darted around. Her solution to most things was to kill it. But the god they hunted wasn't here and while bound she could do nothing. What had that vile slug done to them? Where *were* they?

As if in answer, she felt their body, still in vaxion form, flitter in and out of consciousness. She caught a glimpse of a sun awash with the sky's dawn and one, blissful sun. A rush of cold air slapped their fur.

She hissed. Their prey had sent them back to the real world. And they were *falling*.

"Girl!" Zara barked. "Give me control, *now*!"

But the girl didn't hear her. She was crying now, a sight that made Zara desperately wish she'd torn that god in two. "Stop your screaming!" Zara ordered, yanking hard at the chains that bound her once more. "Give me control before we both die!"

The girl rolled onto her side, and Zara feared she was lost to pain, but then she slapped her hand on the ground. Teeth gritted, she dragged herself an inch closer to Zara, then two. Zara reached out, nearly choking on the chain around her neck, but she took a breath and forced herself forward, fingers splayed.

With a grit and determination Zara admired, the girl grabbed Zara's hand, holding it fiercely. She smiled, her last words nearly lost as a blue sky replaced the darkness of the girl's mind and wind whipped around Zara's fur.

Zara's eyes snapped open, back in her body once more as a huge black vaxion slammed into her. They tumbled through the air, narrowly missing the hole in the waterstone's ceiling. Instead they slammed into its rune-etched exterior, sliding down its curve at deadly speed. She unsheathed her claws, ready to strike the vaxion who clung to her until she realized it was trying to wrap its paws around her.

She fought not to roll her eyes. Lukas was as clumsy in his vaxion form as he was in his human one.

Lukas yipped when they broke away, his cub-like claws skittering against the stone, sparking but finding no purchase. In seconds, he was sliding away from her. The gigantic waterstone curved until it became almost vertical, and Lukas picked up speed, the ground rushing to meet him. At this rate, the fool would break his neck.

Zara sighed.

She sheathed her claws, the stone sliding so quickly under her belly it burned, but she ignored the pain.

Lukas' coils flailed in his panic, and he fought to slow his fall while she straightened her body so it shot down like an arrow, pulling up alongside him.

She growled a warning to be still, not waiting for him to answer before leaping on top of him. He yelped, but she bit down on the scruff of his neck, holding him in place. With a jerk she unsheathed all her claws at once, digging them into the rock. Several caught on the waterstone's jagged runes, ripping out painfully, but she only pressed down harder.

Realizing what she was trying to do, Lukas followed suit, and four claws became eight, the stone sparking like fireworks, nearly blinding her.

A bloodied trail followed their descent.

They slowed, but not quickly enough. She waited until they passed the tree line, branches scratching against her back.

Wait, she told herself, remembering what she had told the parasite about the difference between a predator and a hunter. A branch the size of her arm dug into her flesh, snapping as they whizzed past it.

Wait.

At the last second, she bit down hard enough on Lukas to draw blood and *leaped*.

They didn't fly through the air. They limped through it, narrowly missing a scarlet sunder as Zara hit the ground, curled around Lukas protectively. They tumbled over one another, dirt and stone flying through the air until they came to a slow, aching stop.

Winded, Zara struggled to breathe around several cracked ribs.

Lukas recovered first, his dark tendrils turning blond, his flesh becoming hair. Still half-vaxion, half-human, he limped over to Zara. "Are you all right? That was… *insane*. I mean…" He touched the back of his neck, grimacing when his hand came away bloody. "I could have done without the new neck tattoo, but still."

Zara's bones snapped, her torso shortening as her fur sucked back into her human flesh with a squelch. A shudder ran through her as the coils that burst from the back of her skull molded into her neck, becoming skin once more. There had been a time when she'd felt more comfortable on four paws than on two legs, but now she breathed in a sigh of relief when she was able to straighten up, human once more.

She'd been a child the last time she'd shapeshifted, back before her… time with Magnus. It had been a slow, arduous process that needed all her concentration. Now, however, it took mere seconds.

She hadn't transformed for over a decade. She'd thought it was her own choice, one she'd made to spite her family. Now she realized it had been another of Magnus' lies. What better way to ensure she never transformed, never saw how lightning quick she could change as a *mongrel*, than to trick her into thinking she didn't need her vaxion form?

Flexing her human fingers, Zara realized she and Lukas were the last in the world who could transform into vaxion. The realization carried a weight to it that she wasn't ready to unpack.

"… I've only ever seen waterstones in the *sky*. What the vaxion are doing *living* in one… I suppose it's cheaper than building their own house but…"

Zara grimaced. The cub was still babbling.

She sat up, flexing her fingers. Several of her nails were gone, the tips bloodied. Other than her ribs, and a ruined ankle, she was fine, yet she couldn't shake the feeling something was wrong. It took her a moment to realize the problem was her mind and how quiet it was.

The parasite was gone.

Lukas held out a hand.

Zara ignored it, getting to her feet. "Second Dawn," she said.

"What?"

"At Second Dawn tomorrow, we are going for a run. It is past time you learned how to use your beast properly."

Limping slightly she walked past him, sure the entrance to the waterstone was on the other side.

Epilogue

"You think Mister Lazander will be back before the Freylen mare gives birth?" Garret asked, handing Eternity one of the sandwiches his mother had prepared for them that morning.

Eternity gratefully bit into it, ravenous after hours of backbreaking work. She sighed with happiness at the salted pork and cheese filling, happy she no longer had to check every scrap of food Garret and his family offered her for poison.

They'd proven themselves trustworthy ten times over.

"I'm sure he will," Eternity reassured him. "I know he's been… gone a lot, but there's no one who loves his horses more than…"

"ABOVE."

At the sound of Gallow's voice, Eternity stood, her sandwich falling to floor, forgotten.

"Eternity? Is everything okay?" Garret asked, his mouth still full.

Without a word, Eternity ran out of the stable doors, head craned back, searching the skies. Around her, people no longer darted out of her way or whispered about Gallow's famed Chosen—between helping out at the stables, buying rounds for journeymen at the new, much smaller, Resplendent Farrow, and the men's clothes she had taken to wearing, she no longer caused a ruckus by stepping outside. In fact, other than the odd look she got at her walking backward, head high, no one even glanced at her.

"Eternity? Miss, what's wrong?" Garret appeared at her side, protectively grabbing her sleeve. She should tell him to get inside, but she knew it wouldn't matter.

It would be far too late.

In the blue sky above, a dark shape appeared. She frowned, watching it grow in size, and realized it was heading for the Ivory Keep at speed. One of the king's soldiers, to their credit, noticed it first, but by the time the alarm rang out, the creature's two wings were visible.

A bird? What type of bird can grow to such lengths?

"Stay next to me," Eternity said quietly, putting her arm around Garret.

Against the backdrop of the clanging alarm, people looked up, crying out in fear when they saw the gigantic bird hurtling toward them. Panic ensued, as she knew it would, but the king's soldiers had seen their fair share of battle. They ordered people to one side, funneling them all through the same entrance while the rest were kept clear for the mages who streamed into the courtyard, their purple robes bright against the white cobbles.

Eternity forced her hands to remain still. She didn't know what the beast was, or where it had come from, but Gallow had warned her about it for a reason. Catapults were rolled out, too big and unwieldy to hit the creature, Eternity guessed. The king appeared at her side, his white armor shining, his hand on his sword.

"An evacuation has been ordered, Lady Eternity, and you are no exception," he said, dipping his head respectfully. She smiled but shook her head, relieved when the king's attention snapped back to the monster.

It drew up above them, wings of blue flame stretching the length of the Ivory Keep. Even from this distance, she could feel the *heat* from it. Mages flung spells of ice and flame at it, but they dissipated along with the few arrows that managed to strike it, mere mosquitos against its might. She felt the beast's white hot eyes lock onto her.

Heart pounding, Eternity waited.

The monster pulled back its wings, then swept them forward at speed in a rush of blistering heat. Fire burst from its body, flying toward the Ivory Keep. The strange blue flames struck the walls and freshly tiled roof of the Resplendent Farrow, but it didn't go up in flames as its predecessor would have—enforced magical stone had been woven into the new buildings, on the king's orders. A ball of fire the size of Eternity hit the ground next to her, but she didn't move, not even when Garret yelped, pressing his face into her stomach, his arms wrapped around her waist.

There were shouts for water, the courtyard a flurry of men and women handing out buckets and loading catapults with grim determination. Still, Eternity waited. She wouldn't move until she was ordered to. She'd learned her lesson.

As if sensing this, she felt Gallow reach out, relief flooding her body at his two simple words.

"SAVE THEM."

Eternity raised a single hand above her head, palm out. Taking a deep breath, she opened the door between her and Gallow.

Her eyes darkened, turning as black as the Void, the God of Judgment's power flowing through her. Her skin crawled with his words, his symbols wrapping around her body like the finest of silks.

The cobblestones beneath her feet, freshly laid only the week before, cracked. Garret whimpered, but she held his face against her.

"Kneel. Cry. *Beg*," she said, her voice not her own as Gallow spoke through her. From her palm, a small dark orb appeared. It grew in size, doubling, then tripling, hanging above her like a dark sun.

The monster pulled its wings back once more, ready to unleash its flames.

"For you are not worthy," she intoned.

The orb shot from her palm, leaving a trail of darkness in its path as it hurtled toward the creature—piercing its heart.

She expected the creature to fall, she knew her aim had been true, but instead it burst into a flurry of flames that curled in on itself and *vanished*.

The entire thing had taken less than five minutes, but Eternity knew this was only the beginning of a war that was about to consume the entire world. Breathing hard, she slammed the door between her and Gallow shut, covertly wiping a trail of blood from her nose. "It's safe now," she whispered to Garret, even as Gallow spoke in her mind, warning her the wallow-tail would be back.

Of course, she thought, *killing one of the Tyrant's soldiers wouldn't be this easy.*

She knelt down, hugging Garret close, gratitude filling her heart. The silence that followed the wallow-tail's disappearance grew, and she relished it, knowing what would come next. A clatter of armor made her raise her head. Around her, mages and soldiers alike stared at her with wide eyes while the king approached with the caution of a frightened animal, a full guard at his back. The respect she'd seen in his eyes only moments ago was gone, replaced by a look she'd seen countless times.

Fear.

She sighed, trying to feel grateful for the taste of "normal" life she'd had, even if it was painfully brief.

"The Tyrant has struck first," she said, getting to her feet. "And it is up to us how we answer."

***

The four Champions of Gallow camped silent, and contemplative. Well, some were contemplative. Imani was shadow boxing, dodging around imaginary enemies. Vivek stood, eyes narrowed as he scanned the forest. Malik sat on the ground, his legs crossed, the picture of ease as he settled back against a log.

Lazander knelt, eyes closed, focusing on his breathing. He was no longer a Gilded Knight, that life felt far away, almost like it belonged to another person. But he was still grateful for it. It had taught him much—how to push his body to the absolute limit, then push some more. How to take a blow, then hit back harder. And how quiet his mind before a battle. Or in this case, a slaughter.

"You all right, brother?" Malik asked for the second time.

Imani answered in his stead. "He is, and if you ask him again, I'll punch your lights out myself, Malik."

"For once, I agree with little Imi," Vivek said, smiling broadly when Imani whirled on him at the use of her nickname. "His heart is rock. His soul steady. He will not waver."

Malik laughed quietly to himself, a throaty chuckle. "How quickly they grow up, eh?" he said, nudging Lazander playfully.

The new Champion smiled. He'd thought the Gilded Knights and Gallow's Champions were so different before.

He almost laughed at the thought now.

"It's time," Malik announced, getting to his feet. As one they moved, gliding like ghosts to the cliff edge. In the distance a cave lay nestled, almost hidden by a curve in the landscape and the ice cold waves that struck its side. They'd been tracking the rebels who'd escaped Evergarden for days now, waiting for the perfect opportunity to strike.

"Who awaits us?" Malik asked.

"Ravenna and those foolish enough to serve her," Lazander replied.

"And who is Ravenna?"

Imani rolled her eyes, but Lazander smiled. Malik might love his little lessons, but he meant well. "One of the old gods from before Calamity's fall. She stood by while he wrought destruction, her followers' prayers falling on deaf ears while she hid from his wrath—eager to save only herself."

"Now she bids her followers to poison wells, murder royalty, and sow chaos. Why?"

"She plans to usurp Gallow and throw herself at Calamity's mercy in the hopes he'll spare her."

Malik nodded in approval. "She'd kill Gallow himself if she could. Since there's as much of a chance of that happening as there is of her finally growing a spine, she's settled for chaos instead. She spits on Gallow's name and spreads lies about our savior. So what are we going to do about it?"

Lazander drew his sword, pointing it at the cave, a flash of light betraying the people hidden within.

"We're going to kill her and her little disciples," he said.

Malik clapped his hand on Lazander's shoulder. "That's my boy."

***

Zara couldn't sleep. Her mind raced, and her bandages itched, but she knew Jaza would yell at her if she removed them. So instead of lying and staring at the ceiling in furs she hadn't skinned herself, as had been custom when she was a child, she stood beneath the stars.

The waterstone made her nervous in a way she couldn't explain. Almost as nervous as the vaxion who openly sobbed over the dead. Who bandaged each other's wounds and shared food and water among themselves instead of hoarding their own kills.

These were not the vaxion she remembered.

"It is safer inside, little star," Ashira said behind her, the woman moving silently despite her broken ankle.

"Call me that again, and I'll rip your throat out," Zara replied. She'd heard Ashira come outside, heard the hitch in her breath when she saw Zara, and had hoped her aunt had the courtesy to leave her in peace.

Alas, Ashira wasn't known for her manners.

Her aunt limped closer to her, and Zara's dug her nails into her arms, fighting the urge to swipe at Ashira. Couldn't she see Zara wanted to be left in peace?

"I used to wander at night when I couldn't sleep. But Jaza has shown me that when the mind is heavy, it's better to share the burden," Ashira said awkwardly, shifting uncomfortably.

Zara closed her eyes. She thought hell itself would freeze over before her aunt would offer her ear as a bosom buddy. The silence stretched on until Ashira limped away. Zara was happy to let her leave, but the parasite's words came to her, unbidden.

I wish you'd see not everyone is your enemy.

Zara sighed. "You... this place... isn't what I remembered."

The older woman nodded, returning to stand by Zara's side. "We had to change in order to survive. *I* had to change."

"The Ashira I saw today, who risked her life to save mine, would be butchered by the one I knew."

"The Ashira you knew hadn't lost everything. That tends to change a person."

Zara felt the rare urge to cry. She stamped it out with what she knew best—anger. "You're not the one who lost everything. *I* did."

Ashira nodded calmly. "You did." Zara waited for her to say more, but her aunt was silent.

Zara's eyes were drawn to the fresh scars that marked Ashira's tattoos. When she'd been a girl, her aunt's tattoos were prizes, each a sign of a battle won or an enemy conquered. While Zara could understand vytrex, calligraphy made it so illegible, it usually looked like gibberish to her. But even she could read the tale of Ashira's new tattoos. A story of loss, and grief, each one the name of someone her aunt had failed.

Zara turned away when she spotted her own name along Ashira's forearm.

"I'm not asking for your forgiveness," Ashira said finally, and Zara almost smiled. She might have changed, but she was still Ashira. "For I do not deserve it."

Zara turned in shock.

Ashira was staring up in the sky, resolutely not looking at her. "But know that I am... sorry."

She limped away, head bowed while Zara tried to process the three words she'd have bet her left kidney Ashira would never say. She waited for the parasite to speak up, to tell Zara to run after Ashira.

But she was silent.

Zara stayed outside until the sky began to brighten, the stars above fading in the fire-red brushstrokes of dawn. She should go, she knew. The day was starting, and injured or not, Ashira would be hauling stone along with the others at First Dawn. Zara should help and stop her aunt from ripping her stitches open.

But she couldn't move.

Her mind was silent, her body her own. She should be *happy*. But she'd lied to Ashira. She wasn't awake because she was thinking about the decimated, clawless vaxion she'd once called kin. She was awake because she was thinking about that wretched parasite and her final words when she'd reached out, clasping Zara's hand tightly.

"Calamity won't let me go... unless I obey," she said, smiling as tears of pain filled her eyes. "Take your body... and forget about me."

Zara was free of the mage and still breathing despite the blood-debt that bound her to him. She had her freedom, her *life* back. The sane, rational thing meant doing as the parasite wished. Forgetting her and the fact that she was destined for a life of endless pain at the behest of a slug.

To be broken as Magnus once tried to break Zara.

Zara screwed her eyes up tight, but her treacherous mind kept showing her memories. Memories of the parasite babbling at her from the darkness, the only companionship Zara had had in a decade. Tearing open her own forearm, promising Zara she'd free her from Magnus. Holding up the stone that threatened to crush Ashira, only worried about Zara's freedom and not her own pitiful life.

"*Shek*!" Zara cursed, screaming at the top of her lungs. A group of witterflies angrily burst from the trees. She watched them until they flew into the distance, then turned on her heel, eagerly marching into the waterstone.

She found Lukas in what used to be the training hall, some smooth stones serving as tables where people still ate murky *grobz* for breakfast. He sat apart from the other vaxion, with only Jaza next to him. Their heads were bowed, and Zara watched Jaza reach out, squeezing Lukas' hand gently. Lukas was wiping tears from his eyes, hiding the movement by shoving *grobz* into his mouth.

Zara appeared at his shoulder. "Pack your bag, cub," she barked.

Lukas stared up at her, his mouth full. "What? Why?"

"We're going to save that stupid, wretched parasite."

END OF BOOK TWO

REVIEWS

Thank you, thank you, thank you for making it this far. I was so nervous starting book two (I'd never written a sequel before) and went into it knowing how I wanted the book to end but not knowing how to get there. And boy, did Zara, Lazander, and everyone else have OPINIONS on what should happen. It's what I love about being a pantser, even if it sometimes (often) blows up in my face—I get as many surprises writing it as I hope you all did reading it.

If you enjoyed my brain baby, please consider leaving a review on Amazon. It feeds the algorithm gods (they're starving), helps people find the book, and lets me keep doing this whole "author" thing (still feels so strange to write that! In the best way!)

Also… if you can't wait for book three, find me on Ream. You'll find all of book three there before anyone else, PLUS some super surprises. Otherwise, I hope to see you in book three—the grand finale of the Knights of Eternity trilogy!

Love,

Rachel Ní Chuirc
CHAOS GREMLIN

WANDERING WARRIOR

By Michael Head

Punishment for the guilty is coming – carried by the armored fist of Judge James Holden

He's reached the limits of his power, and in the process, he's brought justice to nineteen entire worlds. But now, cast across time and space to his twentieth planet, something's wrong.

The darkness runs deeper than ever before, those in power corrupt those beneath them, and the concept of honor is twisted and long lost to those who should know better.

James has had enough, and as the chosen weapon of the gods, he'll bring balance to this world again, or die trying.

If somebody needs to be sent to their gods for that to happen? Well, that's a sacrifice he's willing to make.

It's time for judgement.

https://mybook.to/WanderingWarrior

QUEST ACADEMY

By Brian J. Nordon

A world infested by demons.
An Academy designed to train Heroes to save humanity from annihilation.
A new student's power could make all the difference.

Humans have been pushed to the brink of extinction by an ever-evolving demonic threat. Portals are opening faster than ever, Towers bursting into the skies and Dungeons being mined below the last safe havens of society. The demons are winning.

Quest Academy stands defiantly against them, as a place to train the next generation of Heroes. The Guild Association is holding the line but are in dire need of new blood and the powerful abilities they could bring to the battlefront. To be the saviors that humanity needs, they need to surpass the limits of those that came before them.

In a war with everything on the line, every power matters. With an adaptive enemy, comes the need for a constant shift in tactics. A new age of strategy is emerging, with even the unlikeliest of Heroes making an impact.

Salvatore Argento has never seen a demon.
He has never aspired to become a Hero.
Yet his power might be the one to tip the odds in humanity's favor.

https://www.amazon.com/Quest-Academy-Brian-J-Nordon-ebook

SCARLET CITADEL

By Jack Fields

Gormon Hughes is 19, thin as a broom, and has—not for the first time in his life—been swept into the path of trouble. Poor, recently heartbroken, and indebted to the sort of people who file their teeth into needle points and devour wriggling bloated spiders for fun, Hughes sets his sights on salvation.

That salvation is the Scarlet Citadel, a wealthy organization of pageant fighters, monster hunters, and secret keepers. With the aid of strange oracles, rare good fortune, and a unique power that bubbles like champagne in the core of Hughes' being, he must join the Citadel and advance himself.

But the ladder of progression is harsh and dark. The rungs are slippery.

And falling means disaster…

https://mybook.to/ScarletCitadel

ARISE ALPHA

By Jez Cajiao

When you steal a hundred grand from some very bad people, the best way to survive is to stay small and quiet...

Possibly its not to save a pair of drowning girls, not go 'viral' on social media and certainly not to let the local police take your passport, trapping you on a small 'party' island in the middle of the Mediterranean Sea.

But Steve isn't the average guy, he's ex-military, ex-enforcer and ex-human.

He's a one-man nanite fueled nightmare for those that cross the line, and he's decided that it's time to clean up his act. He's going to make up for the things he's done, and save 'the little guys'.

It's a nice fantasy, but even he has to admit, it's really just a justification, because he's a very bad man, with horrifying abilities, and he's only just learning what he's capable of. He needs a reason to not go to the dark, and if that's hunting down the creatures of the night and beating them to death with their own femurs?

Well, he's just the man for the job.

Stolen money. Greek Islands. Werewolves and Enforcers...
What could possibly go wrong?

https://www.amazon.com/Arise-Alpha-Dark-LitRPG-Adventure-ebook

SOMNIA ONLINE

By K.T. Hanna

Discover the class you were born to play.

Wren, a seasoned healer, is dismayed when Somnia Online automatically assigns her character, Murmur, to the Enchanter class. Determined to overcome the unexpected setback, she assembles her guild, intent on the coveted #1 spot. Twelve keys stand between her and victory but finding them is only part of the puzzle. Armed with telepathic abilities, Murmur rises to the challenge. However, old rivals have followed her to Somnia Online desperate for revenge. Intricate quest lines become more dangerous as NPCs absorb powerful artifacts, and Murmur begins to wonder just what sort of AI controls the world.

Murmur questions her sanity as the real and virtual worlds mesh together. Everyone is keeping secrets from her, even the AI, and Murmur's determined to uncover them.

https://www.amazon.com/Initializing-Somnia-Online-Book-1-ebook

FACEBOOK AND SOCIAL MEDIA

I have a very fancy author page if you'd like to reach out and chat! I can't promise you witty banter, but I *can* promise you terrible memes:

OR

There is a FB group where I often lurk, like Valerius in a library. It's dedicated to two very simple rules:

1: Lets spread the word about new and old brilliant LitRPG books.
2: Don't be a dick!

Come join us!

www.facebook.com/groups/litrpglegion

There are also a few really active Facebook groups I'd recommend you join, as you'll get to hear about great new books, new releases and interact with all your favorite authors!

www.facebook.com/groups/LitRPGsociety/

www.facebook.com/groups/LitRPG.books/

www.facebook.com/groups/LitRPGforum/

www.facebook.com/groups/gamelitsociety/

LITRPG!

To learn more about LitRPG, talk to other authors including myself, and to just have an awesome time, please join the LitRPG Group

www.facebook.com/groups/LitRPGGroup

LITRPG LEGION

I am published by The Legion Publishers, a fabulous (and wonderfully chaotic) trio. Jez, Chrissy, and Geneva are taking on new authors, as well as experienced ones, focusing primarily on the LitRPG. They are guided by one simple rule:

Don't be a dick.

That's it. They're also up front and open about their contracts, which you can find here:

www.legionpublishers.com/legioncontract

Got a LitRPG that's been sitting on your desktop, looking for the perfect home? Well, look no further. Submit here!

www.legionpublishers.com/contact-and-submissions

www.ingramcontent.com/pod-product-compliance
Lightning Source LLC
Chambersburg PA
CBHW062113280426
43661CB00118B/1488/J